T0330402

Advances in Organizational Justice

Advances in
Organizational Justice

edited by

Jerald Greenberg

and

Russell Cropanzano

•

Stanford University Press
Stanford, California
2001

Stanford University Press
Stanford, California

Printed and bound by CPI Group (UK) Ltd,
Croydon, CR0 4YY

Library of Congress Cataloging-in-Publication Data

Advances in organizational justice / edited by Jerald Greenberg and Russell
Cropanzano.
    p. cm.
   Includes index.
   ISBN 0-8047-4132-8
    1. Operational justice. I. Greenberg, Jerald. II. Cropanzano, Russell.

  HD6971.3 .A38 2001
  302.3'5--dc21
                                     00-045046

Last figure below indicates year of this printing:
09 08 07 06 05 04 03 02 01

Contents

Dedication

To my best pal.
—J. G.

To Josh and Timmy.
—R. C.

Preface

WALK INTO ANY office or retail establishment and start talking to the employees. Before you know it, the topic of conversation is sure to turn to fairness and justice. Questions about the fairness of pay, the rules used to schedule vacation time, and treatment by bosses are just a few of the topics likely to arise—and everyone has an opinion about them. It would be misleading to suggest, however, that concerns about fairness are unique to the rank-and-file. Indeed, matters of justice routinely consume the attention of top executives, who must attend to such concerns as the fairness of their labor policies, advertising campaigns, and corporate contributions. Indeed, at any level, it is safe to say that concerns about justice on the job are ubiquitous.

The field of *organizational justice*—the study of people's perceptions of fairness in organizations—is dedicated to understanding these issues. When the senior editor of this book first coined the term *organizational justice* in 1987, he and other scientists focused unabashedly on announcing its relevance to the world. They were on a mission to establish the legitimacy of organizational justice in the competitive marketplace of social scientific ideas. However, it is now clear that they have been successful beyond their wildest imaginations. Not only has there been an outpouring of books and journal articles about organizational justice (including many by the contributors to this book!), but there also have been several important international conferences devoted to the topic in recent years. Organizational justice as an area of study has grown so popular, in fact, that for several years, it was the most popular topic of papers submitted to the Organizational Behavior Division of the Academy of Management. Given all this attention, it is not surprising that interest in organizational justice has spread from the basic disciplines of sociology and social psychology, where much of it is rooted, to the applied fields of industrial/organizational psychology, human resources management, organizational behavior, consumer behavior, and legal studies.

Clearly, it is easy to lose oneself in this tide of scholarship—especially when one considers the highly focused, routine matters to which social scientists must devote their attentions. When confronting the routine tasks of collecting data, testing hypotheses, and writing grant proposals, scientists can easily lose sight of changes in the passing landscape. We liken this to sleeping in one's parents' car during a childhood vacation. While your eyes are closed, you are taken someplace new and different. There is a pleasant jolt upon awakening: You don't know exactly where you are, but you know that things have changed.

Unlike children in the backseat of their parents' car, organizational justice researchers have no all-knowing source to guide their travels. They have no roadmaps—only a loose set of ideas that, once applied, quickly take on a life of their own. As today's justice researchers struggle to locate their coordinates on the intellectual landscape, they find themselves at a spot bustling with noisy enthusiasm—the downtown of a bustling metropolis. Along with the obvious opportunities comes confusion, the result of a constant proliferation of concepts, paradigms, measures, and research directions. As organizational justice scholars face uncertainty about what to study and how to do so, the possibility looms that they will lose focus and wander aimlessly, threatening to leave unfulfilled the field's potential.

We assembled this book motivated by our unwillingness to accept this fate. Our objective is clear—to provide the beacon needed to identify directions that organizational justice researchers are taking. To accomplish this, we sought contributions from scholars whose body of work has been most influential in steering organizational justice onto its current course. We asked them to identify their latest thoughts about the field in an effort to describe the state of the science as they see it. The contributors were not intellectually constrained in any way. We invited them to share with us their ideas, no matter how controversial. This book is the result—a rich and variegated collection of state-of-the-science contributions by the acknowledged leaders in the field of organizational justice.

Not surprisingly, because the chapters are written at a high level, professors and doctoral students are likely to comprise our major audience. Specifically, we envision that this book will be of considerable interest to applied researchers and practitioners in the fields of industrial/organizational psychology, organizational behavior, human resources management, communication, consumer behavior, and legal studies, as well as basic scientists in the disciplines of sociology and social psychology.

The present set of chapters provides an accurate representation of the scope of conceptual issues—both broad and narrow—to which today's scientists are devoting their energies. For example, in our opening chapter, *Fairness Theory: Justice as Accountability,* Folger and Cropanzano present a comprehensive, overarching framework that integrates and synthesizes various concepts that have dotted our intellectual landscape over the years—notably, distributive justice, procedural justice, and retributive justice. Chapter 2, *Fairness Heuristic Theory: Justice Judgments as Pivotal Cognitions in Organizational Relations* by Lind, is equally broad but takes a different direction. Specifically, Lind lays out, for the first time in full form, his theoretical analysis of how people use fairness judgments as heuristics to guide their reactions to organizations and organizational authorities.

The next two chapters, more focused in scope, examine the conceptual interrelationships between various forms of organizational justice. For example, in Chapter 3, entitled *Interactional (In)justice: The Sacred and the Profane,* Bies, who first described interactional justice in the late 1980s, presents a definitive review and analysis of this concept by assessing evidence bearing on its validity. The next contribution, Chapter 4, by Cropanzano and Ambrose, also takes a closer look at specific forms of organizational justice. Specifically, their chapter, entitled *Procedural and Distributive Justice Are More Similar than You Think: A Monistic Perspective and a Research Agenda,* argues that previous research has underemphasized some important similarities between distributive and procedural justice. After reviewing these similarities, they discuss several new research directions that are suggested by this monistic view.

Our next three chapters focus on the social and interpersonal antecedents of justice judgments. Specifically, in Chapter 5, entitled *Anticipatory Injustice: The Consequences of Expecting Injustice in the Workplace,* Shapiro and Kirkman analyze the influence that expectations of justice and injustice can have on work-related attitudes and behavior. Their conceptualization focuses on the anticipation of injustice and group-level constructions of justice. Then, in Chapter 6, entitled *When Do Elements of Procedural Fairness Make a Difference? A Classification of Moderating Differences,* Brockner, Ackerman, and Fairchild present a model of the determinants and consequences of normative beliefs about justice in organizations. Making their contribution noteworthy, they place special emphasis on the role of cross-cultural norms. The role of culture is revisited in Chapter 7, entitled *Ethnic Diversity and the Viability of Organizations: The Role of Procedural Justice in Bridging Differences.* In this chapter, Huo and Tyler examine the potential impact of diversity and multiculturalism on the viability of organizations. They present the basic arguments underlying a relational model of authorities and explore how those dynamics are likely to be influenced by the heterogeneity of the organizations involved.

Finally, we close the book with Greenberg's contribution, *The Seven Loose Can(n)ons of Organizational Justice.* In this piece, Chapter 8, the author identifies seven canons of organizational justice and argues that in the absence of additional conceptual refinement, they may operate as loose cannons that threaten the existence of justice as a viable construct in the organizational sciences.

Taken together, these contributions promise to provide the very kind of road map we earlier identified as routinely missing from the glove box of organizational justice researchers. Indeed, this book will help bring readers up to date on the latest conceptualizations in the field of organizational justice and will identify some promising new directions worthy of taking. As such, its benefits as a scientific navigational aid cannot be underestimated. A roadmap is just a tool, however, and we suspect that many of this book's readers will use the present set of chapters not as a beacon guiding them to safe haven, but as an aid to identifying the lay of the land before taking off on their own off-road adventures. This is precisely what we hope. After all, if a book like this stimulates the creativity of other scientists, we will have met our objective.

Jerald Greenberg
Russell Cropanzano

Contributor Biographies

JERALD GREENBERG holds the Irving Abramowitz Memorial Professorship in Business Ethics at the Fisher College of Business at the Ohio State University. He received his Ph.D. and his M.A. in industrial/organizational psychology from Wayne State University and his B.A. in psychology from the State University of New York at Buffalo. His research interests focus on organizational justice, deviant workplace behavior, human responses to technology, organizational research methods, and performance management. Professor Greenberg is the author or coauthor of several books, including *Behavior in Organizations (7th edition)*, *Antisocial Behavior in Organizations*, and *Organizational Behavior: The State of the Science*, and more than 100 scholarly journal articles published in such outlets as the *Journal of Applied Psychology* and *Organizational Behavior and Human Decision Processes*.

RUSSELL CROPANZANO is an Associate Professor of Industrial/Organizational Psychology at Colorado State University. Dr. Cropanzano is a member of the Academy of Management, the American Psychological Society, and the Society for Organizational Behavior. He is a fellow in the Society for Industrial/Organizational Psychology. Currently Dr. Cropanzano serves on the editorial boards for the *Journal of Applied Psychology, Journal of Management, Journal of Personality and Social Psychology,* and *Organizational Behavior and Human Decision Processes*. He has published over 50 scholarly articles and chapters. In addition, Dr. Cropanzano is a coauthor of the book *Organizational Justice and Human Resources Management*, which won the 1998 Book Award from the International Association of Conflict Management. He is also active internationally, having given talks in Australia, France, New Zealand, and the United Kingdom.

GRANT ACKERMAN is on the Faculty of Management at Rutgers University in New Brunswick, where he teaches *Organizational Behavior, Strategic Human Resource Management, Leadership and Negotiations,* and *Managing Conflict and Consensus within and between Firms.* His research focus is on managing conflict and consensus within and between firms and across cultures and issues in organizational justice. Recent papers and publications include "Treating Subordinates with Dignity and Respect: Does It Always Matter? The Moderating Effect of Power Distance," *2000 Academy of Management,* "Culture's Influence on Preferences for and Reactions to Elements of Procedural Justice," *2000 Society of Industrial and Organizational Psychology,* and "Further Evidence of Culture's Influence on Employees' Reactions to Participation in Decision Making: The Effects of Uncertainty Avoidance and Power Distance," *1997 Academy of Management.* His educational background includes a B.A. in Foreign Service and International Relations with a Certificate in Russian Area Studies, Pennsylvania State University, 1978; a J.D., University of Pittsburgh, 1982; an MBA, Columbia University, 1992; and a Ph.D., Columbia University, 2000.

MAUREEN L. AMBROSE is Professor of Management in the College of Business at the University of Central Florida. She received her Ph.D. in 1986 from the University of Illinois at Urbana-Champaign. Her research interests include organizational fairness, cognitive processes, and ethics. Her work has appeared in the *Academy of Management Review, Journal of Applied Psychology, Academy of Management Journal, Journal of Management, Organizational Behavior and Human Decision Processes,* and *Administrative Sciences Quarterly.*

ROBERT J. BIES is Associate Professor of Management in the McDonough School of Business, Georgetown University, Washington, D.C. Professor Bies received his B.A. degree (1975) and M.B.A. degree (1977), both from the University of Washington in Seattle. He received his Ph.D. (1982) from Stanford University. Professor Bies's research interests include organizational (in)justice, revenge in the workplace, trust and distrust dynamics, and the delivery of bad news. His research has been published in the *Academy of Management Journal, Academy of Management Review, Journal of Applied Psychology, Journal of Management, Research in Organizational Behavior, Research on Negotiation in Organizations, Organization Science,* and *Organizational Behavior and Human Decision Processes.*

JOEL BROCKNER is the Phillip Hettleman Professor of Business at Columbia Business School. He received his Ph.D. in social/personality psychology from Tufts University in 1977 and his B.A. in psychology from the State University of New York at Stony Brook in 1972. His research interests include organizational change, organizational justice, self-processes in work organizations, decision making, and cross-cultural differences (and similarities) in work attitudes and behaviors. Works describing these interests have appeared in two books and numerous journal articles in psychology (e.g., *Journal of Personality and Social Psychology, Psychological Bulletin*) and in organizational behavior (e.g., *Administrative Science Quarterly, Organizational Behavior and Human Decision Processes*. He also is the Faculty Director of Columbia Business School's Executive Education program, entitled, "Leading and Managing People."

GREGORY FAIRCHILD is Assistant Professor of Business Administration at the University of Virginia Darden School. In addition to his work on organizational justice, he studies management fashions and entrepreneurship in developing economies, both domestic and international.

ROBERT FOLGER is the Freeman Professor of Research and Doctoral Studies at the A. B. Freeman School of Business, Tulane University. He received his Ph.D. in 1975 from the University of North Carolina. Previously he taught at Southern Methodist and at Northwestern University. Folger's publications include articles in the *Academy of Management Journal, Academy of Management Review, Journal of Applied Psychology, Journal of Personality and Social Psychology,* and *Psychological Bulletin*. This work reflects his research on motivation and reactions to work conditions, including topics such as performance appraisal, layoffs, trust in the workplace, perceptions of unfair treatment, retaliation by disgruntled employees (e.g., workplace violence), and ethical decision making. He also coauthored *Controversial Issues in Social Research Methods* (with Jerald Greenberg) and *Organizational Justice and Human Resources Management* (with Russell Cropanzano).

YUEN J. HUO is Assistant Professor of Psychology at the University of California, Los Angeles. She received her Ph.D. from the University of California, Berkeley. Prior to joining the UCLA faculty, she was a Research Fellow at the Public Policy Institute of California. Her research deals with how identification processes and justice concerns influence social relations within groups and organizations. Her work has appeared in such journals as *Psychological Science, Journal of Personality and Social Psychology, Personality and Social Psychology Bulletin,* and *Social Justice Research*. She along with H. Smith, T. Tyler, and A. Lind is the recipient of the 1997 Otto Klineberg Award from the Society for the Psychological Study of Social Issues for their research on the management of diversity in the workplace.

BRADLEY L. KIRKMAN is assistant professor of Business Administration at the Joseph M. Bryan School of Business at the University of North Carolina-Greensboro. He received his Ph.D. in Organizational Behavior from the Kenan-Flagler Business School at the University of North Carolina-Chapel Hill. Kirkman's research interests include organizational justice, team effectiveness, international management, and organizational change. His publications appear in the *Academy of Management Journal, Academy of Management Review, Organizational Dynamics*, the *International Journal of Conflict Management, Social Justice Research*, and others. He is the author of *High Performance Work Organizations: Definitions, Practices, and an Annotated Bibliography* (Center for Creative Leadership, 1999).

E. ALLAN LIND holds the Thomas A. Finch Jr. Chair in Business Administration at the Fuqua School of Business at Duke University. Prior to coming to Duke, he worked at the American Bar Foundation and the RAND Corporation and held faculty positions at the University of Illinois and the University of New Hampshire. Professor Lind holds a Ph.D. in social psychology from the University of North Carolina in Chapel Hill. He is the coauthor of *The Social Psychology of Procedural Fairness*, and he has published numerous papers over the last 25 years on the psychology of fairness.

DEBRA L. SHAPIRO is the Willard Graham Distinguished Professor of Management and Associate Dean for Ph.D. Programs at the Kenan-Flagler Business School at the University of North Carolina at Chapel Hill. She received her Ph.D. from the Kellogg Graduate School of Management at Northwestern University. Shapiro's research focuses on how to manage conflict in organizations (e.g., change resistance, perceived injustice and mistreatment, team conflicts, cultural differences, and relational and outcome effects of different negotiation strategies). Her publications appear in *Administrative Science Quarterly, The Academy of Management Journal, The Academy of Management Review, Organizational Behavior and Human Decision Processes, Journal of Applied Psychology, Journal of Personality and Social Psychology, The Negotiation Journal*, and others.

TOM TYLER is a professor of Psychology at New York University. He is also an adjunct professor at the New York University school of law. His work explores authority relations in legal, political, and managerial groups. His past books include *The social psychology of procedural justice* (Plenum, 1988, with E. Allan Lind); *Why people obey the law* (Yale,

1990); *Trust in organizations* (Sage, 1996, with Roderick Kramer); *Social justice in a diverse society* (Westview, 1997, with Robert Boeckmann, Yuen Huo, and Heather Smith); *The psychology of the social self* (Erlbaum, 1999, with Roderick Kramer and Oliver John); *Cooperation in modern society* (Routledge, 2000, with Mark Van Vugt, Mark Snyder, and Anders Biel), and *Social influences on ethical behavior in organizations* (Erlbaum, 2001, with John Darley and David Messick).

List of Figures and Tables

Tables

Advances in Organizational Justice

Fairness Theory: Justice as Accountability

Robert Folger
and
Russell Cropanzano

WHAT IS FAIRNESS? What do people mean when they say that they've been treated rightly or wrongly? In this chapter, we try to answer such questions by presenting a new model of justice called *fairness theory*. The theory presumes that the central topic of social justice is the assignment of blame. When people identify an instance of unfair treatment, they are holding someone accountable for an action (or inaction) that threatens another person's material or psychological well-being. If no one is to blame, there is no social injustice. For this reason, the process of *accountability*, or how another social entity comes to be considered blameworthy, is fundamental to justice. When people ascertain the fairness of someone's actions, they are trying to decide whether to hold that person accountable for those actions.

Despite the pivotal role played by accountability in feelings of injustice, previous research has been surprisingly silent on the topic. Some theories of organizational fairness begin one step back from the accountability

The authors would like to thank Kees Van den Bos for his helpful comments on various theoretical ideas presented in this chapter. The authors are accountable for errors and omissions, however.

decision and emphasize those aspects of the situation that eventually lead to blaming someone else. Other theories go one step forward, emphasizing the consequences of blaming someone. Nevertheless, the central role of accountability is at least implicit in many theories of justice.

Referent cognitions theory (RCT) is an example of a "one step back" theory. As discussed by Folger (e.g., 1987, 1993), RCT maintains that people are most likely to experience a sense of injustice when they are disadvantaged in relation to some point of comparison (such as another person; for details, see Folger & Kass, in press; Kulik & Ambrose, 1992). The role of accountability, however, is not explicit in RCT. Nor, as we will indicate, does RCT take into account all of the conditions necessary to attribute blame. Similarly, Lind and Tyler's (1988) *group value model of authority* (which was later elaborated as a relational model by Tyler & Lind, 1992) holds that a sense of justice is engendered when decision makers address individuals' relational concerns. These concerns can be addressed by being trustworthy and benevolent in intention, by recognizing other people's standing as group members, and by showing neutrality (Lind, 1995). These three rules make accountability implicit, especially with regard to intention.

Equity theory (e.g., Adams, 1965) is "one step forward" in that it tends to emphasize the consequences of holding someone accountable for unfair treatment. Adams (1965), for example, asked whether a disadvantageous inequity would result in more than mere feelings of dissatisfaction. Anger toward the perpetrator, he noted, could lead to equity-restoration attempts, which might include such actions as work slowdowns and theft.

An interesting mixed model was introduced by Bies and Moag (1986) and Bies (1987) with the concept of *interactional justice*. According to Bies, decision makers know that they might be held accountable for aversive events. Thus, they devise explanations that they hope will allow them to avoid retaliation from the person who feels unfairly treated. Interactional justice research is especially important for our purposes here because it explicitly notes that authority figures (and, more generally, anyone whose conduct has implications for others' welfare) often risk being blamed. The model goes on to describe tactics by which decision makers avoid being held accountable (for recent reviews see Bies, this volume; Bobocel, McCline, & Folger, 1997). Consequently, Bies (1987) emphasized the role of accountability, although he did not describe the process by which it occurs.

This brief review suggests that although the construct of accountability is ubiquitous, no justice theories have explicitly emphasized the process by which accountability judgments are made. In the following section, we try to plug that gap by introducing and explicating a model of accountability called *fairness theory*. Fairness theory focuses on the implications of accountability for fairness judgments. Briefly previewed, fairness theory maintains that accountability has three interrelated components. One component is the existence of an unfavorable condition (a negative state of events, relative to a given frame of reference). In other words, there must be something of an aversive nature for which someone might be held accountable.[1] Second, the event must be due to the volitional, discretionary actions of the target person whose accountability is assessed. An individual who had no feasible alternatives, for example, is ordinarily not held accountable. Third, those harmful actions (responsible for the negative conditions) must violate some ethical principle of interpersonal conduct—a normative standard of justice. People ordinarily do not, for example, consider a dentist unfair who bears responsibililty for painful conditions caused by a tooth extraction. Though the treatment may hurt in the short run, the dentist has behaved in an ethically fair manner and therefore is not accountable for a charge of injustice.

The following pages describe the model in two parts. The first lays out the three elements of fairness theory. The second part integrates fairness theory with previous justice research.

The Three Elements of Fairness Theory

Imagine arriving at work one morning. Unexpectedly and without cause, your supervisor approaches you with a specimen jar in hand. She orders you to go to the bathroom and, while accompanied by an observer, to provide a urine sample for a random drug test. There is a good chance that you might feel a sense of uneasiness (Konovsky & Cropanzano, 1993), but do you hold your supervisor accountable for having treated you unfairly?

Figure 1.1 shows the three elements of fairness theory: (a) an injurious condition or state of affairs (circumstances considered disadvantageous), (b) attributable to someone's discretionary conduct that (c) violates an applicable moral tenet. For example, many people would have negative thoughts about a random drug test, especially one performed in an invasive fashion. When such events are experienced in that aversive fashion, the first element of accountability is in place. On the other hand, had the organization been less punitive, more supportive, and more respectful of employee privacy, then the test might have seemed less aversive (Cropanzano & Konovsky, 1995), and there would have been less reason to consider assigning blame.

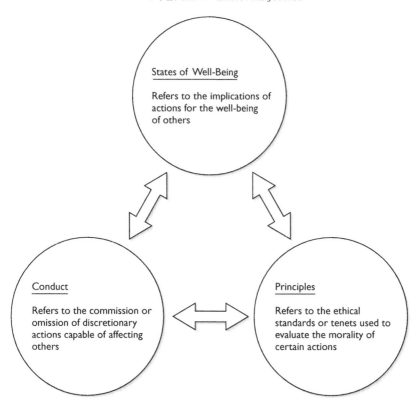

Figure 1.1. Fairness Theory Model of Accountability.

Now consider the second element. Although your supervisor handed you the urine-specimen jar, she might not be the person whom you blame. Perhaps you suspect that she had no choice because the order came from her superiors. If your supervisor was forced to administer the test, then you might not hold her accountable.

Finally, note the relevance of normative precepts as a third element of accountability. When the supervisor is held responsible for her conduct, such a behavior may or may not be a violation of prevailing ethical norms. Certainly, violating the privacy of a well-performing employee might seem morally questionable or problematic to at least some people. There might be a justification for that action, however, that would make it morally legitimate. Perhaps there have been serious safety problems in your company. Your supervisor, though perhaps a tad zealous, is motivated by a concern for others' well-being. Hence, though your supervisor may well be accountable for an odious incident, she may not be accountable for an *unfair* incident.

This example illustrates our three conditions of accountability, which we have modeled after what Schlenker (1997; Schlenker, Britt, Pennington, Murphy, & Doherty 1994) has called the "triangle" nodes of responsibility: (a) injury, (b) discretionary conduct, and (c) moral transgression. More important, it illustrates the interplay among the three (also following Schlenker's emphasis on links among those nodes): For a person to be held accountable for an injustice, that person must harm another person by behaving in a way that violates some ethical principle of social conduct. The fully interconnected chain linking these elements needs to be maintained. If the chain is broken in any place, then a social injustice has not occurred.[2] In effect, an individual composes a sense of accountability from these three judgments—injury, conduct, and standards are the constituent elements from which blame is built.

In the next section we discuss the nature of these three judgments. We argue that all three involve a prototypical form of contrastive thinking. In discussing how that contrastive mode of thought operates, we draw from the most comprehensive descriptions available, as found in the psychological literature on counterfactuals and related topics, such as the *simulation heuristic* (Kahneman & Tversky, 1982) and *norm theory* (Kahneman & Miller, 1986).

When we use the term *counterfactual,* we mean exactly what we say. Counterfactual thinking is "contrary to the facts," as Roese (1997, p. 133) aptly puts it. The point of departure for counterfactual thinking could be any event that someone experiences. If the event is important or at least salient, the person will try to make sense out of it. The person attempts to ascribe some meaning to the occurrence. Meaning is not intrinsic to an event. It is something assigned to an incident by a human observer or observers. In other words, meaning is added during or after the fact. What people add is their own thoughts, interpretations, perceptions, and ideas. In a word, they add their imagination. Among other things, they assess what the nature of the experience *would have been* like if the event had not occurred or had unfolded differently (Roese & Olson, 1995).

When people contemplate an actual event, they often mentally alter certain parameters or change certain facts for a contrastive perspective that acts as a frame of reference. These changed elements are "counterfactual" because, as just mentioned, they run counter to the actual event. The use of counterfactuals creates new, alternative scenarios, and these alternatives provide a frame of reference. In short, people place what "is" side by side with "what might have been." This juxtaposition is the essence of counterfactual thinking (Roese, 1997).

In fairness theory, counterfactual thinking has wide utility. Each of the three central judgments in fairness theory is decided by comparing reality with the corresponding aspect of a counterfactual scenario. From the point of view of cognitive processing, it matters relatively little which of the judgments is being made. Counterfactual thinking is implicated whether we are attempting to understand states, behaviors, or principles. From the point of view of establishing human meaning, on the other hand, each judgment is quite different. First, an aversive state involves implicit comparison with a more beneficial state. This entails a question about what an alternatively experienced state *would* have felt like if a different type of event or situation had occurred—one with more positive implications for well-being than those that were actually encountered. Second, discretionary conduct refers to another person's choices among feasible alternatives. Hence, the contrast between what another person actually did and an alternative course of action involves the behaviors that *could* have transpired. Third, judging another's discretionary conduct by moral principles implies the contrast between what was done and what *should* have been done. *Would, Could,* and *Should* (henceforth capitalized) are the essential elements of accountability.

Would Perceptions: Counterfactual Thinking and Injury (Reduced or Threatened Welfare)

> *When one has been threatened with a great injustice, one accepts a smaller as a favor.*
> —Mrs. Thomas Carlyle

It is easiest to describe fairness theory by beginning with consequences as implications for well-being. What do people mean when they say that they have been injured or harmed? To answer these question, we need to introduce the idea of *states of being.* A state is a condition of existence. For example, wealth and poverty refer to economic states, whereas feelings such as contentment and emotional exhaustion are psychological states. Health is a physical state, and the quality of being respected is a social state. When a person has been injured, some state of being has been worsened or made problematic, even if only as a threatened prospect that jeopardizes future welfare. Malevolent intentions by an antagonist who constitutes a threat to someone's well-being therefore constitute injurious consequences for that person as we use the term *injury.*

Consider, for example, a female employee who submits to a blood test as part of a routine company physical. Unbeknown to the individual, the firm uses the sample for genetic screening, drug screening, and a host of other medical tests (see Stone & Stone, 1990, for an excellent discussion of this and similar issues). Subsequently, the employee is terminated because her genetic tests suggest that she might be prone to some costly illness. How might her state of being be affected? Her economic state is likely to worsen due to the loss of pay. Unemployment is apt to batter her social status as well. Finally, if she becomes ill and cannot draw on company benefits for health care, then her physical state might deteriorate. Clearly, the employee will see the testing and firing as an injurious event. Harm is defined as damage to some state of being, although often justice researchers tend to focus on economic, psychological, and socal states.

Determining Whether Injury Has Occurred

The counterfactual contrast between well-being and injuries such as pain or financial loss seems fairly straightforward in principle, but in fact judgments of injury can be more problematic than they first appear. People are sometimes uncertain whether they have been harmed. This is because it takes a ruler to measure something. To gauge injury, this "ruler" incorporates a referent standard as a point of comparison (Folger, 1984; Folger & Kass, in press; Kulik & Ambrose, 1992). By referring to a referent standard as a ruler, we intend to connote variations in magnitude rather than absolute "yes/no" categories. People can feel a little disadvantaged or quite a lot. In this way, the referent standard acts as a ruler. Generally speaking, a very serious event is one with a large discrepancy between the actual event and the well-being standard. A less serious event has a smaller discrepancy. In any case, it is the rift between a consequence and a comparison point that determines the extent of felt injury.

Harder (1992), for example, documented that pay inequity exists even among highly paid major-league baseball players. Though all of these individuals are far better compensated than the average American, there is still a good deal of variability in their earnings, and, additionally, players do not always get what they want in salary negotiations. From their standpoint, some players see themselves as doing better than their peers. It should be emphasized that this finding is not limited to the unique sample of professional athletes. In fact, considerable evidence suggests that standards of comparison are important in decisions of pay satisfaction (e.g., Cowherd & Levine, 1992; Summers & Hendrix, 1991; Sweeney, McFarlin, & Inderrieden 1990).

An especially intriguing example was discussed by Martin (1981). Martin pondered the circumstances of women working in management. It has been well-documented that women in management earn less than men of similar experience and tenure (Brett & Stroh, 1997; Lyness & Tompson, 1997). However, women managers also earn more than most other female workers, who tend to be overrepresented among lower-paying jobs (Peterson, 1994). This presents female managers with a question: To what extent have they been "injured" by their pay? As Martin observed, if they compare themselves with male managers, then they have been hurt. If they compare themselves with the typical female worker, then they are doing reasonably well. For this reason, some women may be slow to claim discrimination, even when they are clearly not being compensated equitably (for a fuller discussion of this and related phenomena, see Crosby, 1984; Martin, 1986). Parenthetically, we should note the obvious: Federal law requires that women be paid relative to men in their job class and with similar competence, *not* based upon their gender. The managers considered by Martin, therefore, were in fact being discriminated against.

Not only do different people use different referent standards, but the same person can alter his or her standards over time. For example, Stepina and Perrewe (1991) measured workers' standards with respect to four facets of their jobs: compensation, job complexity, security, and supervision. Two years later they surveyed the same individuals again. Those who experienced Time 1 discrepancies often changed their referents at Time 2. These referent changes were most frequently observed for the following three facets: job complexity, security, and supervision. This new, typically lower, referent led to greater satisfaction. Interestingly, however, workers did not change their compensation referent during the two-year interval. Thus, pay satisfaction tended not to change as a result of discrepancy reduction.

Standards for Gauging the Favorability of Procedural Justice

So far we have considered only the case where individuals attempt to assess the damage due to some outcome. However, the decision-making process is also evaluated relative to referent standards for such processes. Indeed, the same procedure could be seen as reasonable at one time but unreasonable at another. Consider the following passage:

> When Thierry feels the blade bite through his flesh,
> And sees the blood upon the grass run red,
> Then he lets drive a blow at Pinabel.

Down to the nasal he cleaves the bright steel helm,
Sheers through the brain and spills it from his head,
Wrenches the blade out and shakes him from it dead.
With that great stroke he wins and makes an end.
Then the Franks all cry: "God's might is manifest!
Justice demands the rope for Guenes's neck,
And for his kinsmen who set their lives in pledge!"

—from the *Song of Roland,* stanza 286

The preceding passage is taken from the French national epic. The knight Pinabel battles on behalf of Guenes and those who betrayed Roland to the Saracens. The knight Thierry battles on behalf of their rivals. The dispute between these factions is settled in a "trial by combat." Whoever wins the fight is presumed to have God on his side and therefore to be in the right. In the end justice requires not only Pinabel's untidy death but the death of Guenes and kinsmen as well. By comparison, organizational downsizing is considerably tamer.

To modern readers it seems odd that civil justice and God's glory are served by cutting a man's head in half. Trial by combat yields the advantage to the biggest and meanest, not to the kindest and most thoughtful. Even the bold and faithful Franks were distressed by this possibility: "Fight Pinabel? Who'd be so rash? Not me!" (stanza 275). Nevertheless, trial by combat was considered a perfectly acceptably procedure for settling disputes, and it persisted for many years. We find that even the Emperor Charlemagne, who was Roland's uncle, is subordinate to the law. Rather than simply having the alleged traitors executed, Charlemagne supports the trial and implies a willingness to abide by its results. For the French in the eleventh century, trial by combat was not considered to be an unfavorable process. (Roland was probably killed in 778. However, the epic we are quoting did not take its modern form until the 1000s.) In trial by combat we see a practice that was once appropriate but is now considered inappropriate. Whether we look backward in time or across the oceans to different cultures, we see many examples of this same phenomenon.

This suggests that judgments concerning procedural events are also made relative to some referent standard. Once more, when the standard changes, so does one's evaluation. This has been less widely discussed in the literature, but it is apparent from the empirical evidence. For example, in one experimental study, Grienberger and Rutte (1996) let some subjects choose the task on which they worked. Other participants were not allowed this choice. Grienberger and Rutte found that the lack of choice, per se, did not engender a sense of injustice. Rather, subjects felt that the task-selection process was unfair to the extent that they were denied participation while another group of individuals were given a choice. The issue of process and referent standards is discussed elsewhere in this book by Cropanzano and Ambrose. We will not belabor the point here. Our only point is that referent standards for procedures determine whether a given procedure seems undesirable.

The Cognitive Operation of Would Counterfactuals

To illustrate Would counterfactual thinking, which operates to determine assessment of both outcomes and procedures, we refer to an example presented by Kahneman and Tversky (1982):

> Mr. Crane and Mr. Tees were scheduled to leave the airport on different flights at the same time. They traveled from town in the same limousine, were caught in a traffic jam, and arrived at the airport 30 minutes after the scheduled departure time of their flights.
> Mr. Crane is told that his flight left on time.
> Mr. Tees is told that his flight was delayed, and just left five minutes ago.
> Who is more upset? (p. 203)

Kahneman and Tversky reported that a full 96% (p. 203) of those surveyed believed that Mr. Tees would be more unhappy because he has an easier time imagining how things *would* have been different. In other words, Mr. Tees need change only one element in the drama to reach a different conclusion. The easier it is to imagine a positive alternative, the more likely it is that a negative event will cause distressful emotion. In other words, the same consequence can seem more or less pernicious depending upon the imagined alternative.

Earlier work (such as Referent Cognitions Theory or RCT; e.g., Folger, 1987) has been influenced by Kahenman and Tversky's (1982) research. The tacit assumption has been that the simulated referent standard was constructed and compared consciously. In fact, more recent research suggests that these comparisons can occur at the unconscious level (for a summary see Bargh, 1997). In other words, the juxtaposition between referents and actual events can take place without a mental alternative's being brought to mind as a conscious act of will. Referents can function as part of the process that Bargh (1997) calls *automaticity*. It is conceivable that these automatic counterfactuals might have an even greater impact than those produced by the conscious simulation of imagined scenarios. This could be expected if the conscious mental process took more effort and had to be deliberately initiated in order to bring the preferred alternative to mind, whereas the automatic counterfactual made the preferred alternative come to mind even when the person tried to avoid thinking about it. Regardless of whether the simulation is built consciously or automatically, our larger points stand: (a) people respond to discrepancies between a counterfactual and an actual event, and (b) the magnitude of the discrepancy is related to the emotional and motivational strength of responses to it.

Could Judgments: Counterfactual Thinking and Feasible Behaviors

> *Corruption never has been compulsory.*
> —*Anthony Eden*

A Would counterfactual contrast—between a referent standard and an experienced event—establishes the degree of a negative event's aversiveness, regardless of whether mental representations of the event code it as procedural or distributive. The counterfactual processing of events, however, is not limited to Would assessments. In particular, crucial questions about fair social relations would remain unanswered if people did not make other counterfactual comparisons as well. Fairness theory postulates that people must also ask themselves a Could question: Could a (target) person have behaved differently? This Could judgment presupposes a target of judgment as the object of a perceiver's attention. Typically another person becomes a judgment target for Could assessments either because that other person's actions constitute the event being experienced (e.g., rude behavior) or else because those actions preceded the event in ways that seem to have led to it. Either way, issues of fairness in social relations imply making judgments about another person's conduct and therefore imply a social target (moral agent) upon which people focus attention.

For example, suppose that you are a White male who was passed over for promotion. You suspect that your supervisor recommended a co-worker in order to achieve an affirmative action goal. You have a clear target for your (potential) resentment—your boss. There is also a negative event, of course—your having not received the desired position. This places you in a position to ask the Could question: *Could* your supervisor have behaved differently?

When people answer the Could question, they are trying to determine whether an alternative action was a feasible, viable option for the target person. Is it reasonable to suppose that this individual could have taken a different course of action? If it is not, then to some extent the person's action was not discretionary. The individual did not have reasonable choices available. In the lack-of-promotion example, even if your supervisor's actions seem unfair in their consequences for you (being denied a job you deserved), you might not respond with hostility toward that person if you perceive that he or she was coerced into making the decision. Could counterfactuals refer to aspects of someone's conduct that involve feasible options and discretionary control over them.

Could Judgments and Causal Accounts

Probably the clearest evidence for the importance of Could judgments comes from research on causal social accounts. A *social account* is an explanation given by a harmdoer that follows a hurtful action. The purpose of the account is to explain or explain away some injury (Bies, 1987; Bies, Chapter 3; Bobocel et al., 1997; Tyler & Bies, 1990). Social accounts are important for this reason: If Could judgments partially drive the sense of injustice, then when a person does not have control over a situation, that person cannot be held accountable. Therefore, an account that demonstrates the inability to exert discretionary control (a type of incapacity for which someone cannot be held responsible) will tend to prevent feelings of social injustice—even when harm has been experienced—if this exculpatory account applies credibly as an explanation for the actions of the person seen as the source of the harm. A causal social account is an explanation that concerns the reasons that an action occurred. Sitkin and Bies (1993) also call this a "mitigating account." When giving a causal or mitigating account, the harmdoer admits that things did not go well (i.e., things Would have been different otherwise). The harmdoer also maintains, however, that there were extenuating circumstances that made the action necessary or unavoidable. "Yes," the besieged decision maker concedes, "things *would* have been better, but they *could* not have been."

A good example of a causal account can be found in a vignette study conducted by Bobocel et al. (1996). In the experimental scenario, a manager resolved a dispute in a way that was unfavorable to an employee. The research participant's job was to take the role of the employee and indicate how much injustice the employee experienced. Bobocel and her colleagues found that when the manager deflected blame by using a causal account, participants reported less ill will. In other words, although a negative consequence occurred, the manager was not seen as having control. Lacking such a viable choice, the blame had to rest elsewhere. Other research evidence also attests to the usefulness of causal accounts (e.g.,

Bies & Shapiro, 1988; Bies, Shapiro, & Cummings, 1988; Folger, Rosenfield, & Robinson, 1983; Shapiro, 1991).

The key point is this: It makes no sense to hold people morally responsible for the implications of events that they could not control or could not
reasonably be expected to have anticipated. When harmdoers provide a
causal account, they strive to acquit themselves by pleading a lack of control. A causal account works like an excuse. It tells the listener that someone or something else is ultimately responsible for the deleterious consequence. Codes of moral conduct must entail actions that people can
implement. Thus, to hold people responsible for what they *should* have
done (a moral failing), one must first ascertain whether they could have
done something. In the end, a successful causal account preserves a sense
of justice even in the face of misfortune (Bies & Sitkin, 1992).

Could Judgments and Sins of Omission

It is probably easiest to think about Could judgments when someone has
done some harm and would like *not* to accept responsibility—a "sin of
commission." Consider an incident of losing your temper and shouting at
a colleague. On the face of it, that act might be viewed as interpersonally
insensitive and therefore at least potentially unfair (Greenberg, 1993;
Tyler & Bies, 1990). However, if this ill-tempered behavior were attributed to the work situation ("We have all been under a lot stress lately"),
then it might not be seen as unfair. Yes, the shouting was aversive (the
Would part of the fairness theory), but the rage was not your fault (the
Could part of the fairness theory). Most justice research has examined sins
of commission.

People can also be guilty of "sins of omission." That is, they may withhold certain helpful acts and, in so doing, cause harm to other people. Col-
loquially, this might be referred to as "passive aggression," though this
term is a bit too loose for the idea we are trying to convey here. A person
can withhold assistance in order to deliberately hurt someone (passive
aggression) or simply out of ignorance. As we discuss later, ignorance may
or may not lead to liability. In any case, individuals can be held accountable for sins of omission as well as those of commission. This could occur,
for example, if a person neglected to assist an overworked co-worker or if
a supervisor failed to provide suitable developmental opportunities for
subordinates. In each case it is not so much what the individual did, but
what the individual did not do, that raises the issue of accountability.

Sins of omission pose a difficult problem. When one inflicts injury on
another, the responsibility is direct and easy to spot. However, with a sin

of omission, the responsible individual is not the one who actually did the damage. He or she merely stood to one side while someone else committed the transaction. Metaphorically, in a sin of commission the harmdoer pulls the trigger; in a sin of omission the harmdoer "merely" lets the gun go off.

How do people assign blame for a *non* intervention? The counterfactual task is formidable. When a person commits a harm, one can construct a counterfactual scenario by simply changing a particular act. On the other hand, there are a potentially infinite number of behaviors that a person *could* have committed. To forge a serviceable counterfactual, one must ascertain which part of this myriad was feasible and then append it to one's cognitive scenario. For this reason, it might be easier mentally to exclude a pernicious act than to attach an advantageous one. The method of assigning blame for nonintervention is greatly in need of future research. We propose that people are most likely to be held responsible for sins of omission when there is a clear normative expectation that a certain beneficial action be taken. For example, a supervisor who does not give appropriate positive feedback may be every bit as insensitive as one who gives too much destructive negative feedback. Likewise, a nurse who does not answer the call of a sick patient would probably also be held responsible. Otherwise, the problem is less tractable and would greatly benefit from new research.

Could Judgments and the Problem of Ignorance

U.S. citizens learn the common-law saying that "Ignorance of the law is no excuse." For example, suppose the speed limit on a certain street is 35 miles per hour. One day it is lowered to 25. A person who is caught driving 30 miles per hour could not legally plead ignorance. That person could be held accountable even though the mistake was an "innocent" one. Although this is a convenient legal contrivance, it is likely that many of us would sympathize with this unwitting speeder. We suspect that under the circumstances we have described, police officers might even offer a de facto "grace period" before ticketing those who drove 25–35 miles per hour. The same problem faces people when they try to hold someone accountable if that persons's behavior resulted from a genuine lack of knowledge. In these cases people have to decide not only whether a person had the necessary information but also whether that person could reasonably have been expected to be knowledgeable.

An example might help. Suppose one day at work you have a heart attack. Lacking the necessary skills, no one offers emergency CPR, and you barely manage to survive. While recovering from your illness, you attempt to decide whether your co-workers' ignorance of CPR constitutes an injustice. In most cases you would probably be understanding. Most people do not know CPR, so it is not reasonable to expect this of your co-workers. On the other hand, if your heart attack had occurred in the midst of the coronary care unit of a major regional medical center, then you would probably blame the staff if they lacked basic CPR skills. This is because having certain skills is supposed to be part of these nurses' and doctors' training. Unfortunately, most situations are not as clear as the incident described here. There are many gray areas where certain bits of knowledge may or may not be expected.

It is important not to confuse the issue of ignorance with the sins of omission that we described earlier. In fact, a person can either perform or not perform a critical behavior based upon ignorance. Another medical example illustrates the point. Consider the case of a misinformed obstetrician. Obstetricians are supposed to keep apprised of new medicines that can assist their patients. Let us suppose that one doctor has not. As a result, he erroneously prescribes a dangerous drug to a pregnant woman and thereby causes a birth defect in her baby. This is a sin of commission. Because the doctor is an obstetrician, he could reasonably be expected to have had the necessary knowledge. Thus, even though his actions were not deliberate in the strict sense, he could be held accountable. Now let us consider a different obstetrician. Suppose this other doctor fails to prescribe a new drug that might have prevented a miscarriage. As a result, one of her pregnant patients experiences the death of a baby. This is an "innocent" sin of omission, but again the obstetrician could conceivably be held accountable.

COULD JUDGMENTS AND THE RESPONSIBLE MANAGER   Another problem of Could judgments concerns the issue of supervision. When are people responsible for the actions and nonactions of others? For example, suppose you decide to change your health-care coverage and consult your benefits office. The benefits counselor offers inadequate advice and this misinformation costs you financially. Certainly, in this case the counselor could feasibly have known the alternative health-care plans. As such, the counselor is likely to be held accountable (pending the Should judgments, of course). But what about the counselor's supervisor? In this case, could the supervisor be liable as well? Perhaps judgment in this case might depend on the feasibility of the supervisor's knowing. However, this is difficult to ascertain. It is unclear when authority figures are held responsible for their subordinates, which makes that a topic for future research.

COULD JUDGMENTS AND JURISTIC PERSONS   People make Could judgments in deciding who might be responsible. But who is "who"? Organizational justice research has been heavily influenced by the individualistic foci of social and industrial/organizational psychologists (see Cropanzano & Greenberg, 1997; Greenberg, 1990). As a result, justice is often thought of as a person-to-person affair. Although important, this one-to-one approach is limited. Modern society is largely dominated by corporate actors. These are large, social institutions—such as work organizations and government agenciencies—that have a legally recognized "life" of their own (Coleman, 1993).

Because these institutions are legally recognized as "persons" but do not have a flesh-and-blood body, Coleman (1982) calls them "juristic persons" or simply "corporations." A business organization is a good example of a juristic person. The structure of the firm, from the line worker to the CEO, is a collection of positions. These corporate actors can transact business among themselves (e.g., when Ford buys steel from USX) or between themselves and regular people (e.g., when a corporation sues an individual). In these respects juristic persons are much like real persons. But there are differences as well. Corporations have longer life expectancies. When real persons die or leave, the juristic person goes on. Consider, for example, major-league baseball. With free agency, players hop from team to team, but the teams do not stop existing. The owners simply find someone else to fill the empty positions.

When we consider juristic persons, we see that justice researchers actually have two types of social actors to consider: corporations and the rest of us. Because either of these social actors can interact with the other, we can derive the 2 × 2 matrix diagrammed in Figure 1.2. This matrix is adapted for our purposes from a more general one presented by Coleman (1982). As the matrix shows, individual persons can interact with other individual persons (the usual focus of justice research) or with juristic persons. Likewise, juristic persons can interact with individual persons or with other juristic persons. This provides four sets of circumstances within which the need for accountability might arise. We briefly examine each.

Cell 1: Individual Person to Individual Person   Cell 1 represents cases in which the actions of a potential harmdoer are evaluated by another individual person. For most organizational justice researchers, this is probably the most familiar circumstance. Likewise, this is the only cell that this chapter has discussed so far. Given that a substantial body of work has already explored this condition, we do not dwell on it further.

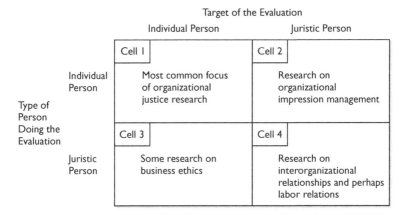

Figure 1.2. "Could" Judgments for Individual People
and Juristic Persons.

Cell 2: Individual Person to Juristic Person   In Cell 2 an individual must make a Could decision regarding the actions of a juristic person. One can imagine that this circumstance is especially familiar to community activists. For example, when an individual tries to prevent a chemical company from locating a hazardous waste dump near her home, she finds herself in Cell 2 (though one suspects that this is the least of her worries).

Cell 2 has been the subject of recent research. In one interesting line of inquiry, Gatewood, Gowan, and Lautenschlager (1993) noted that it is often not individuals but organizations that have to explain their actions. This topic has been studied under the rubric of organizational impression management (Ginzel, Kramer, & Sutton, 1993). Considerable research has shown that organizations often provide social accounts for their behavior in a way that is quite similar to the tactics used by individuals (e.g., Dutton & Dukerich, 1991; Elsbach, 1994; Elsbach & Sutton, 1992).

Cell 3: Juristic Person to Individual Person   This is a condition in which we have been unable to locate any relevant empirical research. In Cell 3 an organization is deliberating on the actions of an individual. Although this case might be unusual within the organizational justice literature, it is probably familiar to business ethicists. In fact, every time a firm sets up any sort of ethical guidelines and then identifies people who are not in compliance, it is in Cell 3. For example, if a manager were found guilty of sexual harassment and summarily dismissed, then this would entail a Cell 3 transaction. The same would be true if a field representative were disciplined for making a sale by bribing a foreign official. Cell 3 is an open area for future work. In doing such research one might conceivably integrate the organizational justice literature with work in organizational theory and business ethics.

Cell 4: Juristic Person to Juristic Person   Cell 4 represents another possibility for future inquiry. In this circumstance two juristic persons have transacted business. One is now deciding whether to hold the other accountable for potential harm. Although this cell has not been widely explored by justice researchers, it certainly has received its share of attention. For example, Howard (1994) has raised questions about the alleged difficulties that businesses (one type of juristic person) have in complying with the dictates of government regulatory agencies (another juristic person). Similarly, considerable attention has been given to the relationship between organizations and large labor unions. A justice researcher interested in Cell 4, therefore, could benefit from cross-disciplinary observations by other scholars.

THE COGNITIVE OPERATION OF COULD COUNTERFACTUALS   As seen earlier, Could counterfactuals can be exceedingly complex. Holding people responsible for their actions requires that alternative actions be feasible. It also requires, of course, that alternative behaviors be cognizable (i.e., occur to the perceiver) in the first place. Moreover, there are many situations in which we simply do not have enough research. For example, we know little about when ignorance is or is not an excuse, about how nonactions are judged, or about the accountability of supervisors for their subordinates' actions. Given this dearth of knowledge, we cannot answer any of these questions here. We propose that the path to understanding these issues, however, might be through a better comprehension of Could counterfactuals. The purpose of the current section is to provide an initial inquiry into these issues.

Essentially, people more often hold someone accountable if they can easily imagine a Could counterfactual. We suggest that Could counterfactuals are more likely to be constructed when a questionable action is novel or has extreme consequences. We discuss each of these possibilities next, although we caution that this list is not exhaustive. Like many of the topics this chapter discusses, this one would benefit greatly from more research attention.

Could Counterfactuals and Novel Behavior   A novel, and especially an unexpected, behavior would seem most likely to induce Could counterfactual thinking. If the action is expected or has a long tradition, then it is less likely that an observer will mentally construct an alternative. Unusual events, on the other hand, can be undone simply by substituting the old action for the new one. We would suspect, therefore, that these sorts of situations would be especially fertile grounds for counterfactual thinking.

Could Counterfactuals and Extreme Consequences   Felt harm is very important. It tells us that an event is important or significant to us. Consistent with the Would judgment, injury focuses a search for meaning that often brings about Could thinking. Because the relative automaticity of heuristic or peripheral processing about social stimuli can make people constantly aware of other persons' presumed capabilities for action, however, some Could judgments might actually precede Would judgments as foregone conclusions (e.g., stereotypes about disabled persons). Regardless of temporal order, moreover, Would and Could evaluations do not seem to be independent. When a Would counterfactual makes a set of consequences seem exceedingly harmful, people are more likely to seek some social actor to blame. This "would/could" link is probably most clear from research on the "just-world" phenomenon. Lerner and his colleagues (e.g., Lerner, 1980; Lerner & Miller, 1978) have shown that people are motivated to maintain their belief that the world is basically fair, even when events conspire against them. Thus, if something bad occurs to another person, observers seem to infer that the individual brought it upon himself or herself (i.e., the person could have acted otherwise and therefore deserves to suffer).

Worse still, this tendency to blame the victim becomes stronger as the consequence becomes more aversive. For example, in research reviewed by Carli (1991), participants were presented with vignettes describing interactions between a man and a women. The only difference between these two scenarios was the ending: In one vignette the woman was raped, and in the other vignette the man proposed marriage. In the case of the rape, the woman was more likely to be blamed. In the case of the marriage, this was less so.

Should Judgments: Counterfactual Thinking and Moral Standards

> *Moral qualities rule the world, but at short distances the senses are despotic.*
> —*Ralph Waldo Emerson*

This section on Should judgments begins with an example. Suppose that your performance appraisal ratings are not as positive as you had hoped, but you have to concede that you were treated well during the annual review session. Perhaps your boss listened carefully to your viewpoint, made accurate ratings, and treated you with the utmost sensitivity throughout. How do you feel about your supervisor and about the organization? If research by Taylor, Tracy, Renard, Harrison, and Carroll (1995) is any indication, you probably do not feel unfairly treated. In fact, you may well have a high opinion of your manager and remain firmly committed to your employer (for additional evidence see Cropanzano & Prehar, 1997; Folger & Lewis, 1993; Greenberg, 1986; Korsgaard & Roberson, 1995). Of course, no one is saying that all of that nice treatment makes you forget about the disappointing ratings. You would no doubt still have preferred a more advantageous consequence (Folger & Konovsky, 1989). The point is that some of the ill effects can be remedied by fair treatment.

In terms of fairness theory, this poses an important question. Consider Taylor et al.'s (1995) research participants who received negative ratings and knew what it *would* have been like to get positive ratings (e.g., based on the inflated appraisals that had occurred previously). In fact, the control group in the Taylor et al. field experiment was composed of employees randomly assigned to that previous appraisal system, and those employees *did* receive higher ratings than the ones in the procedurally fair condition. Likewise, it is probably not hard to imagine a supervisor's being more lenient (e.g., being reluctant to be the bearer of bad news by giving harsh ratings), and such leniency is also likely to seem feasible. Such situations provide "yes" answers to both the Could and the Would questions. But the example suggests that Would and Could do not seem to produce injustice by themselves; something else is needed.

The missing ingredient involves what *should* have transpired. The Should issue drives home the sense of injustice. *Should* things have been different than they actually were? By Should we mean the moral or ethical tenets that are violated when someone behaves unfairly. A justice judgment is one that has special moral gravity. It is about right and wrong, good and bad. Something is not unfair until it violates moral tenets by which people *should* act.

Should Judgments and Ideological Accounts

Evidence about the importance of Should judgments comes from work on ideological social accounts. Earlier we mentioned that social accounts explain why something aversive took place. We discussed how causal accounts short-circuit the Could judgment by pointing to mitigating circumstances. Another type of social account is the ideological account

(Bies, 1987). When decision makers provide an ideological account, they admit that something ill occurred (things Would have been better in other circumstances) but maintain that these ill effects are justified by the need to achieve a higher goal. For example, an affirmative action program might ordinarily offend the sensibilities of some White males. After hearing about the need to right historic wrongs, however, these same White males often become more tolerant (Bobocel & Farrell, 1996). There is considerable evidence attesting to the effectiveness of ideological accounts (e.g., Bies & Shapiro, 1988; Schaubroeck, May, & Brown, 1994).

Let us consider Would, Could, and Should judgments in view of these ideological accounts. The Would remains intact. Both the decision maker and the victim agree that something noxious took place. Could also remains in place, at least in principle. The potential harmdoer might openly admit that he or she Could have acted otherwise. In fact, the decision maker might well express pride in the chosen course of action! The ideological account exerts its effects on the Should judgment. In effect, the decision maker is saying "Darn right I *should* have done that! To have acted otherwise would have been immoral."

The Cognitive Operation of Should Counterfactuals

As with Would and Could judgments, a Should judgment involves using a standard. With Should, however, the standard is an ethical or a moral one. An action must be consistent with basic moral tenets if it is to avoid provoking a sense of injustice. Ethical standards likely make for efficient counterfactual production. In other words, it is probably relatively easy to think about the mental substitution of an ethical act for an unethical one—consistent with the *norm theory* prediction (Kahneman & Miller, 1986) that the abnormal and exceptional tend to evoke the normal and typical as counterfactual replacements for a transgressive reality. Of course, just because people can easily make Should judgments does not mean that they always do. People do not always use "right" and "wrong" as a lens for viewing the behavior of others.

Because justice perceptions appear to affect many aspects of work life, it is easy to assume that every event is evaluated with respect to fairness. Research in ethics suggests, however, that sometimes people do not make Should judgments. For example, Jones (1991) has argued that only some events are evaluated with respect to right or wrong. It is as if people have an "ethical tool kit"[3] used only on some occasions. In fact, one goal of training in business ethics is to encourage students to think in terms of morality.

The work of Jones (1991) raises the question of when Should counterfactuals will be more or less likely. Unfortunately, the paucity of research necessitates the mere speculation that highly salient events are more likely to demand a Should evaluation. Thus, we predict that when consequences are very negative, very novel, or occur in a context that calls attention to them (e.g., they stand in sharp relief to other aspects of the context, in figure/ground fashion), they are more often compared to moral standards. Clearly, this topic needs further inquiry.

ONE SOURCE OF SHOULD COUNTERFACTUALS: NORMATIVE PHILOSOPHY
As Greenberg and Bies (1992) have noted, organizational justice and business ethics are fertile grounds for integration. That comment shows the relevance of Should counterfactuals. According to Brady (1985; 1986; 1987) business people's orientations toward ethics can be divided into two broad categories: utilitarianism and formalism. Utilitarianism is teleological. For a utilitarian the "right" or ethical action is the one that produces the greatest good for the greatest number of people. Thus, utilitarianism is outcome oriented. Formalism is based on the act itself. Certain acts are said to be right or wrong for their own sake (for a review of this literature, see Cropanzano & Grandey, 1998). For this reason, formalism emphasizes personal behavior and choices. Formalism is more process focused (Schminke, Ambrose, & Noel, 1997), and it is also more focused on the deontological criteria of rights and duties emphasized by Immanuel Kant's ethical philosophy.

Using that distinction, Schminke et al. (1997) assessed the utilitarian and formalistic orientations of managers. As predicted, utilitarians tended to be more concerned with outcome distributions, whereas formalists were more concerned with process. These findings are significant for two reasons. First, they suggest that individuals sometimes use their ethical standards in making fairness judgments. Second, Schminke et al. further show that both outcomes and processes can be influenced by ethical inclinations. Sometimes people evaluate the morality of distributions, whereas at other times they evaluate the morality of processes.

A SECOND SOURCE OF SHOULD COUNTERFACTUALS: PSYCHOLOGICAL CONTRACTS Because we speak of ethical proclivities as a source of Should counterfactuals, the reader might infer that moral standards are carried around by each individual and are unlikely to change from situation to situation. No doubt that is partially true, but only partially. In fact, people often define right and wrong by agreement. That is, as we move to new organizations and work with different people, we form "psychological contracts" (Rousseau, 1995). These contracts are explicit or implicit agreements as to what constitutes appropriate treatment in a given setting.

We have already noted that psychological contracts change across times and places, suggesting that justice is relative. All people might share a common interest in fairness, but what they presume to be fair varies widely. One can envision two people perceiving the same situation in the same way but reaching very different conclusions regarding justice. This could occur either because the two people share different contracts with a decision maker or because they share the same contract but perceive it differently. Likewise, a single person can be treated in the same way at different times but have different fairness perceptions during the two events. This could occur because the person has different psychological contracts in each circumstance. To the extent that justice is defined in reference to a psychological contract, justice is *relative*. This is not, however, the same thing as maintaining that justice is *arbitrary*. To the extent that the terms are not determined in a random fashion, there could be a lawfulness to contracts and a resulting lawfulness to justice perceptions.

Although a thorough review of the psychological contract is well beyond the scope of this chapter, it is noteworthy that there are different types of contracts with different terms for the individual (Rousseau & Parks, 1993). According to Rousseau (1995, especially her Chapter 4) and Shore and Tetrick (1994), the various types of contracts can be conceptualized as resting on a continuum that ranges from transactional to relational. A transactional contract is based on economic exchange. Individuals in transactional contracts tend to have agreements that are narrow in scope and involve easily monetizable outcomes and "tit-for-tat" exchanges. A relational contract, on the other hand, has a wider scope and involves the whole person. In relational contracts the time period is more open ended and less bounded. The outcomes exchanged may be economic but also tend to be more social (e.g., confer a sense of status and dignity) and emotional (e.g., convey feelings of friendship and love). Each type of psychological contract affords a different answer to the Should question. Different things are important for fairness when one is in a transactional contract than when we are in a relational contract. This is perhaps most notable in the case of procedural justice. When one uses a fair process, one tends to treat someone with dignity and respect (Lind, 1995; Lind & Tyler, 1988); thus procedural concerns should be greatest when one has a relational contract with a group or an authority figure.

This idea has not been tested directly, although it is consistent with recent research. For example, Tyler and Degoey (1995) surveyed citizens about water conservation decisions. Citizens who identified strongly with their community also showed stronger procedural justice effects than did those who identified less strongly. This effect has been replicated several times (Brockner, Tyler, & Cooper-Schneider, 1992; Holbrook & Kulik, 1996; Huo, Smith, Tyler, & Lind, 1996). Unfortunately for the present idea, none of this work has examined relational contracts per se. Rather, these studies have examined the effect of group identity or commitment. One might assume that identity accompanies a relational contract, of course, but this needs to be independently verified and not simply assumed.

HOW NORMATIVE PHILOSOPHY AND CONTRACTS WORK TOGETHER There is a certain duality in justice perceptions. On the one hand, people often tend to worry about justice more when it is in the context of a close group. As we have just seen, people show more profound relational concerns when an injustice comes at the hands of a group with which they identity (Brockner et al., 1992; Holbrook & Kulik, 1996; Huo et al., 1996). For all that, justice does not stop at the door of a cohesive in-group. Even though the effect seems to be less profound, people can also be moved by the injustices experienced by strangers. To take several extreme examples, the Holocaust, Jim Crow segregation in the American Southeast, and the genocide committed by Pol Pot are crimes against all of us, not only against the particular groups that were directly effected. Moreover, various types of unjust events can incense many of us even when the context does not involve those types of victimized groups. We can feel outrage when a mother kills her children and sheds "crocodile tears" in seeking public help, through the news media, for "finding my babies' killers" (as happened in the South Carolina case of Susan Smith). We experience righteous indignation when a professional athlete spits in an umpire's face or chokes a coach. Indeed, "person as referee" (moral sanctioner) might join the panoply of *homo ludens, homo economicus,* and other characterizations of the human race.

Thus, there is a certain duality about human concerns—they can be most profound when things involve an important in-group but also often (though perhaps not often enough) present for the suffering of strangers. This duality is captured by the two sources of our Should counterfactuals. Psychological contracts bind us most closely when they are relational and, therefore, most closely to those with whom we have a relational contract. On the other hand, the normative philosophies of formalism and utilitarianism, among others, apply to people in general. They tell us how people *overall* should be treated. We human beings do not always live up to our ethical standards. Nevertheless, when we do, we can empathize with the injustice of people all over the world—even those whom we never meet.

A RESIDUAL TOPIC: THE NORMATIVE MIXTURE OF FAIRNESS MODELS   Finally, this discussion would be incomplete without briefly mentioning yet another fertile area for future research associated with counterfactual reasoning about morality. As indicated earlier, standard approaches tend to split the world into halves and give each a label such as "relational" and "transactional." This calls to mind Robert Benchley's remark that there are two kinds of people in the world—those who think there are two kinds of people in the world, and those who don't. Although we called for research on relational-contract situations, we do not want to be "two kinds of people" (or two kinds of situational contexts) theorists. Rather, we suspect that most situations involve a mixture of motives (cf. Folger et al., 1995). Fiske (1991) has amassed considerable evidence for four distinct mental models concerning human relations: *communal sharing, authority ranking, equality matching,* and *market pricing.*

Equity theory (Adams, 1965) taps only the last of those, whereas some aspects of the other three seem relevant to procedural and interactional justice. Fiske (1991), like Folger et al. (1995), has argued that most social situations invoke mixed models. Further integration of the organizational justice literature might usefully borrow from Fiske's work. Note, for example, the challenge to organizational justice conceptions framed by one of Fiske's illustrations. He pointed out that in workplace settings, fairness norms drawing from all four models are prevalent—even in the same setting.

Faculty members assessing the fairness of their salaries, for example, might draw upon equity conceptions about the market pricing exchange of labor for pay. "What is the return on investment in the marketplace for my labor? How has my employer priced that labor, relative to the price paid by the same employer for other employees' labor or the price paid by other employers?" When considering resources shared as "public goods" among colleagues (e.g., access to a building in which to work together as colleagues), however, the same faculty member would not argue for differentiating among colleagues on the basis of merit. In some sense, the norm might invoke the mental model of equality matching for social relations. The size of offices, the types of telephones put into each faculty office, and so on, might be identical across most and perhaps all the professors within a given academic unit. On the other hand, the authority ranking model could just as easily come into play. Sources of rank differentiation involve not only hierarchical chains of authority per se, of course, but also other grounds for status ranking (e.g., amenities possessed by teaching members of professional schools often seem more luxurious than those granted to their colleagues who teach liberal arts). Finally, the mental model for communal sharing suggests that efforts and resources be pooled for the good of the whole (oneness as a shared trait of the whole, suggesting an indivisible, common identity of colleagues or comrades— like kinship). Freely allowing professors to avail themselves of needed supplies (as idiosyncratically desired) might fit that model, as would devoting resources to ensuring access for those with handicaps.

Caveats and Conclusions Regarding Would, Could, and Should

In the first half of this chapter we have reviewed the basic components of Fairness Theory: Would, Could, and Should. For ease of presentation, we have simplified the process a bit. In particular, we have presented the components as if the sequence is linear and logical—Would to Could, Could to Should. However, we do not believe that this is the case. In fact, as Figure 1.1 shows, the causal arrows point in all directions. An individual can enter the model at any point and move in either direction to reach the other. For example, suppose an employee hears a manager make a minor, but racist, remark during a private phone conversation. Here the action is probably discretionary, and therefore the Could judgment is relevant. Likewise, it violates widely held moral tenets, so it also has implications for the Should judgment. Finally, although the conversation was in private, the employee might worry that this manager's espoused attitudes will spill over to affect other behaviors—actions that, in turn, might have both short- and long-term implications for the employee's well-being. In this incident, Would might follow last of all, perhaps because of the tendency for this Would judgment of future harm to be more hypothetical than Could and Should. Alternatively, the Would judgment might occur virtually at the same time as the other two if it related to the immediately harsh impact of the racist remark as personally offensive to the employee (like the interactional injustice of an insult). At any rate, an injustice can be perceived even if the employee's cognitions do not follow the same sequence as the order in which we presented the sections of this chapter.

There is another caveat worth noting. In all of our examples we have discussed only negative consequences. It is certainly plausible, however, that these cognitive steps are also taken for positive consequences. After all, people are held accountable when something goes right! In this case, though, we might speak more accurately of using these three cognitions to assign credit rather than blame. Nonetheless, we shall stick with the negative case here because that is the most common phenomenon examined in the organizational justice literature.

Integrating Fairness Theory with Other Models of Organizational Justice

Now that we have described the three basic elements of fairness theory, we describe how our approach may be reconciled with existing models of organizational justice.

Standard Thinking about Organizational Justice and the Benefits of Group Membership

Previous research suggests that fairness judgments have at least two targets or foci: The outcomes of a given decision (distributive justice) and the process by which a decision is made (procedural justice). Both types of fairness judgments affect people's feelings and behavior in work settings. It is not readily clear, however, why this should be the case. Why does justice matter at all? This question is not merely rhetorical. It would seem simpler for people to ascertain the *favorability* of their economic outcomes selfishly and not to worry at all about fairness. And there would seem to be no obviously "rational" reason to care about process (in the sense that economists sometimes use the term *rational*).

This question is central to organizational justice, so considerable effort has addressed it (e.g., see Lind, Chapter 2). Justice often deals with how people are treated by authorities and by members of social groups. Because social relations are important to human beings, so, too, is justice. One way to see why justice matters, therefore, is to examine what people get when they affiliate with others. Based on previous research, Cropanzano and Schminke (in press) have argued that groups and interpersonal relationships supply people with two families of benefits. The first family is economic. This family includes things such as money and consumer goods. The second family contains socioemotional benefits. These include, among other things, treatment by others that conveys respect for one's dignity and intrinsic worth. Socioemotional benefits are often termed *symbolic* because their value is based on what they stand for. Being treated with interpersonal sensitivity, for example, may offer little material advantage. However, kindness does convey that a person has dignity. Justice is important because it signals the present or future attainment of a material or socioemotional benefit. Injustice signals the absence of such valued benefits.

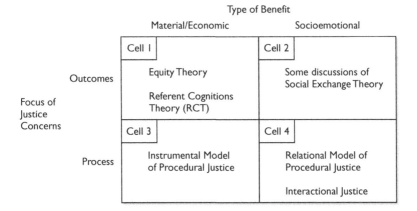

Figure 1.3. The Relationship of Outcomes and Processes to Two
Types of Benefits.

The matter becomes more complicated when one realizes that the same
consequence may have both a material and a socioemotional (or symbolic)
value. For example, money is certainly important for purchasing food and
shelter. Thus, it serves as a material benefit. But money also allows people
to improve their status (e.g., through the purchase of a European luxury
car). For this reason money has both economic and symbolic value. Likewise, voice in decision making signals that one is respected (a socioemotional benefit) and also allows one the opportunity to influence the decision to one's personal advantage (i.e., it offers potential for providing
material benefits).

As we have noted, justice researchers generally think in terms of decision processes and/or decision outcomes. When considering the two types
of group benefits at the same time as process and outcomes, the result can
be diagrammed as a 2 × 2 matrix. This matrix, displayed in Figure 1.3,
helps make two important points. First, either the process or the outcome
can convey material or socioemotional benefits. That point has not always
been emphasized in the organizational justice literature. Second, different
theories of justice tend to fall into one "box" or the other. By that we
mean only that they tend to emphasize primarily either outcome or
process along with either material or socioemotional goods.

CELL 1: USING OUTCOMES TO CONVEY MATERIAL BENEFITS In the
first cell we have placed Adams's (1965; Adams & Freedman, 1976) classic formulation of equity theory. According to equity theory, people for-
mulate ratios of inputs to outcomes. They then compare their ratio to the

ratio for a referent other. If these ratios are approximately equal, then no injustice is experienced. If these ratios do not match, then individuals experience some aversive emotional state. The nature of the emotion varies depending on whether the person is underrewarded or overrewarded relative to the referent other. In the case of underreward, the emotions include anger and resentment. In the case of overreward, feelings such as guilt are more typical. These negative emotions act as an impetus to resolve the inequity.

Equity theory, therefore, is oriented around the outcomes that people receive and says nothing about the processes used to assign those outcomes (other than perhaps implying that outcome-determining deliberations should take relevant inputs into acount and should assess those inputs accurately). As such, it does not specify the determinants of felt injustice fully (see Cropanzano & Folger, 1989; Folger, 1986). Moreover, most studies of equity theory have tended to use pay, usually thought of as a material good, as a determinant of inequity. For this reason, we have placed equity theory in Cell 1.

Note, however, that our placement is not without caveats. As we have already said, pay can be seen as a socioemotional benefit as well as a material one. Additionally, not all tests of equity theory have used the same operationalization. For instance, in one interesting study Greenberg (1988) replicated the over-/underreward effects by manipulating the assignment of office space. Office space is monetizable and concrete. Thus it can be partially seen as a material benefit. On the other hand, it also conveys status and worth. Therefore it is also a socioemotional good. For that matter, some formulations of equity theory (e.g., Walster, Walster, & Berscheid, 1978) have expanded its coverage into the socioemotional domain.

Another theory that could be characterized as fitting into Cell 1 is Folger's (1987) referent cognitions theory (RCT). RCT is a precursor to fairness theory. According to RCT, individuals evaluate their outcomes by comparing them to referent outcomes. A referent outcome is some standard of comparison. The outcomes obtained by some comparison other, for example, could serve as a referent. This is one example of the same type of Would judgment that we have included in fairness theory. In tests of RCT, these outcomes have tended to be material/economic and not socioemotional. When people perceive that their outcomes are poorer than those of their referent, they often wonder whether this state of affairs is as it *should* be. The Should judgment is central to RCT, as it carries the ethical weight that drives the model (foreshadowing the fairness theory emphasis on moral accountability). When things are as they Should be, even if the outcome is unfavorable, people will not feel injustice. When a negative Should judgment is coupled with a disadvantageous outcome, then injustice is experienced. Generally speaking, most of the available evidence supports RCT (e.g., Brockner & Wiesenfeld, 1996; Cropanzano & Folger, 1989; Folger, Rosenfield, Rheaume, & Martin, 1983; Folger et al. 1983; Folger & Martin, 1986).

CELL 2: USING OUTCOMES TO CONVEY SOCIOEMOTIONAL BENEFITS
Social exchange theory appears in Cell 2, although that designation applies more properly to only certain versions of the theory. In particular, social exchange theorists have discussed the allocation of both material and socioemotional goods (Foa & Foa, 1974). Those discussions that emphasize socioemotional benefits, of course, would fit most closely in Cell 2. A good example of this kind of research is provided by Martin and Harder (1994), who had research participants allocate both material goods (e.g., pay) and socioemotional goods (e.g., invitations to a picnic). These researchers found that it was generally seen as fairer to allocate material goods via an equity rule and socioemotional goods via an equality rule. Chen (1995) found that in China managers tended to allocate both types of benefits via equity.

CELL 3: USING PROCEDURES TO CONVEY MATERIAL BENEFITS   According-ing to research on procedural justice, processes can be used as the means for access to material benefits. This has been termed the *instrumental model.* Proponents of the instrumental model maintain that one reason people prefer fair procedures is that in the long run, fair procedures help to ensure the most favorable outcomes (Thibaut & Walker, 1975). For example, having voice improves the odds of influencing a decision in one's own favor. Considerable research supports the instrumental model (Cropanzano & Greenberg, 1997). Nevertheless, as Lind (1995), Lind and Tyler (1988), and Tyler and Lind (1992) have noted, the instrumental model is also limited. In particular, it does not discuss the socioemotional benefits that can be obtained through fair processes. Perhaps it would be best to say that the instrumental model is correct insofar as it goes but that it does not go far enough.

CELL 4: USING PROCEDURES TO CONVEY SOCIOEMOTIONAL BENEFITS
We have situated the relational model (e.g., Lind, 1995; Tyler & Lind, 1992) in Cell 4. According to this model, people are concerned with their status and dignity in social groups. Tyler and Lind (1992) refer to these as "dignity concerns." Certain behaviors are fair because they convey respect

to individuals and affirm the status of membership in a valued group. Fair processes boost one's self-esteem and afford one a measure of social acceptance. People especially like decision makers who are trustworthy, unbiased, and affirming of people's status as full-fledged group members (see Huo & Tyler, Chapter 7; Lind, 1995). The relational model is clearly about the socioemotional benefits from fair procedures.

Bies's work on interactional justice emphasized relational concern (e.g., see this volume), so it also is in Cell 4. Bies noted that people care about the interpersonal treatment they receive. When individuals are presented with explanatory social accounts (Bies, 1987; Bies et al., 1988; Bies & Sitkin, 1992) and are treated with interpersonal sensitivity (Bies & Moag, 1986), such behavior signals that their dignity and intrinsic worth have been honored.

SUMMARY   As Figure 1.3 illustrates, several important theories of organizational justice can be arrayed in a 2 × 2 matrix. We do not want to imply by this characterization, however, that all four cells in the matrix have received equal amounts of attention. Generally speaking, recent research in organizational justice has tended to emphasize Cell 1 (distribution and material benefits) and Cell 4 (process and socioemotional benefits). Some attention has been paid to Cell 3, but very little recent organizational justice research exists for Cell 2. If only Cells 1 and 4 are considered, then the foci of justice would be perfectly correlated with the type of benefit. In other words, distributive justice would be based on the fairness of the *material* goods, whereas procedural justice would be based on the fairness of the *socioemotional* goods. Within the organizational justice literature, we would argue that this type of confounded comparison has dominated discussions about distributive and procedural justice.

Figure 1.3 also illustrates another limitation of the organizational justice literature. This is the one with which we opened this chapter: *There is no explicit consideration of accountability.* As we noted earlier, the one possible exception to this can be found in Bies's (1987; Chapter 3; Bies & Moag, 1986) model of interactional justice. Regardless, the matrix typology does not in itself provide any details about the steps taken to judge accountability.

Absent a theory of accountability, the matrix has no role for ethics or moral intentions. It ignores sources of justice standards, which makes it hard to link the organizational justice literature with psychological contracts and business ethics. Additionally, the standard model displayed in Figure 1.3 has no mechanism for applying justice beyond in-group boundaries, addressing the needs of strangers. By omitting, or at least deemphasizing, this important mechanism, research and theory risk fostering an ethnocentric perspective on organizational justice and thereby institutionalizing forms of in-group bias. But if a sense of fairness were always limited to one's in-group, then "being fair" would be consistent with such excesses of nationalism, for example, as ethnic cleansing. Surely fairness must mean more. Surely there must be a role for what Folger (1998) has called fairness as a moral virtue.

There is another problem here as well. By filling four cells with five different theories, we may risk masking some underlying similarities in the way justice judgments are made. For example, according to the fairness theory (the integrative model we propose in this chapter), a variety of different judgments are made using the same basic mechanism—counterfactual scenarios. Similarities and common building blocks are not readily apparent when different theories address different topics that all exist within the same overall domain (viz., justice).

Fairness Theory and the Two Types of Benefits

Fairness theory attempts to address the aforementioned limitations by articulating a general model by which justice decisions are made. As we have emphasized, fairness is based on accountability. Accountability, in turn, is based on three judgments—Would, Could, and Should. When we consider these three judgments in conjunction with the two types of benefits (material and socioemotional), we get the 2 × 3 matrix displayed in Figure 1.4. As we have described throughout this chapter, our new model emphasizes the central role of accountability. It thereby links the justice literature to work on ethics and psychological contracts, and it highlights the commonalties among the three judgments (e.g., the use of counterfactuals). In doing so, the fairness theory provides a broader context within which we can re-organize all of the previously mentioned theories.

Unfortunately, this reorganization is somewhat more controversial than the model presented in Figure 1.3. This is because previous theories, especially those concerned with procedural justice, often imply the presence of accountability without actually specifying its role or addressing related issues in explicit detail. Taking a closer look at the Would row in Figure 1.4, we can see that the pure distributive justice theories fit under material benefits (for equity) and socioemotional benefits (for social exchange theory). Likewise, the instrumental model of procedural justice also fits nicely under the Would heading. The instrumental model emphasizes what an outcome Would be like if obtained under a "fair" process as opposed to an "unfair" process. Thus, social exchange theory, equity theory, and the

Type of Benefit

	Material/Economic	Socioemotional
	Cell 1	**Cell 2**
"Would"	Equity Theory Instrumental Model of Procedural Justice Referent Cognitions Theory (RCT)	Some discussions of Social Exchange Theory Relational Model of Procedural Justice Interactional Justice (Interpersonal Sensitivity)
	Cell 3	**Cell 4**
"Could"	Instrumental Model of Procedural Justice Interactional Justice (Causal Accounts)	Relational Model of Procedural Justice Interactional Justice (Causal Accounts)
	Cell 5	**Cell 6**
"Should"	Referent Cognitions Theory (RCT) Interactional Justice (Ideological Accounts)	Relational Model of Procedural Justice Interactional Justice (Ideological Accounts)

Figure 1.4. The Relationship of the Three Accountability Judgments
to Two Types of Benefits.

instrumental model tend to focus on the outcomes a person would receive
if treated like some comparison other (e.g., had she possessed a different
exchange partner, or had there been a different process). Referent cognitions theory requires two cells, but it can also be classified in a straightforward manner. Research on RCT fits easily into Cell 1 (what Would have
happened) and Cell 5 (what Should have happened). This illustrates that
the fairness theory is an expansion and a refinement of the earlier referent
cognitions framework. The relational model and interactional justice are
more difficult to classify unambiguously and without the categorization's
being subject to controversy about possible alternative interpretations.

The relational model of procedural justice strongly emphasizes such
socioemotional benefits as personal identity, dignity, self-esteem, status
recognition, and inclusion within a valued group. Because such benefits
derive from fair procedures, some aspects of the relational model fit well
in Cell 2 (Would socioemotional). However, the relational model is too
rich for a single cell. Although missing an explicit role for accountability,

the relational model strongly implies that accountability—as the decision maker's intent—is important. For example, Tyler (1984) and Shapiro (1993) have written about the importance of consideration. That is, fairness requires that a decision maker must at least try to be fair (see also Lind & Tyler, 1988). More to the point, Lind (Chapter 2; Van den Bos et al., in press) argues that individuals seek to infer an authority figure's intentions through the use of a "fairness heuristic." In this respect, the relational model would seem to have quite a bit in common with the fairness theory. Because the relational model is more focused on intentions and less on feasibility, we have placed this theory in Cell 6 (Should socioemotional). When our placement of the relational model (Cells 2 and 6) is considered with our placement of the instrumental model (Cell 1), we can see why procedural factors are so important to workers. Processes are used to allocate both material and socioemotional benefits. As if that were not enough, they also convey a sense of ethical treatment and moral justice. Further, it should be emphasized that this analysis is conservative. Some researchers consider interactional justice an aspect of process (e.g., Tyler & Bies, 1990). If this were the case, then procedural justice considerations would fit into every single cell in Figure 1.4; for that reason, we have included the relational aspects of procedural justice in Cell 4.

As was the case with the relational model, interactional justice theory is problematic for our matrix because of its breadth. For example, social accounts vary depending upon the type of account. As mentioned earlier, causal accounts are claims about a lack of control over outcomes (e.g., excuses based on mitigating circumstances as conditions beyond personal control). These are directed toward Could judgments of feasibility and fit into Cells 3 and 4. On the other hand, ideological accounts provide justification by refering to the Should of a greater good, which puts them in Cells 5 and 6. Finally, the interpersonal sensitivity aspect of interactional justice is clearly socioemotional (i.e., concerned with dignity more than with economic benefits). It is also Would oriented, however, because insensitive behavior is allocated as a distributive good (see Cropanzano & Ambrose, Chapter 4; Greenberg, 1993). To perceive treatment as being insensitive implies a contrast with what it would be like to enjoy sensitive treatment instead (a referent state at least implicit, if not explicitly pondered).

Thus, much of the organizational justice literature can be organized into a 2 × 3 matrix by considering the three judgments of the fairness theory along with two types of benefits. The fairness theory can be seen as a broad framework that builds upon but does not contradict previous research. In addition, the fairness theory does more than supply a new taxonomy; it also provides the means for reinterpreting previous findings. In the next section we demonstrate one aspect of reinterpretation by taking another look at the Outcome × Process interaction.

Fairness Theory and the Outcome × Process Interaction

Previous research has identified an interaction between process and outcomes (for reviews see Brockner & Wiesenfeld, 1996; Cropanzano & Folger, 1991; Cropanzano & Greenberg, 1997; Folger, 1987, 1993). This work suggests that the sense of injustice and accompanying emotions such as resentment are likely to be strongest when outcomes are unfavorable (or unfair—there is some operational and conceptual ambiguity here) and when the process is unfair. Put differently, the degree of process unfairness is most closely tied to the negativity of reactions when the outcome is unfavorable, and the degree of outcome unfavorability is most closely tied to the negativity of reactions when the process is unfair. In an important review, Brockner and Wiesenfeld (1996) suggested various theoretical interpretations of this phenomenon, including those that expanded beyond the original prediction of that interaction by RCT (e.g., Folger, 1987). We suggest yet another type of explanation (although ours also represents an expansion built upon RCT as the original base from which predictions of this interaction have been derived).

Considering Figure 1.4 and omitting the Would row for the moment, it becomes clear that procedural justice theories can be placed in Cells 3 (causal social accounts), 4 (causal social accounts and the relational model), 5 (ideological social accounts), and 6 (ideological social accounts and the relational model).[4] Given that categorization, then process is at least concerned with Could and Should. (We argue that it is also concerned with Would, but we postpone that discussion momentarily.) Because previous work has not tended to separate Could and Should judgments, let us collapse them together for convenience and call them Could/Should. We are now in a position to reinterpret the Outcome × Process interaction. In research on this interaction, outcomes tend to be operationalized as "material outcomes." This fits neatly into the Would row, especially Cell 1. In fairness theory terms, the Outcome × Process interaction is a Would (negativity) by Could/Should (accountability) interaction. As such, that interaction is in accordance with the perspective taken here.

Fairness Theory and the Two-Factor Model: The Case of Embedded Main Effects

Note that procedural justice is not subordinate to outcome favorability or fairness. That is to say, procedures are more than simply a moderator of reactions to outcomes. In fact, procedural justice often exerts main effects as well. Generally speaking, process fairness affects employee attitudes toward the organization and toward authority figures. Outcome fairness tends to influence reactions toward the particular outcome in question (Lind & Tyler, 1988). Sweeney and McFarlin (1993) have dubbed this the "two-factor" model.

At first glance the two-factor model might appear inconsistent with the fairness theory. After all, the fairness theory predicts an interaction among Would, Could, and Should (or Would and Could/Should) as crucial judgments. A close look at Figure 1.4, however, suggests why no inconsistency exists. Examining the instrumental model, interpersonal sensitivity, the relational model, and interactional justice shows that measures of procedure can actually pull together all three types of judgments. Embedded in process fairness may be an evaluation of one's future material outcomes (the instrumental model), one's current dignity (the relational model and interpersonal sensitivity), Could (interactional justice as causal accounts), and Should (moral dictates somewhat implied by interactional justice and the relational model).

Thus, returning to a metaphor we used earlier, a summary measure of procedural justice is "one step forward" from the three accountability judgments. By the time the subject completes questionnaire items assessing procedural justice, he or she might have already made the Would, Could, and Should evaluations as a function of deciding on the response to give. When that occurs, the interaction exists, but it is embedded in the measure.

Broader Implications of Fairness Theory

Fairness theory radically alters the distinction between outcome and process in two ways. First, it argues for similarity where the field of organizational justice has emphasized difference. Traditional views have separated distributive, procedural, and interactional justice, whereas the fairness theory emphasizes counterfactual similarities that all three have in common (see also Cropanzano & Ambrose, Chapter 4; Folger & Skarlicki, 2001). Counterfactual contrast is the underlying psychological mechanism for all three types of justice perceptions. The same counterfactual logic of Would, Could, and Should applies whether the injustice is distributive, procedural, or interactional. This radical reorientation is essential, we believe, to achieving a truly unified perspective on (in)justice. In contrast, the field is currently littered with isolated theories applied to separate domains (e.g., an inequity theory of distributive justice, the relational model of procedural justice, and impression-management analyses of social accounts applied to interactional justice).

A second reorientation offers a new differentiation while still avoiding the previous fragmentation tendencies. Whereas the first reorientation stresses counterfactual commonality across Would, Could, and Should, this second aspect differentiates Would on the one hand from Could and Should on the other. Unlike outcome versus process, differentiating Would from Could and Should still fosters integrative synthesis because the same counterfactual logic still applies across all three (or the two sets, when treated as Would vs. Could/Should).

Distinguishing Would from Could/Should also maintains contact with the familiar distinction between outcome-as-ends (reinterpreted in terms of Would) and process-as-means (reinterpreted in terms of Could/Should). Theory and research using the process-outcome distinction, however, reified the terms by identifying each with a *separate type* of event. In contrast, the fairness theory stipulates that *any* given event can be analyzed *both* in terms of Would (adversity for Person A) *and also* in terms of Could/Should (Person B's responsibility for that adversity). Would relates loosely to qualities of events formerly classified as distributive. The Could/Should implications correspond loosely to qualities of events formerly classified either as procedural or as procedural and interactional. Note, however, that no one-to-one correspondence exists either for Could with Procedural and Should with Interactional or for Could with Interactional and Should with Procedural. *Unlike the fairness theory, the traditional orientation refers to separate events rather than to separable aspects of the same event.*

The radical reorientations implied by the fairness theory require further elaboration. We want to show that fairness theory can refer to the same events as the traditional perspective but put those events in a new light. In the following section, we illustrate that point by examining the same sequence of events from both perspectives. Our example, drawn from Bies and Moag (1986; cf. Gilliland, 1996), involves a sequence of events occurring when an academic author receives reviews from a journal editor. First we refer to the Bies and Moag description, which labels three segments of the sequence by using the traditional distinctions among procedural, interactional, and distributive justice. Then we consider the same three stages of events a second time, using the fairness-theory lens of a Would and Could/Should analysis to yield a different perspective. By comparing the fairness theory with the traditional perspective, we illustrate not only their similarities but also their differences.

Journal Reviewing as Event-Sequence Segments Labeled with Traditional Justice Terms

Bies and Moag (1986) introduced the concept of interactional justice by referring to it as one of three distinct stages or segments within an ongoing event sequence: "In taking this perspective, we view an allocation decision as a *sequence of events* in which a *procedure* generates a process of *interaction* and decision making through which an *outcome* is allocated to someone" (p. 45, italics in original). Although subsequent analyses have enriched and modified the interactional justice concept (e.g., Bies, 1987; this volume), the original description still fits with common usage often seen in the literature. Also, common practice also still frequently refers to procedural, interactional, and distributive justice in terms of different *types* of events, and so an illustration that identifies different types of events as stages in a sequence has usefulness as an example of what we call the traditional model.

Bies and Moag (1986) diagrammed PROCEDURE → INTERACTION → OUTCOME, then commented as follows: "Each part of the sequence is subject to fairness considerations and thus, every aspect of an organizational decision (procedure, interaction, outcome) may create a potential justice episode" (p. 46). Note, therefore, that separate fairness judgments might be made regarding each part of the sequence, although an extreme judgment about any one segment might color someone's overall reaction to the entire sequence. Insulting interpersonal treatment, as the fairness judgment about the interactional-justice segment, might create such an effect (cf. Bies, Chapter 3; Folger & Cropanzano, 1998; Gilliland, 1996).

Bies and Moag (1986) argued that such effects show the importance of distinguishing interactional justice from distributive and procedural justice. As they put it, considering interactional justice "might . . . explain why people feel unfairly treated even though they would characterize the decision making procedures and the outcome to be fair" (p. 46). Moreover,

> The journal review process provides a relevant setting. . . . For example, we might feel that multiple expert reviewers and a blind review are fair procedures. Similarly, we may view the recommendation for a minor or even a major revision to be a fair outcome, given the problems inherent in research and writing. Yet, we may feel unfairly treated because a reviewer engaged in personalized attacks of our ideas or failed to provide an adequate justification for the suggested revision. (Bies & Moag, 1986, p. 46)

In the next section we use the same example (in slightly modified form) to show how fairness theory appraisals—Would as an assessment of a person's adversity and Could/Should as an assessment of another social agent's role (causal and moral) with respect to that adversity—apply to events usually labeled with the traditional justice terms.

Journal Review Redux: Analyzing Each Segment with All Three Fairness-Theory Appraisals

We illustrate the two radical reorientations of fairness theory by contrasting its analysis with the preceding depiction of the journal-reviewing situation. The traditional analysis paired a Segment 1 and a Segment 2 with two aspects of process—procedural and interactional justice, respectively. Segment 3, as the final outcome, goes with distributive justice. In contrast, the fairness theory analyzes each of the three segments by using the counterfactual logic of Would and also analyzes each segment by using the counterfactual logic of Could/Should.

PROCEDURAL ASPECTS AS METHODS FOR THE STAGE OF DELIBERATIVE REVIEW ON A MANUSCRIPT   Recall what Bies and Moag (1986) said about Segment-1 procedural justice: "[W]e might feel that multiple expert reviewers and a blind review are fair procedures" (p. 46). An author, knowing that a manuscript review used flawed methods (e.g., inherently inconsistent; prone to inaccuracy when applied), has its counterfactual opposite as a possible frame of reference: What *would* it be like to know that unflawed (e.g., consistent, accurate) methods were used?

Bies and Moag (1986) referred to multiple expert reviewers as a fair procedure. For simplicity, consider merely the number of reviewers as one methodological dimension of review procedures. Suppose, for example, Person A is an author who gets an editorial judgment based on three reviews enclosed with the editor's own comments. The author might not give it a second thought if that seemed routine. Or perhaps the editor also enclosed a copy of the journal's editorial statement, and the author reads that obtaining three reviewers is standard operating procedure. Any of a variety of such conditions might give the *actual* number of reviewers legitimacy, thereby removing the potential that some *counterfactual* number comes to mind. When Bies and Moag wrote that "we might feel that" some number of "multiple . . . reviewers" is one example of "fair procedures" (1986, p. 46), therefore, they implicitly relied on the reader's own actual/counterfactual appraisal of Would. What does it feel like to receive copies of three outside reviews? What would it feel like to receive only one, or even none, instead? Although we have not emphasized this point until now, obviously an unfair counterfactual can make the actual event seem fair, in the same manner that a fair counterfactual can make the actual event seem unfair. Alternatively, legitimacy tends to accompany routine events, which sometimes might not evoke any counterfactual at all.

Now we consider another aspect of fairness theory, namely, Could appraisals. *Could* the editor have used a different number of reviewers? Again, any of a variety of circumstances might elicit a counterfactual alternative. Note, however, a contrast with the Would appraisal just described: Would appraisals refer to states-of-being experienced by Person A (e.g., author), whereas Could appraisals refer to actions taken by a "Person B" (e.g., the editor; some institutional source as a "juristic person").

The counterfactual of a Could appraisal refers to something that Person B—the relevant social agent who might conceivably have had some willful impact on Person A's adversity—could have done but did not. In the case of the review, for example, the author (Person A) must at least implicitly infer the extent to which it was possible for the editor (Person B) to obtain some other number of reviewers. The author might think that the use of only two reviews would tend to jeopardize accuracy but that it is virtually impossible to get many more than three on a consistent basis. Knowing that three were used, this author again might simply not even stop to think about whether the editor could have obtained more. If the author did make the effort to simulate some mental counterfactuals about Could (for whatever reason), he or she might readily conclude that editors normally have a limited ability to get larger numbers of reviewers per manuscript and that this ability diminishes rapidly past the number three.

Finally, we turn to Should appraisals. *Should* the editor have obtained more than three reviewers? Answering this type of question about the morality of someone else's actions requires ethical criteria for judging behavior in an interpersonal transaction. For this part of the review sequence as Segment 1, such criteria address procedural aspects of the transaction (e.g., methods on which the editor relies to make informed deliberations about a manuscript's acceptability for publication). We noted in first discussing Should appraisals that they can involve utilitarian or formalistic criteria. The author who appraises the editor's actions using utilitarian criteria might, for example, focus on the likely accuracy of using various numbers of reviewers. The author who uses a criterion based on formalism might instead consider an act that displays consistency or a lack of bias as right for its own sake and an act that displays inconsistency or bias as wrong in and of itself. The author as a utilitarian moralist, therefore, might consider the editor's actions legitimate if appropriately driven by concerns for accuracy (i.e., not think that the editor should have tried harder to get more reviewers but instead think that making sure to get at least two was the legitimate degree of effort). The author as a formalist might, on the other hand, think that the editor's Should requirements were met by using three reviewers simply because such an action was consistent with stated editorial policy.

DISTRIBUTIVE ASPECTS AS RESULTS AT THE ENDING STAGE OF REVIEW TRANSACTIONS A manuscript review can go through multiple cycles, each a separate transaction. For now we skip the intermediate aspect of such transactions, to which Bies and Moag (1986) referred in illustrating interactional justice. Instead we focus on one such transaction's ending, when the author receives comments about a manuscript and a preliminary evaluation from the editor. We use the Bies and Moag example of a preliminary evaluation that the manuscript cannot yet be accepted but must instead first go through at least one revision.

To simplify, we refer only to a requirement for a statistical reanalysis as the author's outcome. The author in this instance had originally analyzed the data a different way from the one now required by the editor. Those two ways stand in opposition to one another as a natural pairing of actual and counterfactual events. Assume the editor has said that the manuscript is provisionally accepted, subject only to reporting the results of the reanalysis in addition to the results already reported (with acceptance guaranteed even if the analyses produce differing results). In actuality, then, the accepted manuscript will have the additional results reported (assuming that the author wants the manuscript accepted and therefore complies with the editor's demand). The author knows that a certain amount of effort is actually required to do the reanalysis (and write about it), which that author can now compare with the counterfactual of having had the manuscript accepted without that effort's being required.

To make this example distributively fair, as in the Bies and Moag example, assume that this actual/counterfactual contrast is not aversive. Many authors, for example, expect never to have the very first version of a manuscript accepted as is. (Yes, such a result would feel great! On the other hand, being guaranteed an acceptance for doing a reanalysis might easily seem not so very much worse—hence, perfectly within the range of reasonable and fair outcomes.)

Moreover, any concerns might evaporate after Could or Should considerations. Perhaps one reviewer was a statistical expert who the publications board has insisted must have the final say on certain types of issues.

The editor essentially had no choice but to require the reanalysis that this consulting reviewer demanded. Moreover, suppose the author decides that the statistical expert was correct. If so, the editor was constrained not only on the could-not-do-otherwise grounds of policy but also on the should-not-do-otherwise grounds of correctness.

INTERACTIONAL JUSTICE ASPECTS AS COMMUNICATIONS ACCOMPA-NYING A TRANSACTION   We have followed the Bies and Moag (1986) example by describing the separate Would, Could, and Should appraisals consistent with their having referred to a distributively and procedurally fair review. Recall, however, the further comment included in that example: "Yet, we may feel unfairly treated because a reviewer engaged in personalized attacks of our ideas or failed to provide an adequate justification for the suggested revision" (1986, p. 46). As a communication accompanying the review transaction, examples of interpersonal treatment such as a personalized attack illustrate violations of interactional justice.

Suppose, for instance, the editor not only demanded a statistical reanalysis but also commented derisively about the author's failure to have performed it initially. Imagine comments such as "I'm not sure how even some idiot graduate student could have been so stupid as to analyze the data the way you did" or "you stupid fool" sprinkled throughout the letter. How would it feel to be the recipient of such comments? By comparison, how *would* it feel not to be subjected to them? Obviously such Would appraisals can make instances of interactional injustice seem aversive to the author as Person A.

How about the editor's behavior? *Could* he or she have acted otherwise? In cases of demeaning and insultingly rude comments such as the examples given, it certainly seems easy to imagine how anyone could have thought of a more polite way to point out someone else's mistakes. *Should* that have been the case? Again, social norms—such as those pertaining to polite conduct—often come readily to mind. Once brought to mind, social norms of conduct thereby provide the Should counterfactuals that condemn the editor as "out of line."

Attributional Ambiguity: Are Could/Should Appraisals Always Equally Easy to Make?

We like the Bies and Moag (1986) example because it also provides a way to discuss how the fairness theory distinguishes among distributive, procedural, and interactional justice in terms of attributional ambiguity. We present only a brief discussion; the interested reader should consult Folger and Cropanzano (1998) for a prior description of essentially the same point. Because we have addressed the issue elsewhere and must use limited space here, we link our discussion to the editorial review example of Bies and Moag (1986) for convenience.

In that example, the interactional injustice left a bad taste in the author's mouth despite distributive and procedural justice. We have speculated (Folger & Cropanzano, 1998) that such occurrences might be quite common, indicating why violations of interactional justice can be especially noteworthy in terms of appraisals about Could and Should. We speculated about an underlying rank-order among the three forms of justice on an ambiguity continuum: the ease or readiness of making clear-cut judgments about accountability for injustice. The rank-order of ambiguity runs from distributive justice as the most difficult judgment about which to have conclusive accountability evidence readily at hand (under most normal circumstances), followed by procedural justice as a midpoint and then interactional justice as the easiest judgment (ordinarily least ambiguous). Van den Bos, Lind, Vermunt, & Wilke (1997) expressed— independently of our speculations—somewhat related ideas about ambiguity differences between distributive and procedural justice. As was the case when we addressed the broader idea of a continuum involving all three types of (in)justice (Folger & Cropanzano, 1998), the following section not only adds interactional justice to the mix but also grounds it in a fairness theory approach regarding the attributional ambiguity of accountability judgments.

DOES ATTRIBUTIONAL AMBIGUITY VARY ALONG DISTRIBUTIVE-PROCEDURAL-INTERACTIONAL LINES? The study of organizational justice has raised questions about when distributive justice matters and when procedural and/or interactional justice might matter more. The fairness theory raises a parallel question regarding attributions of intention and responsibility: Does the extent to which someone blames another person for adversity differ depending on whether the issues involve distributive, procedural, or interactional injustice? The fairness theory answers "yes" about differences with regard to inferring intent. Reading harmful intent into a maldistribution of goods, for example, is often problematic (cf. Van den Bos et al., 1997) because far too many forces ordinarily combine to influence the distribution of goods. Income inequalities within nations certainly stem at least in part from government taxation policies, for example, but a great many other influences combine indiscriminately under such umbrella-like headings as "the workings of the market." When "market forces" yield distributive injustice, who is most directly to blame? Because of the difficulty in placing the blame squarely (and exclusively) on the shoulders of any given social agent (e.g., the representatives of government or of a company's management), the connection between the extent of the adversity and the direct source of the adversity seems muddled. Given that attributions of intentional harm or malfeasance seem problematic, variations in the extent of adversity are less likely to be associated directly with levels of hostility and resentment (about unfair treatment) directed toward any given party as social agent.

The situation is just the opposite when it comes to insult, and instances of procedural injustice represent something of a midpoint case between the extreme poles of distributive and interactional injustice. Consider insulting interpersonal insensitivity as the paradigmatic violation of interactional injustice. Who's to blame when someone calls you "a name" or humiliates you in front of peers? Often the possibilities for finger pointing easily resolve in a single direction: The person who made the insulting remark is obviously the one and only source of the derogatory impact. Moreover, truly demeaning insults do not often occur on a coincidental or accidental basis. The Could inference of intentional control over discretionary conduct therefore seems clear. Moreover, the act itself tends not to qualify as a true insult unless it involves the violation of Should as well: To treat another person in such a manner is exactly the essence of Should prescriptions, which refer to the legitimacy of conduct.

Procedures seem to occupy a middle-ground position when it comes to inferences of intent. On the one hand, someone "in charge" usually has relatively clear responsibility for adopting whatever design features govern a given set of deliberations. On the other hand, several types of considerations might mitigate such a person's accountability. Sometimes, for example, procedural methods and regulations derive as policies made by a committee rather than a single person. Sometimes they have an unknown past; they remain in effect by tradition, but perhaps no one knows how those procedural traditions got started (i.e., where the accountability lies). Also, a procedure can have both instrumental and relational impact (Tyler & Lind, 1992). In instrumental terms, it is more like distributive justice—because judging procedures in instrumental terms involves primarily utilitarian (or "consequentialist") criteria of fairness. In relational terms, it is more like interactional justice—because judging procedures in relational terms involves primarily deontological (rights-and-duties-oriented) criteria of fairness. For that reason as well, therefore, procedures might tend to occupy roughly a midpoint position on a distributively and interactionally bounded continuum.

ANOTHER IMPLICATION: RELATING "WOULD" TO RELATIONAL EFFECTS BASED ON GROUP IMPORTANCE To illustrate how fairness theory conceptionalization of Would sheds new light on other perspectives, consider the relational model's assumption that treatment from the leader of a group conveys an indication of inclusion as a full-fledged member (versus the leader's unfair treatment of a group member, which sends a message of exclusion as if that person were a nonmember). If group affiliation constitutes an important basis for establishing self-identity and feelings of self-worth, then the fairness of a leader's behavior along the relational dimensions of trust, neutrality, and standing will be of paramount significance. In particular, such relational concerns have greater impact from the leader of a valued in-group than when variations along those same three relational dimensions involve behavior toward oneself from the leader of some less-valued group or from an out-group's leader.

The reasoning adopted by fairness theory does not use those relational assumptions about threats to self-esteem, yet it can account for relational findings in terms of assumptions regarding how Would counterfactuals affect evaluation of an event or situation on dimensions such as goodness-badness (value judgments). Some groups are valued more than others for various reasons that include one emphasized by relational models: Belonging to a group can have important implications for self-esteem and self-identity. If identity and esteem hinge on feedback originating from a group in which a person cherishes membership, then the magnitude of perceived adversity can vary greatly as a function of (unfair) relational treatment by the leader of that group. The impact on experienced adversity will not vary so strongly as a function of relational treatment by the leader of some other group, whose membership is a matter of indifference for the person exposed to that treatment by the other leader.

The evidence from studies of this effect as a relational-model prediction, therefore, simply reduces to variation on the same theme of severity-of-adversity as a function of actual/counterfactual discrepancies (the Would factor). The absence of fair relational treatment by the leader of a valued in-group merely constitutes another type of actual adversity, which in turn yields the experience of suffering when juxtaposed with the superior quality of the counterfactual referent (the presence of fair relational treatment). The presence-versus-absence of fair relational treatment by in-group leaders rather than out-group leaders produces a larger impact on severity simply because a more extreme discrepancy exists in the former case than in the latter. A loss (e.g., of treatment as a full-fledged group member, with the respect and dignity to which all such members are entitled) seems severe in comparison with the state of being characterized by no loss. Within a valued in-group, the no-loss state of fair relational treatment has more importance (precisely because of the significance for self-identity and esteem) than the corresponding no-loss state of fair relational treatment from the leader of a less-valued group.

Conclusion

In this chapter we described fairness theory as a new model of organizational justice. We articulated the model and then described its relationship with previous research. By contrast with other models, the fairness theory emphasizes that justice is a social process in which people assign one another blame and credit. Justice helps human beings to deal with mixed-motive, interdependent interactions. Fairness precepts of social conduct promote civil order and aid in the management of conflicting interests. How we adapt to or become alienated from others involves the accountability of evaluating other people by standards of fair conduct.

Fairness theory treats the severity of an adverse experience (Would judgments) in conjunction with inferences about the conduct of other people (Could and Should judgments). Would judgments reflect differences between actual and counterfactual (i.e., referent) events as two classes of experience. An actual *un*fairness, whether distributive, procedural, or interactional, differs from *fairness* as the counterfactual. Distributive or procedural justice norms as counterfactuals make possible the experience of distributive or procedural injustice; interactional injustice as insensitive treatment entails sensitive treatment as the counterfactual that makes the insensitivity seem so adverse by contrast.

An exclusive focus on personally undeserved adversity (a negative Would for which the perceiver does not feel responsible), however, omits vital details about the role of other people in an event's origins—the Could and Should details that go to the heart of justice's role in social interaction. "I didn't get what I deserved" is an incomplete picture of social justice that tells but half the story—the part about not blaming people for their own unwarranted misfortune (personally undeserved adversity). The fairness theory addresses both the issue of personally unwarranted adversity and the issue of its social origins in the interpersonal conduct of others; by addressing the accountability of interpersonal conduct, it puts the two halves of the fairness story together into an integrative model. This synthesis is the story of how mutually restrained social conduct can sustain a moral community.

NOTES

1. We address only negative (aversive) events or conditions. The scope of the fairness theory extends easily enough, however, to positive (advantageous) events or conditions. Such an extension follows directly from the very nature of accountability itself, which can involve assigning either blame or credit. We focus solely on blame in this chapter for the sake of brevity. Moreover, evidence for the asymmetry of cognitive and emotional reactions to negative events versus positive events indicates the value of emphasizing the former because of the especially significant motivational impact they tend to have. Also notably, our attention on negativity represents a difference in perspective from some other approaches to the study of justice-motivated behaviors. For instance, a focus on positivity seems more evident in writings by Lind and by Tyler that develop a relational approach to authority (e.g., Lind & Tyler, 1988; Tyler & Lind, 1992). The thrust of their analysis focuses on the degree of positive action by authority as fair conduct and on the extent to which positive reactions might be expected from people affected by the decisions of authorities. In particular, a positive theme underlies the emphasis on predicting such reactions as the extent of the willingness to obey authority, to evaluate the authority positively and offer a corresponding degree of supportiveness, and to voluntarily comply with authority.

2. Social fairness differs from the private sense of fairness-as-deservingness that requires no knowledge about any other social being's state (neither their conduct nor a social comparison with their outcomes). Tending a garden and harvesting crops can take a great deal of effort, for example, and it might seem unfair for an entire season's crops to be ruined by an unprecedented freeze. Harm done by the impersonal forces of nature can effect the personal sense of deserving of a lone individual (e.g., crops grown in isolation by a hermit).

3. The authors would like to thank Marshall Schminke for this metaphor.

4. We are here treating interactional justice as a form of procedure justice. However, it is important to emphasize that some have argued that interactional justice remain separate from procedural (Bies, this volume). Our intent here is not to take a position on this issue. Interactional justice fits into Figure 1.4, Cells 3–6 regardless of whether one considers it a procedure. For this reason, interactional justice does concern itself with *could* and *should*, regardless of how it may be related to process. In the end, it makes no difference to the present analysis whether interactional justice is considered an aspect of procedure or whether it is considered something different.

REFERENCES

Adams, J. S. (1965). Inequity in social exchange. In L. Berkowitz (Ed.), *Advances in experimental social psychology* (Vol. 2, pp. 267–299). New York: Academic Press.

Adams, J. S., & Freedman, S. (1976). Equity theory revisited: Comments and annotated bibliography. In L. Berkowitz (Ed.), *Advances in experimental social psychology* (Vol. 9, pp. 43–90). New York: Academic Press.

Bargh, J. A. (1997). Automaticity in social psychology. In E. T. Higgins & A. W. Kruglanski (Eds.), *Social psychology: Handbook of basic principles* (pp. 169–183). New York: Guilford.

Bies, R. J. (1987). The predicament of injustice: The management of moral outrage. In L. L. Cummings & B. M. Staw (Eds.), *Research in organizational behavior* (Vol. 9, pp. 289–319). Greenwich, CT: JAI Press.

Bies, R. J., & Moag, J. S. (1986). Interactional justice: Communication criteria for fairness. In B. Sheppard (Ed.), *Research on negotiation in organizations* (Vol. 1, pps. 43–55). Greenwich, CT: JAI Press.

Bies, R. J., & Shapiro, D. L. (1988). Voice and justification: Their influence on procedural fairness judgments. *Academy of Management Journal, 31,* 676–685.

Bies, R. J., Shapiro, D. L., & Cummings, L. L. (1988). Causal accounts and managing organizational conflicts: Is it enough to say it's not my fault? *Communications Research, 15,* 381–399.

Bies, R. J., & Sitkin, S. B. (1992). Explanation as legitimation: Excuse-making in organizations. In M. L. McLaughlin, M. J. Cody, & S. J. Read (Eds.), *Explaining one's self to others: Reason-giving in a social context* (pp. 183–198). Hillsdale, NJ: Erlbaum.

Bobocel, D. R., Agar, S. E., Meyer, J. P., & Irving, P. G. (1996, April). *Managerial accounts and fairness perceptions in third-party conflict resolution: Differentiating the effects of shifting responsibility and providing a justification.* Paper presented at the annual meeting of the Society for Industrial and Organizational Psychology. San Diego, CA.

Bobocel, D. R., & Farrell, A. C. (1996). Sex-based promotion decisions and interactions fairness: Investigating the influence of managerial accounts. *Journal of Applied Psychology, 81,* 22–35.

Bobocel, D. R., McCline, R. L., & Folger, R. (1997). Letting them down gently: Conceptual advances in explaining controversial organizational policies. In C. L. Cooper & D. M. Rousseau (Eds.), *Trends in organizational behavior* (Vol. 4, pp. 73–88). Sussex, England: John Wiley & Sons.

Brady, F. N. (1985). A Janus-headed model of ethical theory: Looking two ways at business/society issues. *Academy of Management Review, 10,* 568–576.

Brady, F. N. (1986). Aesthetic components of management ethics. *Academy of Management Review, 11,* 337–344.

Brady, F. N. (1987). Rules for making exceptions to rules. *Academy of Management Review, 12,* 436–444.

Brett, J. M., & Stroh, L. K. (1997). Jumping ship: Who benefits from an external labor market strategy? *Journal of Applied Psychology, 82,* 331–341.

Brockner, J., Tyler, T. R., & Cooper-Schneider, R. (1992). The influence of prior commitment to an institution on reactions to perceived unfairness: The higher they are, the harder they fall. *Administrative Science Quarterly, 37,* 241–261.

Brockner, J., & Wiesenfeld, B. M. (1996). An integrative framework for explaining reactions to decisions: The interactive effects of outcomes and procedures. *Psychological Bulletin, 120,* 189–208.

Carli, L. L. (1991). Gender, status, and influence. In E. J. Lawler & B. Markovsky (Eds.), *Advances in group processes: Theory and reserach* (Vol. 8). Greenwich, CT: JAP Press.

Chen, C. C. (1995). New trends in rewards allocation preferences: A Sino–U.S. comparison. *Academy of Management Journal, 38,* 408–428.

Coleman, J. S. (1982). *The asymmetric society.* Syracuse, NY: Syracuse University Press.

Coleman, J. S. (1993). The rational reconstruction of society. *American Sociological Review, 58,* 1–15.

Cowherd, D. M., & Levine, D. I. (1992). Product quality and pay equity between lower-level employees and top management: An investigation of distributive justice theory. *Administrative, Science Quarterly, 37,* 302–320.

Cropanzano, R., & Folger, R. (1989). Referent cognitions and task decision autonomy: Beyond equity theory. *Journal of Applied Psychology, 74,* 293–299.

Cropanzano, R., & Folger, R. (1991). Procedural justice and worker motivation. In R. M. Steers & L. W. Porter (Eds.), *Motivation and work behavior* (5th Ed., pp. 131–143). New York: McGraw-Hill.

Cropanzano, R., & Grandey, A. A. (1998). If politics is a game, then what are the rules?: Three suggestions for ethical managers. In M. Schminke (Ed.), *Organizations and ethics: Morally managing people and processes* (pp. 133–152). Mahwah, NJ: Erlbaum.

Cropanzano, R., & Greenberg, J. (1997). Progress in organizational justice: Tunneling through the maze. In I. T. Robertson & C. L. Cooper (Eds.), *International Review of Industrial and Organizational Psychology* (Vol. 12, pp. 317–372). New York: Wiley.

Cropanzano, R., & Konovsky, M. A. (1995). Resolving the justice dilemma by improving the outcomes: The case of employee drug screening. *Journal of Business and Psychology, 10,* 221–244.

Cropanzano, R., & Prehar, C. (1997, June). *Procedural justice, leader–member exchange and the consequences of performance evaluation.* Paper presented at the 1997 meeting of the Australian Psychological Society's Industrial and Organizational Psychology Conference. Melbourne, Victoria, Australia.

Cropanzano, R., & Schminke, M. (2001). Using social justice to build effective work groups. In M. Turner (Ed)., *Groups at work: Advances in theory and research* (pp. 143–171). Hillsdale, NJ: Erlbaum.

Crosby, F. (1984). The denial of personal discrimination. *American Behavioral Scientist, 27,* 371–386.

Dutton, J. E., & Dukerich, J. M. (1991). Keeping an eye on the mirror: Image and identity in organizational adaption. *Academy of Management Journal, 34,* 517–554.

Elsbach, K. D. (1994). Managing organizational legitimacy in the California cattle industry: The construction and effectiveness of verbal accounts. *Administrative Science Quarterly, 39,* 57–88.

Elsbach, K. D., & Sutton, R. I. (1992). Acquiring organizational legitimacy through illegitimate actions: A marriage of institutional and impression management theories. *Academy of Management Journal, 35,* 699–738.

Fiske, A. P. (1991) *Structures of social life: The four elementary forms of human relations.* New York: Free Press.

Foa, U. G., & Foa, E. B. (1974). *Societal structures of the mind.* Springfield, IL: Charles C. Thomas.

Folger, R. (1984). Perceived injustice, referent cognitions, and the concept of comparison level. *Representative Research in Social Psychology, 14,* 88–108.

Folger, R. (1986). Rethinking equity theory: A referent cognitions model. In H. W. Bierhoff, R. L. Cohen, & J. Greenberg (Eds.), *Justice in social relations* (pp. 145–162). New York: Plenum.

Folger, R. (1987). Reformulating the preconditions of resentment: A referent cognitions model. In J. C. Masters & W. P. Smith (Eds.), *Social comparison, justice, and relative deprivation: Theoretical, empirical, and policy perspectives* (pp. 183–215). Hillsdale, NJ: Lawrence Erlbaum Associates.

Folger, R. (1993). Reactions to mistreatment at work. In K. Murnigham (Ed.), *Social psychology in organizations: Advances in theory and research.* Englewood Cliffs, NJ: Prentice-Hall.

Folger, R. (1998). Fairness as a moral virtue. In M. Schminke (Ed.), *Managerial ethics: Morally managing people and processes* (pp. 13–34). Mahwah, NJ: Lawrence Erlbaum Associates.

Folger, R., & Cropanzano, R. (1998). *Organizational justice and human resource management.* Thousand Oaks, CA: Sage.

Folger, R., & Kass, E. (in press). Social comparison and fairness: A counterfactual simulations perspective. In J. Suls & L. Wheeler (Eds.), *Handbook of social comparison: Theory and research.* New York: Plenum.

Folger, R., & Konovsky, M. (1989). Effects of procedural and distributive justice on reactions to pay raise decisions. *Academy of Management Journal, 32,* 115–130.

Folger, R., & Lewis, D. (1993). Self-appraisal and fairness in evaluations. In R. Cropanzano (Ed.), *Justice in the workplace: Approaching fairness in human resource management* (pp. 107–131). Hillsdale, NJ: Lawrence Erlbaum Assocates.

Folger, R., & Martin, C. (1986). Relative deprivation and referent cognitions: Distributive and procedural justice effects. *Journal of Experimental Social Psychology, 22,* 531–546.

Folger, R., Rosenfield, D., Rheaume, K., & Martin, C. (1983). Relative deprivation and referent cognitions. *Journal of Experimental Social Psychology, 19,* 172–184.

Folger, R., Rosenfield, D., & Robinson, T. (1983). Relative deprivation and procedural justifications. *Journal of Personality and Social Psychology, 45,* 268–273.

Folger, R., Sheppard, B. H., & Buttram, R. (1995). Three faces of justice. In J. Rubin & B. Bunker (Eds.), *Cooperation, conflict, and justice.* San Francisco: Jossey-Bass.

Folger, R., & Skarlicki, D. P. (2001). Fairness as a dependent variable: Why tough times can lead to bad management. In R. Cropanzano (Ed.), *Justice in the workplace: Vol. 2. From theory to practice* (pp. 97–118). Mahwah, NJ: Erlbaum.

Gatewood, R. D., Gowan, M., & Lautenschlager, G. J. (1993). Corporate image, recruitment image, and initial job choice decisions. *Academy of Management Journal, 36,* 414–427.

Gilliland, S. W. (1996). Procedural and distributive justice in the editorial review process. *Personnel Psychology, 49,* 669–690.

Ginzel, L. E., Kramer, R. M., & Sutton, R. I. (1993). Organizational impression management as a reciprocal influence process: The neglected role of the organizational audience. In L. L. Cummings & B. M. Staw (Eds.), *Research in organizational behavior* (Vol. 15, pp. 227–266). Greenwich, CT: JAP Press.

Greenberg, J. (1986). Determinants of perceived fairness of performance evaluations. *Journal of Applied Psychology, 71,* 340–342.

Greenberg, J. (1988). Equity and workplace status: A field experiment. *Journal of Applied Psychology, 73,* 606–613.

Greenberg, J. (1990). Organizational justice: Yesterday, today, and tomorrow. *Journal of Management, 16,* 399–432.

Greenberg, J. (1993). The social side of fairness: Interpersonal and informational classes of organizational justice. In R. Cropanzano (Ed.), *Justice in the workplace: Approaching fairness in human resource management* (pp. 79–103). Hillsdale, NJ: Erlbaum.

Greenberg, J., & Bies, R. J. (1992). Establishing the role of empirical studies of organizational justice in philosophical inquiries into business ethics. *Journal of Business Ethics, 11,* 433–444.

Grienberger, I. V., & Rutte, C. G. (1996, March). *Influence of social comparisons of outcomes and procedures on fairness judgments*. Paper presented at the Kurt Lewin Institute Workshop. Schiermonnikoog, the Netherlands.

Harder, J. W. (1992). Play for pay: Effects of inequity in pay-for-performance context. *Administrative Science Quarterly, 37,* 321–335.

Holbrook, R. L., Jr., & Kulik, C. T. (April, 1996). *Strength of membership influences on reactions to bank loan procedures*. Paper presented at the annual meeting of the Society for Industrial and Organizational Psychology. San Diego.

Howard, P. K. (1994). *The decline of common sense: How law is suffocating America*. New York: Random House.

Huo, Y. J., Smith, H. J., Tyler, T. R., & Lind, E. A. (1996). Superordinate identification, subgroup identification, and justice concerns: Is separatism the problem? Is assimilation the answer? *Psychological Science, 7,* 40–45.

Jones, T. M. (1991). Ethical decision making by individuals in organizations: An issue-contingent model. *Academy of Management Review, 16,* 366–395.

Kahneman, D., & Miller, D. (1986). Norm theory: Comparing reality to its alternatives. *Psychological Review, 93,* 136–153.

Kahneman, D., & Tversky, A. (1982). The simulation heuristic. In D. Kahneman, P. Slovic, & A. Tversky (Eds.), *Judgments under uncertainty: Heuristics and biases* (pp. 201–208). New York: Cambridge University Press.

Konovsky, M. A., & Cropanzano, R. (1993). Justice considerations in employee drug testing. In R. Cropanzano (Ed.), *Justice in the workplace: Approaching fairness in human resource management* (pp. 171–192). Hillsdale, NJ: Erlbaum.

Korsgaard, M. A., & Roberson, L. (1995). Procedural justice in performance evaluation: The role of instrumental and non-instrumental voice in performance appraisal decisions. *Journal of Management, 21,* 657–669.

Kulik, C. T., & Ambrose, M. L. (1992). Personal and situational determinants of referent choice. *Academy of Management Review, 17,* 212–237.

Lerner, M. J. (1980). *The belief in a just world: A fundamental delusion*. New York: Plenum.

Lerner, M. J., & Miller, D. T. (1978). Just world research and the attribution process: Looking back and ahead. *Psychological Bulletin, 85,* 1030–1051.

Lind, E. A. (1995). Justice and authority relations in organizations. In R. Cropanzano & M. K. Kacmar (Eds.), *Organizational politics, justice, and support: Managing the social climate of the workplace* (pp. 83–96). Westport, CT: Quorum Books.

Lind, E. A., & Tyler, T. R. (1988). *The social psychology of procedural justice*. New York: Plenum.

Lyness, K. S., & Thompson, D. E. (1997). Above the glass ceiling? A comparison of matched samples of female and male executives. *Journal of Applied Psychology, 82,* 359–375.

Martin, J. (1981). Relative deprivation: A theory of distributive justice for an era of shrinking resources. In L. L. Cummings & B. M. Staw (Eds.), *Research in organizational behavior* (Vol. 3, p. 53–107). Greenwich, CT: JAI Press.

Martin, J. (1986). The tolerance of injustice. In J. M. Olsen, C. P. Herman, & M. P. Zanna (Eds.), *Relative deprivation and social comparison: The Ontario symposium* (Vol. 4, pp. 217–242). Hillsdale, NJ: Erlbaum.

Martin, J., & Harder, J. W. (1994). Bread and roses: Justice and the distribution of financial and socioemotional rewards in organizations. *Social Justice Research, 7*, 241–264.

Peterson, W. C. (1994). *Silent depression: Twenty-five years of wage squeeze and middle-class decline.* New York: W. W. Norton & Company.

Roese, N. J. (1997). Counterfactual thinking. *Psychological Bulletin, 121*, 133–148.

Roese, N. J., & Olsen, J. M. (1995). *What might have been: The social psychology of counterfactual thinking.* Mahway, NJ: Erlbaum.

Rousseau, D. M. (1995). *Psychological contracts in organizations: Understanding written and unwritten agreements.* Thousand Oaks, CA: Sage.

Rousseau, D. M., & Parks, J. M. (1993). The contracts of individuals and organizations. In L. L. Cummings and B. M. Staw (Eds.), *Research in organizational behavior* (Vol. 15, p. 1–43). Greenwich, CT: JAI Press.

Schaubroeck, J., May, D. R, & Brown, F. W. (1994). Procedural justice explanations and employee reactions to economic hardship: A field experiment. *Journal of Applied Psychology, 79*, 455–460.

Schlenker, B. R. (1997). Personal responsibility: Applications of the triangle model. In L. L. Cummings & B. M. Staw (Eds.), *Research in organizational behavior* (Vol. 19, pp. 241–301). Greenwich, CT: JAI Press.

Schlenker, B. R., Britt, T. W., Pennington, J. W., Murphy, R., & Doherty, K. J. (1994). The triangle model of responsibility. *Psychological Review, 101*, 632–652.

Schminke, M., Ambrose, M. L., & Noel, T. W. (1997). The effect of ethical frameworks on perceptions of organizational justice. *Academy of Management Journal, 40*, 1190–1207.

Shapiro, D. L. (1991). The effects of explanations on negative reactions to deceit. *Administrative Science Quarterly, 36*, 614–630.

Shapiro, D. L. (1993). Reconciling theoretical differences among procedural justice researchers by re-evaluating what it means to have one's view "considered": Implications for third-party managers. In R. Cropanzano (Ed.), *Justice in the workplace: Approaching fairness in human resource management* (pp. 51–78). Hillsdale, NJ: Erbaum.

Shore, L. M., & Tetrick, L. E. (1994). The psychological contract as an explanatory framework in the employment relationship. In C. L. Cooper & D. M. Rousseau (Eds.), *Trends in organizational behavior* (Vol. 1, pp. 91–109). Chichester, England: John Wiley & Sons.

Sitkin, S. B., & Bies, R. J. (1993). Social accounts in conflict situations: Using explanations to manage conflict. *Human Relations, 46,* 349–370.

Stepina, L. P., & Perrewe, P. L. (1991). The stability of comparative referent choice and feelings of inequity: A longitudinal field study. *Journal of Organizational Behavior, 12,* 185–200.

Stone, E. F., & Stone, D. L. (1990). Privacy in organizations: Theoretical issues, research findings, and protection mechanisms. In G. R. Ferris & K. M. Rowland (Eds.), *Research in personnel and human resource management* (Vol. 8, pp. 349–411). Greenwich, CT: JAI Press.

Summers, T. P., & Hendrix, W. H. (1991). Modeling the role of pay equity perceptions: A field study. *Journal of Occupational Psychology, 64,* 145–157.

Sweeney, P. D., & McFarlin, D. B. (1993). Workers' evaluations of the "ends" and the "means": An examination of four models of distributive and procedural justice. *Organizational Behavior and Human Decision Processes, 55,* 23–40.

Sweeney, P. D., McFarlin, D. B., & Inderrieden, E. J. (1990). Using relative deprivation theory to explain satisfaction with income and pay level: A multistudy examination. *Academy of Management Journal, 33,* 423–436.

Taylor, M. S., Tracy, K. B., Renard, M. K., Harrison, J. K., & Carroll, S. J. (1995). Due process in performance appraisal: A quasi-experiment in procedural justice. *Administrative Science Quarterly, 40,* 495–523.

Thibaut, J. W., & Walker, L. (1975). *Procedural justice: A psychological perspective.* Hillsdale, NJ: Erlbaum.

Tyler, T. R. (1987). Conditions leading to value expressive effects in judgments of procedural justice. *Journal of Personality and Social Psychology, 52,* 51–74.

Tyler, T. R., & Bies, R. J. (1990). Beyond formal procedures: The interpersonal context of procedural justice. In J. S. Carroll (Ed.), *Applied social psychology and organizational settings* (pp. 77–98). Hillsdale, NJ: Lawrence Erlbaum Associates.

Tyler, T. R., & Degoey, P. (1995). Collective restraint in social dilemmas: Procedural justice and social identification effects on support for authorities. *Journal of Personality and Social Psychology, 69,* 482–497.

Tyler, T. R., & Lind, E. A. (1992). A relational model of authority in groups. In M. P. Zanna (Ed.), *Advances in experimental social psychology* (Vol. 25, pp. 115–191). San Diego: Academic Press.

Van den Bos, K., Lind, E. A., Vermunt, R., & Wilke, H. A. W. (1997). How do I judge my outcome when I do not know the outcome of others? The psychology of the fair process effect. *Journal of Personality and Social Psychology, 72,* 1034–1046.

Van den Bos, K., Lind, E. A., & Wilke, H. A. W. (2001). The psychology of procedural and distributive justice viewed from the perspective of fairness heuristic theory. In R. Cropanzano (Ed.), *Justice in the workplace (Vol. 2): From theory to practice* (pp. 49–66). Mahwah, NJ: Erlbaum.

Walster, E., Walster, G. W., & Berscheid, E. (1978). *Equity: Theory and research.* Boston: Allyn & Bacon.

2

Fairness Heuristic Theory: Justice Judgments as Pivotal Cognitions in Organizational Relations

E. Allan Lind

IN THIS CHAPTER I describe a theory of the psychology of justice judgments.[1] The theory has developed over several years since its first presentation (Lind & MacCoun, 1992) and initial publication (Lind, Kulik, Ambrose, & Park, 1993), but throughout its development the two basic processes posited by the theory have remained unchanged: 1) Fairness judgments are assumed to serve as a proxy for interpersonal trust in guiding decisions about whether to behave in a cooperative fashion to social situations, and 2) people are assumed to use a variety of cognitive short-cuts to ensure that they have a fairness judgment available when they need to make decisions about engaging in cooperative behavior. The theory seeks, through an analysis of the social and cognitive function of fairness, to explain why justice judgments have such a substantial effect on attitudes and behaviors in organizations and other social contexts (Lind, 1994, 1995a, 1995b; Van den Bos, Lind, & Wilke, in press). My analysis offers some new perspectives on, and some new predictions about, the causes, effects, and dynamics of justice judgments.

This work was supported by the National Science Foundation, the American Bar Foundation, and the Fuqua School of Business.

Nearly three decades of laboratory and field research (for reviews see Greenberg, 1987; Lind & Tyler, 1988; Tyler & Smith, 1997) provides convincing evidence that fairness judgments affect a variety of organizational attitudes and behavior, that these effects are substantial, and that the effects occur across a wide variety of contexts. What has been lacking in previous theory on justice was a coherent and unified account of exactly why justice judgments have such powerful and ubiquitous effects. Fairness heuristic theory takes as a starting point some of the elements of my previous theoretical work—in particular, elements of group value theory (Lind and Tyler, 1988) and the relational model of authority (Tyler and Lind, 1992)—and seeks to explain how and why people use fairness judgments in the ways described in those theories. But the theory also breaks new ground: The scope of the theory expands to include distributive and interactional justice judgments as well as procedural justice judgments, and the theory also explores the cognitive dynamics of justice judgments much more deeply than did either of the previous theories. I focus here on applications of the theory to relations within and between organizations—an important application of the theory and obviously the appropriate focus given the nature of this book—but the theory, if it is in fact an accurate portrayal of justice judgment processes, also has implications for human relations in personal, legal, political, and other contexts.

Some Questions to Be Answered

Over the course of the past 35 years, ever since Adams's (1965) seminal work on the effects of feelings of inequity on work attitudes and performance, a great deal of research evidence has accumulated showing that feelings of just or unjust treatment play an important role in guiding behavior and in shaping social attitudes. Especially since Thibaut and Walker (1975, 1978) extended the domain of justice research and theory to include not only the fairness of outcomes but also the fairness of procedures and social process, a considerable research literature has accumulated on the psychology of justice judgments. Several aspects of the justice judgment literature are particularly important for the theory presented here, either because they represent findings that suggested key parts of fairness heuristic theory or because they raise questions that the theory can answer.

Why Are Justice Judgments Linked to Relationship Concerns?

First, it is important to note that over the years we have learned that justice judgments depend not only on whether one's outcomes are fair but also on nuances of procedure and treatment. In particular, it is now clear that the feeling that one has been treated fairly involves such things as whether the person in question is given an opportunity to voice concerns and needs to authorities, whether the person is treated with respect and dignity, and whether the authority seems to include or exclude the person from the authority's in-group (see, e.g., Lind & Tyler, 1988; Tyler & Lind, 1992; Tyler & Smith, 1997). Because these elements of process and procedure seem to speak more to the nature and quality of one's relationships with others than to more instrumental, material-outcome issues, Tyler and I termed them "relational antecedents of justice" (Tyler & Lind, 1992). We used such terms as "group value" (Lind & Tyler, 1988) and "relational" (Tyler & Lind, 1992) to name our theories of justice because we were convinced that the perception that one is valued by the group or organization and the belief that one's relationship with the group or organization is fundamentally sound are an important part—indeed in our view *the most important* part—of what people mean by fairness. Clearly any new theory of justice judgments and their effects would have to explain why fairness is so tied up with issues of inclusion and belonging.

Just as some of the most important *antecedents* of justice judgments are nuances of procedure and treatment that speak to concerns about inclusion, so too the strongest *effects* of justice judgments are relational, in that they are consequences that are linked to what early social psychologists termed *group cohesion* and *promotive social process*. In the realm of organizational attitudes, for example, positive justice judgments have been shown to promote organizational commitment, to enhance loyalty to and the perceived legitimacy of organizational authorities, to improve trust in co-workers, and to engender favorable attitudes toward organizational policies and actions (for reviews see, e.g., Greenberg, 1994; Tyler & Lind, 1992; Tyler & Smith, 1997). Justice judgments affect not only cognitions but also behaviors, and again the strongest effects are on behaviors relating to the acceptance of group or organizational authority and the subordination of individual interests and goals to group interests and goals. For example, a number of studies have shown that people are much more likely to accept and act in accordance with the decisions of authorities and that they are more likely to engage in organizational citizenship behaviors if they feel they have been treated fairly (Huo, Smith, Tyler, & Lind, 1996; Konovsky & Folger, 1991; Lind et al., 1993; Podsakoff & MacKenzie, 1993; see generally, Greenberg, 1993; Tyler & Lind, 1992; Tyler & Smith, 1997). On the other hand, negative justice judgments have been shown to cause a variety of attitudes and behaviors that are at best self-interested and at worst antisocial. Folger, Robinson, Dietz, McLean-Parks, and

Baron (1998) report a connection between feelings of unfair treatment and workplace assaults; Greenberg and Scott (1996) show that feelings of unfair treatment can lead to theft by employees; and Lind, Greenberg, Scott, and Welchans (2000) show that former workers who feel they were dismissed in an unfair manner are far more likely to sue than are those who feel they were treated fairly. Again any new theory of justice judgments must address these findings, explaining why positive justice judgments lead to cooperative and prosocial behaviors and negative justice judgments lead to self-interested or antisocial behaviors.

What Is the Relationship between Distributive and Procedural Justice?

The findings just described suggested some of the key ideas in fairness heuristic theory, but other findings either converge with implications of the theory or raise questions that can be addressed using the theory. For example, ever since Thibaut and Walker (1975) began the study of procedural justice, there have been questions about the relationship between distributive justice and procedural justice. We have known since the very first procedural justice studies (Walker, LaTour, Lind, & Thibaut, 1974) that both procedures and outcome distributions are sources of justice judgments, but since that time we have also known that measures of procedural and distributive justice are generally correlated (see Tyler, 1994), sometimes quite highly correlated. When we began to look at the fairness implications of social process and behavior outside of formal procedures (Bies & Moag, 1986), some theorists argued that there is a third justice dimension—interactional fairness. Again, empirical studies showed that judgments of this type of fairness were correlated with distributive and procedural justice. What has been unclear all this time is precisely how these dimensions of justice are related, how they are distinct, and when one or another of these dimensions exerts stronger effects on the consequences of justice.

Does Procedural Justice Matter More When Outcomes Are Negative?

Some years ago Brockner and Wiesenfeld (1996) offered an analysis of the relationship between outcomes and procedural justice in which they suggested that procedural justice effects are stronger when outcomes are negative. In my opinion the Brockner and Wiesenfeld conclusion is far too general: It is in fact clear from the research literature that procedural justice effects often occur with equal potency regardless of the favorability of the outcomes involved. To cite just some examples from my own research, unambiguous procedure main effects, unqualified by outcomes, are seen in Walker, LaTour, Lind, & Thibaut, 1974; Walker, Lind, & Thibaut, 1979; Lind, Lissak, & Conlon, 1983; Lind, 1990; Lind, Kurtz, Musante, Walker, & Thibaut, 1980; and Lind et al. 1999). There are even studies showing that under some conditions positive outcomes can enhance procedural justice effects as much as or more than negative outcomes (e.g., Lind & Lissak, 1985; Smith, Tyler, Huo, Ortiz, & Lind, 1998, Study 1). What is needed is a theoretical account that will predict when negative outcomes enhance the importance of procedural justice and when other process-outcome effect patterns will occur.

Fairness Heuristic Theory

When viewed in conjunction with the widespread and often quite impressive effects of justice judgments on cognitive and attitudinal dimensions, the substantial behavioral effects of justice judgments raise a troubling question for organizational justice theorists: Why exactly does fairness matter so much? After all, many fairness effects fly in the face of expectancy and exchange theories of organizational and social behavior—theories that assert that the outcome of behavior and the contingencies between behaviors and outcomes control most of our social behavior. Outcome-oriented explanations of behavior are both reasonable and intuitive, but justice research shows that they fail to account for the fact that people often react more strongly to the fairness of the treatment they receive than to the favorability of the outcomes attached to various actions (for reviews supporting this conclusion, see Lind & Tyler [1988] and Tyler & Lind [1992]). These findings show that in many instances people behave in accordance with their fairness judgments even when they clearly perceive no outcome benefit—or even when they see costs involved—in doing so. This raises the question that motivates much of fairness heuristic theory: Why do impressions of fair or unfair treatment have such substantial consequences for how people relate to others and to the organizations and institutions to which they belong?

Fairness heuristic theory begins with an examination of some features of organizational life—indeed features of all social relations—that pose a dilemma. Next the theory argues that fairness judgments offer a useful and widely employed heuristic for resolving this dilemma. Then the theory uses these insights to examine how people might form and use fairness judgments and to examine the relation between fairness judgments and other important organizational attitudes and behavior.

The Fundamental Social Dilemma

The basis of fairness heuristic theory is the recognition that virtually all social relationships, including most relationships in organizations, involve repeated encounters with a very basic dilemma. On the one hand, by identifying with and contributing effort and personal resources to a social or organizational entity, people can extend their individual capacities to accomplish goals, obtain better outcomes, and, perhaps most important, secure a self-identity that incorporates a broader social meaning than they could ever achieve alone. On the other hand, identification with and sacrifice for a group, organization, or society can limit individual freedom of action, invite exploitation, and open the door to rejection and loss of identity. If, at any given time or with respect to any given social relation, one chooses to cooperate with others and to sacrifice for the common good, there is at least some possibility that this cooperative behavior will be exploited. Similarly, if one links one's identity and sense of self to some larger social or organizational identity, there is always the risk that one will experience rejection by the group and an attendant loss of identity. On the other hand, to choose an independent and self-sufficient course of action and a self-centered mode of thinking about oneself and one's interests almost necessarily entails foregoing the better outcomes, greater accomplishments, and enhanced identity that social entities can provide. I have termed this ubiquitous feature of social and organizational life the "fundamental social dilemma," using the label because this common quandary includes elements of the traditional outcome-oriented social dilemma that has been discussed a great deal in the literature on the social psychology of conflict. That said, I believe that the dilemma as I have just described it actually occurs more frequently and plays itself out at a more basic psychological level than do dilemmas that turn only on outcome issues.

The fundamental social dilemma is "fundamental" because it reflects one of the most basic aspects of human nature. We humans are at once individual and social beings. We live and work in social units, but we maintain a strong sense of self and of our own individuality. It is this tension between social impulses and individual interests that forms the context of much of our social and organizational existence.

Although I originally phrased the fundamental social dilemma in terms of individual versus group interests and identities (Lind, 1994, 1995a, 1995b), the same sort of tension—and, I would argue, much the same psychological process—arises in the face of competing demands and identities posed by multiple group memberships. For example, the competing demands of family and work illustrate just such a dilemma of conflicting demands and identities. Most working people have to make decisions about how to allocate their time and energy between work and family, and we have all made choices, however implicitly, about how much we invest our self-image and self-identity in being a good and successful employee versus being a good mother, father, wife, or husband.

In addition to the competing demands of home and work, there are competing demands from the multiple group identities that exist within and across organizations—identities associated with being a member of a particular department or a given work team or with friendship relations between members of different organizations or organizational components. Identity dilemmas exist in these situations and are familiar to anyone who has served on a cross-disciplinary team or committee or to anyone who deals repeatedly with the same clients or suppliers. Given the current trend toward team-based and matrixed organizational forms, it seems likely that intraorganizational identity conflicts will become more and more common. However much the current rage for teams and teamwork pretends uniformity of purpose across the entire organization, there will always be conflicts between the interests, responsibilities, and identity that one owes the team and the interests, responsibilities, and identities that one owes the larger organization. To the extent that one invests time and energy to outside interests and outside identities, the team is likely to be less successful than it would be if its members were willing to consider only the team's goals. And unless team and broader organizational goals are perfectly aligned, to the extent that one is a good "team player," the interests of the greater organization will take on lesser priority.

The preceding discussion of the fundamental social dilemma hints at a certain duality in the concerns and choices that the dilemma involves and in the implications of those choices. Fairness heuristic theory assumes that people are very much concerned with two aspects of organizational life. One aspect of the fundamental social dilemma—the concern with the material side of investing time, effort, and resources in any social or organizational relationship—reflects a tension between the material rewards of organizational life and the possibility of exploitation. The source of the concern is that, by allowing one's own outcomes to depend on the actions and choices of others, we run the risk that those others will take more than they give. This concern is, of course, the focus of much work on outcome fairness, and it is the target of traditional research and theory on social dilemmas. If one chooses to behave cooperatively, one would like some guarantee—or at least some expectation—that others will not exploit that cooperative behavior.

The other aspect of the fundamental social dilemma is the concern about linking one's identity in a relationship, role, or organization and the danger of rejection that can threaten that identity. To link one's identity with an organization, or with any other social relationship, makes one more than just an individual, but it also runs the risk of the negative identity consequences of being rejected or excluded, conditions that would diminish this aspect of one's self. Taking a job enhances one's personal identity by linking individual identity to a corporate identity, but it also risks the possibility that one will lose some part of one's self-identify if the relationship with the corporate entity is terminated. Even short of such instances of outright rejection as a layoff or a firing, one's personal identity is vulnerable to the implication of exclusion in more modest organizational rejections. If a person's identity is linked to being a member of a given organization or department or team, that person is more vulnerable to being hurt or diminished if expected signs of recognition and inclusion are not forthcoming.

The two concerns are clearly interrelated. There is evidence in traditional social dilemma research that, when people share a social identity, they are more likely to make investments in the common good, suggesting that identity can moderate concerns about exploitation (e.g., Brewer & Kramer, 1986). In addition, research and theory in social justice (e.g., Greenberg, 1993) point to the facts that exploitation carries with it a message of rejection and favorable outcomes carry a message of inclusion.

In line with my previous theoretical work with Tyler (Lind & Tyler, 1988, chapter 10; Tyler & Lind, 1992), I would argue that identity concerns are the more potent of the two. To lose the material payoff or return to which one is entitled is a transient negative experience, but to stake part of one's identity on being a part of one's organization or on belonging to a team or department within the organization and then to be rejected is to have one's very self diminished. I would also argue, along the lines suggested by Greenberg (1993), that much of the sting of exploitative outcomes lies in the identity implications of being exploited. To be taken advantage of is resented so much because it implies that one is the sort of person (an outgroup member or a "loser") that can be taken advantage of.

Viewed in and of itself, the fundamental social dilemma is a problem that is so pervasive in any sort of social relation, again including most organizational relations, that trying to resolve each manifestation of the dilemma would place crippling demands on any person's social knowledge and cognitive processing capacity. Consider, for example, a typical day in the work life of an imaginary busy professional—let's call him Jim. Even before leaving for work, Jim is confronted with questions about whether family obligations can be neglected so he can leave early and prepare for an important meeting. If Jim leaves for work early, he knows he will be shifting to his wife some of his responsibility for getting their children ready for school, and he will be abandoning some potentially interesting and rewarding time with his family in order to do that extra preparation. Is the job really worth it? Will the extra work be appreciated or rewarded? How secure is Jim's job really? If he foregoes his family time in favor of working for his organization, what guarantee does he have that he won't be laid off the next time the company faces a reversal in its fortunes? Jim has heard stories, as we all have, about men and women who missed their children's youth because they were dedicated to their jobs, only to be cast aside in their 50s by employers who wanted younger, cheaper, or more up-to-date talent. On the other hand, how secure is the family? Will extra work or extra time invested in family activities be appreciated?

When Jim gets to work, he rushes to prepare for the meeting. When the time for the meeting—let's say with a potential new client—arrives, Jim is surprised to recognize an old college friend among the client's representatives. It turns out that the old friend has just been assigned to head up the project for the client. The prospect of interacting with an old friend is pleasant, but then the meeting gets a bit tense over issues about which the two organizations have conflicting preferences. Jim's organization wants a long contract to justify development costs of a new product, whereas the client prefers not to incur a long-term obligation until they see how the product sells. Jim's friend finds a chance during a break to ask Jim to support the client's position, arguing that once that is done, he, the friend, will work within the client's organization to make Jim's organization a long-term and exclusive supplier. This would resolve the immediate conflict and might ultimately help Jim's organization (and Jim's position within it), but what will happen if the friend fails to accomplish what he is suggesting? In addition, Jim wonders whether being seen as too "chummy" with his old friend will lead his co-workers to question how loyal he is to his own firm.

After the meeting Jim goes back to work with lots more little decisions: Does he work through lunch or take a break and go to the cafeteria? Does he take the time to help a colleague with a difficult problem or stick to his own work? When planning a business trip, does he take the flights that are most convenient for him or try to save his organization a few dollars? Later another decision comes up. Jim's boss drops by to ask Jim if he is willing to serve on the organization's charity committee, a task that means a lot of volunteer hours, no extra pay, and little personal benefit, but a good showing will help the company's image in the community. As the clock ticks past the normal quitting time, there is the daily decision about whether to leave or to stay and try to get through some more of that mound of papers in the in-box.

The preceding scenario lays out the sort of decisions that anyone might face in a relatively ordinary workday. The decisions to be made are small or large manifestations of the fundamental social dilemma: In each case the choice involves whether to invest time, energy, personal resources, and identity, and in each case the dilemma turns on the possibility that one will be exploited or excluded.

It becomes apparent (when one considers the many and various manifestations of the fundamental social dilemma) that these sorts of decisions are so much a part of the fabric of life that no one can really stop and calculate probabilities and subjective expected utilities for each option every time such a decision arises. Because resolving large or small manifestations of the fundamental social dilemma is such a basic requirement of virtually any social relationship, two interesting questions arise. First, how do people resolve these dilemmas, and, second, what does one type of resolution versus another imply for subsequent attitudes and behaviors?

Fairness as a Social Heuristic

One way that people routinely resolve the fundamental social dilemma, I argue, is by using impressions of fair treatment as a heuristic device. If people believe that they have been treated fairly by others in a given social context, then this prompts a "shortcut" decision to subordinate personal desires to the needs of the group, team, or organization. Fair treatment leads people to respond cooperatively to the demands and requests of others and of the group as a whole. On the other hand, if they believe that they have been treated unfairly, this cooperative orientation is rejected in favor of a self-interested orientation that decides every request on the basis of its implications for short-term self-interest. Only requests or requirements that are of direct and immediate benefit will be acceded to, and any time the actions dictated by group good run counter to those dictated by individual self-interest, the latter will prevail.

I am suggesting that people use overall impressions of fair treatment as a surrogate for interpersonal trust; that they refer to their impressions of fair or unfair treatment as they process the requests, demands, and potential obligations that are so much a part of social and organizational life. People use fairness judgments in much the same way that they would refer to feelings of trust—if they had an independent basis for forming trust—to decide how to react to demands in a long-standing personal relationship. It is important to note that I am not suggesting that people are generally conscious of either the social contract implicit in the foregoing discussion of the fundamental social dilemma or the solution of the dilemma through the use of fairness judgments. I am suggesting instead that over the course of socialization and especially in the course of learning about the potential costs and benefits of associating with and identifying with others, we come to use our impressions of fairness as a guide and to regulate our investment and involvement in various relationships to match the level of fairness that we experience.

Why should people use fairness as a heuristic to resolve instances of the fundamental social dilemma? First, the use of some heuristic allows people to free up cognitive capacity that would otherwise be devoted to trying to calculate the likelihood of all the various potential outcomes associated with complying with or resisting group requests. Analyses of outcome contingencies in the way suggested by classical interdependence theory (Thibaut & Kelley, 1959; Kelley & Thibaut, 1978), if carried out in their entirety, would quickly overwhelm the cognitive resources of even the most astute of social actors, so some shortcut is needed.[2] In addition, the fairness heuristic lends some confidence to action. Not only are the outcome contingencies associated with normal social and organizational life so complicated that they would overwhelm the attentive and cognitive capacity of most people, the probabilities associated with those contingencies are so various and so uncertain that even if the cognitive capacity existed, there would likely be no clearly dominant solution across even a limited range of circumstances. By deciding simply that one will cooperate and make reasonable accommodations to group interest if one is treated fairly and that one will pattern one's behavior on short-term outcomes, if one is not treated unfairly, these problems can be made to disappear.

Of course, the fairness heuristic is an imprecise algorithm for deciding what is the best thing to do, and as is the case with any shortcut, the fairness heuristic can lead one astray. The heuristic is based on *perceived* fairness of treatment, it must be remembered, and perceptions can be at variance to reality. It is certainly possible that one can be misled by *apparently* fair treatment that is in fact just a social control façade. This said, we should recognize that being able to decide to do something is almost always preferable to just sitting and analyzing the "wheels within wheels" that one could see in any social interaction, and the benefits of the heuristic probably far outweigh its potential limitations and abuses (see Lind, 1995a, for a more detailed exploration of this "false consciousness" issue).

The essence of the fairness heuristic process is that fair treatment leads to a shift from responding to social situations in terms of immediate self-interest, which might be termed the "individual mode," to responding to social situations as a member of the larger social entity, which might be termed the "group mode." In group mode there is far less concern with, and far less attention paid to, the individual material payoffs associated with any given behavior. Instead, requests are processed almost automatically if they come from sources appropriate to the group or organizational context. Instead of monitoring and responding to individual material outcomes, people in group mode are primarily concerned with what is good for the group and what they can do to reach group goals. Group mode is "switched on" when one feels one is being treated fairly and "switched off" when one feels one is being treated unfairly.

What I am terming the individual mode is the more familiar of the two to social science researchers because it has been so thoroughly studied and much analyzed theoretically by expectancy theorists, game theorists, and social exchange theorists. It is important to note that cooperative, even group-promotive behavior, can occur when one is in individual mode—all that is needed is for the person in question to have some independent assurance that cooperation or obedience serves his or her short-term self-interest. But this sort of individually motivated cooperative behavior will evaporate if its immediate incentive disappears. Group-mode behavior is a way of behaving that has received more attention in the years since social identity researchers and theorists began to show that individual interests are often subordinated to group identity, but it is still an under-researched area of organizational behavior. The most unique and important element of fairness heuristic theory is that it proposes a mechanism—reference to a generalized feeling of fair treatment—that moderates the switch from one mode to the other. For this reason, I refer to general fairness judgments as "pivotal cognitions" (e.g., Lind, 1995b).

Some recent evidence (Van den Bos, Wilke, & Lind, 1998) supports the idea that fairness judgments are used as a surrogate for interpersonal trust. One would expect, on the basis of fairness heuristic theory, that when one has little information about the trustworthiness of an organizational authority, one would be especially attentive and sensitive to fairness-relevant information. In contrast, when one knows for certain that an organizational authority is either very trustworthy or very untrustworthy, one would be less sensitive to fairness information. In two studies, Van den Bos et al. showed that procedural justice manipulations had stronger effects on the evaluation of an authority's decisions when the perceiver had little independent information about the trustworthiness of the authority than when the perceiver knew the authority to be either trustworthy or untrustworthy.

Fairness is probably not the only construct that can function as pivotal cognition, moving people from individual mode to group mode. The Van den Bos et al. (1998) study suggests that trust functions in this way. Affection and identification are two other constructs that seem to alter behavior in this way, to "flip" orientations from cooperative and prosocial on the one hand to competitive and self-interested on the other. Thus, a strong affective bond will often provoke an unselfish response, as will strong identification with the group, team, or organization. History and literature provide many instances of lovers, parents, or soldiers who, however badly treated, gave their all when called upon to do so. Similarly, personal ideology can provide a shortcut guide to help people respond to the competing demands of self-interest and group interest. There are people, "martyrs" perhaps, who generally respond to the needs of their group or organization whatever their own interests, and there are others, dare I say "economists," who as a matter of ideology reify self-interest and material outcomes.

But there is good reason to focus at least initially on fairness and its use as a relationship heuristic. It is arguable that we know more about the psychology of fairness than we know about any of the other possible heuristics, especially in organizational contexts. We know, for example, of procedural and distributive factors that are powerful antecedents of fairness judgments, and this means we can predict with considerable confidence when people will feel fairly or unfairly treated. This means in turn that we can offer suggestions about how people might be induced to move from one mode to another. Finally, as noted in the next section, we have some evidence that supports fairness heuristic theory, whereas there is as yet no firm evidence that might support (or refute) an "identity" heuristic theory, "affection" heuristic theory, or "ideology" heuristic theory.

Before closing this section and moving on to a discussion of some of the implications of fairness as a social heuristic, it is important to point out one way that my theorizing here differs both from my own previous work on justice judgments and from the conventional wisdom in social and organizational psychology about the distinctiveness of various types of justice judgments. I would argue that the fairness judgment that is used as a heuristic to decide involvement and investment in groups or organizations is an overall judgment of how fairly one has been (and will be) treated in the social context in question.[3] This global judgment of fair treatment draws information from procedural, process, and distributive elements. Previous work by myself and others has generally viewed different forms of justice judgments as rather distinct in both their antecedents and their consequences. I would argue that, at least for the purposes of generating the fairness judgment that serves as a basis for involvement and investment decisions of the sort outlined earlier, the various forms of fairness are far more fungible than one would think from existing work on the organizational and social justice judgments. As I note in the following section, there is reason to suppose that fairness of process and procedure is sometimes more potent in determining how fairly one feels one has been treated in general, but there are clearly instances in which the perception of fair outcomes is also used, and indeed in some circumstances outcome justice experiences can be more powerful than experiences with process or procedural justice.

Development of the Theory

If fairness is used as a social heuristic to determine how a person approaches social and organizational situations, a functional analysis suggests some interesting processes and phenomena. That is, if we suppose that justice judgments are used as described earlier *and* if we assume further that justice judgment processes are such that they serve this use, we can generate some interesting predictions about justice judgment effects. Many of the tests to date of fairness heuristic theory have addressed one or another of these predictions. In addition, the predicted effects have some very important implications for how justice judgments function in organizational contexts. In this section I address these implications and the research that bears on the validity of the implications.

EPISODIC PATTERNING OF JUSTICE JUDGMENT EFFECTS One of the most immediate implications of the idea that justice judgments are used as a heuristic is that the generation and use of fairness judgments will be episodic. In particular, the theory predicts that to be functional as heuristic, justice judgments will be used more than they are revised. At the beginning of a relationship or at times of clear uncertainty or change in the relationship, justice-relevant information will be processed to create or to revise the general justice judgment referred to earlier. This "judgmental phase" will be relatively brief, however, because people need to arrive quickly at a justice judgment in order to have it to guide decisions about cooperation and self-interest. Once a general justice judgment is formed, the theory suggests, there will be a change in processing as the justice judgment is used to guide social decisions and to make sense of incoming information. In this "use phase" the general justice judgment will exert influence on other attitudes and on particular categories of justice judgments, as the information and other judgments are assimilated to the more general, and more stable, general justice judgment. The justice judgment itself will not be the target of much processing and revision. Figure 2.1 shows the general outline of the change in processing.

The logic of this prediction is that the general justice judgment would be of little use as a heuristic if it were itself constantly being revised and updated with new information. There would be little cognitive saving if, instead of trying to calculate all of the outcome and inclusion implications of a given request or action, a person had to try to calculate all of the fairness implications of that request or action. For fairness to function well as a routine basis for deciding actions and conditioning other cognitions, the fairness judgment itself must be relatively stable. I am suggesting that once a general fairness judgment is generated, it will be assumed to be accurate, and any incoming information relevant to the fairness of treatment will be reinterpreted and assimilated to be congruent with the existing general

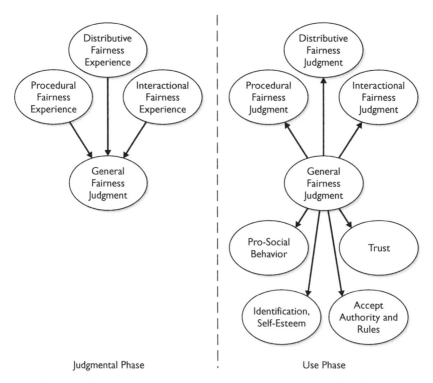

Figure 2.1. A Representation of the Judgmental and Use Phases.

fairness judgment; hence the arrows in the figure from the general fairness judgment to a variety of other cognitions and prosocial behaviors.

PRIMACY EFFECTS   Let us consider first the judgmental phase. The argument is that, because fairness judgments will be needed as one moves into a relationship with other people or with an organization, it is functional for these judgments to be developed quickly at the outset of the relationship. This suggests that fairness judgments will be formed hurriedly, with the first relevant information exercising the greatest influence on feelings of overall fair treatment. In the terminology of social psychology, fairness judgments should show strong primacy effects.

There is some good experimental evidence for just such effects in the justice judgment process. Thompson, Kray, and I (Lind, Kray, & Thompson, 1999) conducted an experiment in which we gave the participants two experiences of fair process and one experience of unfair process in the course of their interaction with a supervisor. The participants worked on three computer-based tasks in a work environment that included some substantial equipment problems on each task. In a "voice" manipulation designed to affect fairness judgments, we told the participants that they could offer explanations of their performance, in terms of relaying to the supervisor the delays caused by the equipment failure, but we also said that the supervisor did not have to accept the information. Each participant received feedback that his or her explanations had been considered on two of the three tasks, and each got a rather rude message denying voice by rejecting the equipment downtime report on the remaining task. The principal experimental manipulation was whether the (unfair) denial of voice occurred on the first, second, or third task.

Figure 2.2 shows the results of the experiment.[4] Even though all of the participants received the same number of positive and negative fairness experiences, those who encountered the unfair experience early in their relationships with their supervisor viewed the supervisor as much more unfair than did those who encountered the unfair experience later. The primacy effect prediction is clearly supported in these findings.

The Lind et al. study suggests not only that justice judgments show a primacy effect but also that the transition from the judgmental phase to the use phase occurs quite quickly. In the experiment, the time difference between the first and the third trial was well under an hour, yet the primacy effect was strong enough to make the subjects who received early unfairness see the supervisor as unfair and those who received the late unfairness see the supervisor as fair. Whether the phase transition occurs this quickly in real-world settings is not yet known, but both this study

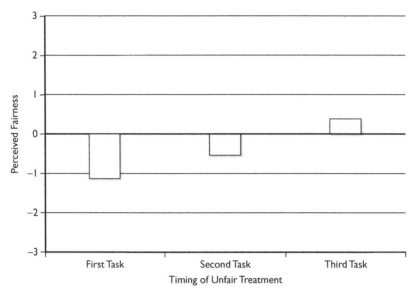

Figure 2.2. A Primacy Effect in Justice Judgments.

and the theory it tests suggest that it is likely that there is probably very little time at the outset of an organizational relationship to establish a feeling of fair treatment.

Fairness heuristic theory also predicts that whatever justice-relevant information is received first will have the greatest impact on the general fairness judgment that forms the basis of the fairness heuristic. Figure 2.1 suggests that procedural, distributive, and outcome fairness experiences will all affect the general fairness judgment during the judgmental phase, but which type of fairness will exert the strongest influence will depend on which information is most readily available at the time the general fairness judgment is being formed. According to the theory, at least one reason that procedural and process fairness seems to play a greater role in affecting fairness-driven attitudes and behavior than does distributive fairness (Lind & Tyler, 1988; Tyler & Lind, 1992) is that procedural and process information is typically encountered before outcome information. The stronger effect of procedure and process is thus a manifestation of the primacy effect: The early process information is processed while the perceiver is still in the judgmental phase, whereas outcome information often does not reach the perceiver until he or she is in the use phase (at which time the perceiver will assimilate the outcome information to the preexisting general fairness judgment; see Figure 2.1). If outcome information were available *before* process information, the theory suggests, then distributive justice experiences would show stronger effects than procedural justice experiences on the general justice judgment and on consequences that flow from the general fairness judgment in the use phase.

Evidence for just this sort of primacy effect is seen in an experimental study by Van den Bos, Vermunt, and Wilke (1997). In one of the first experiments developed explicitly to test fairness heuristic theory, Van den Bos et al. looked at the effects of manipulations of procedural and distributive justice, varying whether the procedural or distributive justice information was received first. They found that when distributive justice information was available before procedural justice information, there was a strong effect on overall fairness judgments for distributive justice and very little effect for procedural justice. On the other hand, when procedural justice information was available first, its effect on overall justice judgments was substantial, and there was very little effect of distributive justice.

Of course these primacy effects are not all-powerful. Strong indications of fairness or unfairness cannot be completely ignored, regardless of when they occur. Rather, what the theory predicts is that early fairness judgments will be especially potent and that there will be a substantial level of inertia in changing these judgments. I return later in the chapter to a discussion of how general fairness judgments can become "unstuck" as people reenter the judgmental phase.

The theory's primacy implication suggests that by far the best time to make a worker a willing and cooperative member of an organization is at the beginning of the worker's relationship with the organization. Manifestly fair treatment early on will pay great dividends later in terms of support, sacrifice, and acceptance of the organization and its authorities. The way to capitalize on the primacy effect is to enact fair process and fair procedures and to provide fair outcomes at the outset of a new employee's experience with the organization.

THE SUBSTITUTABILITY EFFECT   When the judgmental phase ends and the use phase begins, according to the theory, the way that fairness-relevant information is processed undergoes some profound changes. Specifically, the general fairness judgment becomes an anchor and a context used to understand and interpret justice-relevant experiences and cognitions. Consider, for example, the difference in how a given outcome is interpreted during the judgmental phase and during the use phase. In the judgmental phase an outcome that seems to be moderately inequitable will lead to a judgment of distributive unfairness, and this judgment will have a substantial negative effect on the general fairness judgment. Through that judgment the inequitable outcome will have a substantial negative effect on cooperation with organizational goals and authorities. In contrast, if the same moderately inequitable outcome is encountered after fair procedures have created a positive general fairness judgment, the inequitable nature of the outcome may well be explained away in order to preserve the general fairness judgment. The nature of the causal sequence is strikingly different in the two phases. In the judgmental phase, the experienced outcome will cause lower distributive-justice judgments, which will in turn cause lower general-fairness judgments. In the use phase, the experienced outcome will be reinterpreted in light of the favorable general-fairness judgment, so that the general-fairness judgment will exert a generally stronger causative effect on distributive-fairness judgments than vice versa.

This logic leads to another of the implications of fairness heuristic theory—what has come to be called the "substitutability" implication. I noted in describing the primacy implication that it is reasonable in the context of using fairness as a heuristic that people would seize on the first available fairness information, which is often process information, as they build an overall fairness judgment to guide their behavior. It takes only one additional conceptual step to predict that the process will then turn around and work the other way: If a particular type of fairness judgment is missing, people will use other types of fairness to "fill in the blank" as they make fairness judgments. This sequence of effects—procedural fairness impressions to general fairness impressions to distributive fairness impressions—is the way that fairness heuristic theory accounts for what has been called the "fair process effect" (the enhancement of perceived distributive fairness by voice and other procedural fairness variables). Figure 2.3 shows a substitutability effect of this sort. Note that the theory thus predicts the existence of not just "fair process effects" but also "fair outcome effects," of the sort that would occur if early information on the fairness of outcomes enhanced the perceived fairness of later information about the process that generated the outcomes (e.g., see Daly and Tripp, 1996).

In a recent series of experiments, Van den Bos, Wilke, Vermunt, and I tested this implication of the theory by examining when procedural fairness information is used as a substitute for missing distributive fairness information to affect the perceived fairness of outcomes (Van den Bos, Lind, Vermunt, & Wilke, 1997; Van den Bos, Wilke, Lind, & Vermunt, 1998; see Van den Bos, Lind, & Wilke, in press, for a review of these studies). The Van den Bos et al. (1997) study described earlier had shown,

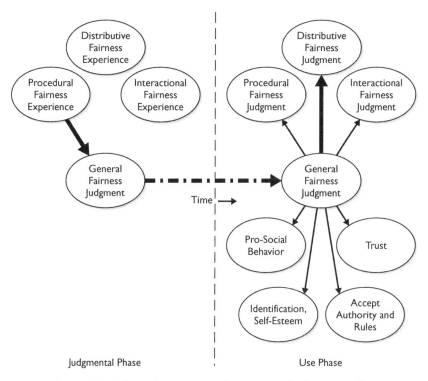

Figure 2.3. The Fair Process Effect as a Substitution Effect.

among other things, that when procedural justice information was available first, not only was there a substantial procedural fairness effect on overall fairness judgments, this effect also carried over to ratings of the fairness of the outcomes. We followed up on this finding with additional studies looking at when procedural justice information—in the form of a voice manipulation—did or did not change perceptions of the fairness of outcomes. We predicted, following the logic of the fairness heuristic, that voice effects would occur when there was an absence of reliable, meaningful distributive fairness information. The first set of studies showed that, as the theory predicted, procedural fairness judgments are used to evaluate outcomes when little equity-relevant information is available. When solid social comparison information about performance and outcomes is available, however, procedural justice judgments have little effect on outcome evaluations (Van den Bos, Lind et al., 1997). The second set of studies showed that, as expected, this substitutability phenomenon works across different types of fairness judgments, but it does not work between fairness and favorability information (Van den Bos, Wilke et al., 1998). In this second set of studies, procedural justice effects on outcome fairness judgments were strong regardless of how much information was available about the favorability of the outcome. As in the Van den Bos, Lind et al. study, however, when information about the fairness of the outcome was readily available, procedural justice effects were much attenuated.

This research showed that the "substitutability effect" does not cross the boundary between fairness judgments and satisfaction judgments. As one would expect from the special role accorded to fairness judgments in the theory, justice judgments can be more or less fungible in the judgmental process, but satisfaction judgments cannot replace or be replaced by fairness judgments. Incidentally, this finding shows that it is necessary to be careful not to view perceived distributive fairness and satisfaction as equivalent (cf. Brockner & Wiesenfeld, 1996).

OTHER FAIRNESS EFFECTS The substitutability effect occurs when information relevant to one type of fairness affects the underlying general fairness judgment during the judgmental phase, and this general fairness judgment then affects judgments of another type of fairness during the use phase. I suspect that there are other cognitions that are similarly affected by being assimilated to the general fairness judgment during the use phase. We know from the Van den Bos, Wilke et al. (1998) study that these assimilative effects do not cross over from fairness to satisfaction judgments, but the logic of the theory suggests that assimilative effects do occur for a variety of cognitions relating to self- and social identity. A strong implication of fairness heuristic theory is that there is a certain class of organizational variables that is especially likely to be affected by fairness. If fairness judgments are important because they serve to move people from individual to group mode, then the most powerful and most obvious effects of fair or unfair treatment should be those that are most sensitive to changes in mode. Attitudes relating to social identity, and those that turn on one's place in the group, are most likely to be altered by the change from individual to group mode. Thus, organizational commitment and organizational identity (and the self-esteem that comes from belonging to a valued group), trust in co-workers and supervisors, and the perceived legitimacy of organizational hierarchy and policy are all attitudes that seem especially likely to be affected by fairness judgments. On the other hand, except for "halo" effects, attitudes that have little to do with the organization as a social entity or with one's place in it will show modest fairness effects. Behaviors that turn on whether one trusts and identifies with the organization will be more strongly affected by fairness judgments than will behaviors that are less closely linked to investment in the organization. Thus, raw individual (and individualized, i.e., not team-based) performance is not likely to be affected by fairness judgments, while performance to goals, team performance, and organizational citizenship behaviors will be much more strongly affected by fairness, as will behaviors that turn on the acceptance of organizational authority.

Evidence in support of this implication of the theory is seen if we look across the entirety of the organizational justice literature. As I noted earlier in this chapter, by far the greatest number of effects, and the strongest effects, of fairness judgments are on attitudes and behaviors related to the group side of organizational life. Consider the findings of a goal-setting study by Lind, Kanfer, and Earley (1990), in comparison with the findings of another performance-oriented experimental study of the effects of voice in performance evaluation, reported by Kanfer, Sawyer, Earley, and Lind (1987). Both studies included manipulations of voice, and both showed strong enhancement of fairness judgments in the voice condition. But the Lind et al. study also showed a voice effect on performance, whereas the Kanfer et al. study did not show any performance effect. The key difference between the two studies, I would argue, is that the performance dynamic in Lind et al. turned on the acceptance of an unpopular goal that had to be internalized by the experimental participants in order for performance to be affected, while the performance dynamic in the Kanfer et al. study involved only individual workers performing for individual gains. The fairness manipulation affected performance in the Lind et al. study because the internalization process could occur only if the worker accepted the authority of the experimenter who set the goal and because the acceptance of authority is a group-mode versus individual-mode issue.

Even if strong justice effects are reserved for the more "relational" of organizational processes, though, there is still plenty of opportunity for the justice judgment processes posited by fairness heuristic theory to have substantial effects on performance in modern organizations. Indeed, with the current culture of teamwork and "flat" organizations, voluntary investment in the team and organization becomes all the more critical, and fairness as a way of promoting this involvement becomes an extremely attractive management principle. This said, however, fairness heuristic theory suggests that fairness cannot do everything. Managing for fairness is a very powerful tool for some particularly important organizational issues, but it is no panacea for all the problems that might arise in organizational life.

PHASE-SHIFTING EVENTS In the discussion concerning the episodic patterning of justice processes, I focused for the most part on the transition from the initial judgmental phase in a new relationship to the use phase, a phase shift that gives rise to the primacy and substitutability predictions. It would be unreasonable to suppose that people never revisit the validity of their fairness judgments, however. Thus, it is interesting to speculate about what might prompt someone to reenter the judgmental phase at some later point in a relationship.

Returning to the functional analysis that underlies much of fairness heuristic theory, we can ask what would be reasonable stimuli to push fairness processes back into the judgmental phase. It seems to me that there are two good candidates: 1) signs that the relationship in question is changing and 2) fairness-relevant events or information that falls far outside what would be expected from the existing general fairness judgment. Both of these types of phase-shifting events seem likely to make the perceiver question his or her understanding of the relationship and its fairness, and it is this questioning that would push the perceiver from use mode back into judgmental mode.

A clear sign that the relationship to which the fairness judgment is attached is changing will almost of necessity call into question the validity of the existing general fairness judgment. The sign, I would argue, can be either actual or symbolic, but it must be noticeable, and it must signal a substantial change in the nature of the relationship. The logic of fairness heuristic theory points to considerable resistance in changing the general fairness judgment, so the relationship change must be more than just normal, day-to-day alterations in the style, outcome, or patterning of interactions. In an organizational context a change in leadership, a merger, or restructuring would likely push people back into judgmental mode. Once the shift back to judgmental mode occurs, one would expect to see the processes that were discussed in the earlier section on primacy: A relatively rapid gathering and processing of fairness-relevant information, the quick formation of a new general fairness judgment, and then transition back to a new use phase.

Some evidence in favor of this line of thought is seen in the growing literature on the justice effects of layoff and other termination experiences. The work that Brockner and his colleagues (e.g., Brockner & Greenberg, 1990; Brockner, Konovsky, Schneider, Folger, Martin, & Bies, 1994) have done on the substantial impact of layoff procedures on the attitudes of layoff survivors, and the work that Greenberg and I (Lind et al., 2000) have done on the behavior of terminated employees both show relatively strong effects for justice experiences encountered during times of organizational restructuring, just as one would expect from the proposition advanced earlier. The work that Greenberg and I did takes the issue one step further by testing empirically whether fairness judgments held prior to the time of the terminations are better or worse predictors of litigation against the company than are fairness judgments generated at the time of termination. The theoretical analysis just presented would predict that it is the judgments formed at the time of restructuring that have the greatest impact on subsequent behavior, and this is indeed what the data showed.

Practically speaking, this means that just as the early days of an organizational relationship are probably critical times for forming general feelings of fair or unfair treatment, so too are times of real or symbolic change in the organization. It is probably no accident that savvy organizational politicians realize that one of the few ways to forge a new relationship with a widely disaffected workforce is to undertake some radical change in the leadership or structure of the organization. What a very obvious "change at the top" does is to push people back into judgmental mode and invite them to consider new outcomes, procedures, or social process as they re-form their fairness judgments. Of course, even the most successful device for pushing people back into judgmental mode is of little value if the subsequent experiences are the same as those that led to the original fairness judgments.

The other type of event that will probably prompt transition back into a judgmental phase is a fairness-relevant experience that falls well outside expectations based on the existing general fairness judgment. Just as the relationship changes discussed earlier would need to be quite substantial, so too the violation of expectations would have to be fairly radical if the usefulness of the general fairness judgment as a heuristic is to be questioned. Shifts back to judgmental mode probably occur when a person encounters an outcome, procedure, or process experience that was radically different from that expected from the general fairness judgment. Less radical outcome, procedure, and process experiences will be "explained away" as the person tries to avoid the refocusing of cognitive effort and the cognitive and social turmoil that accompanies reentry into judgmental phase processing.

Note that the unexpected experience that shifts the perceiver back into judgmental mode can be either positive or negative; what is important is that there be a truly substantial deviation from expectations. Although it is probably true that natural optimism makes negative outcomes, biased procedures, or disrespectful process more unexpected than their positive counterparts (e.g., Kanouse & Hanson, 1972), it is also true that in many social and organizational contexts an extremely positive experience can deviate a great deal from expectations. If a person receives a manifestly equitable outcome, an unquestionably fair and just procedure, or clearly respectful behavior at the hands of someone who had been regarded as an enemy, the perceiver may reenter the judgmental phase and look for new information about the fairness of the other. The outcome, procedure, or process would have to be so far from expectations that it could not be explained away as some Machiavellian tactic, but if this were the case, and if the fair experiences continued through the newly reinitiated judgmental phase, it might be possible for the two to form a new and more positive relationship.[5]

Questions Answered

With the preceding ideas developed in mind, we can return to the questions posed earlier in the chapter. Fairness heuristic theory gives a fresh perspective on the issues raised there.

Why Are Justice Judgments Linked with Relationship Concerns?

A clear implication of the use of fairness judgments as a heuristic in the way I have suggested is that questions of fairness of treatment are most naturally thought of in relational terms. Overall fairness judgments will be used to address concerns about exploitation and identity investment, and these issues are best addressed, I would argue, when what people generally mean by fairness is not a single fair transaction but rather a fair relationship. Put somewhat differently, when people think about fairness, they think about where they stand in long-term, enduring relationships. Indeed, the whole theme of what I have been calling group mode is a reduction of concern with individual transactions in favor of involvement in and identification with the organization or group, so it would make little sense if people were to move into this mode on the basis of their impressions of the fairness of isolated transactions. This means that for both procedural and distributive fairness judgments, great attention will be given to the relational implications of the procedure, process, or outcome. Elsewhere (Lind & Tyler, 1988, chapter 10) I have argued that this is a reason—over and above the primacy processes discussed earlier—for predicting that procedural fairness judgments have greater impact than distributive fairness judgments in determining overall feelings of fair treatment. Process information is more readily interpretable as indicative of one's relationship with authorities and with the organization or group.

Process information, containing as it does nuances of style and politeness, carries a great deal of information about such things as positive or negative regard, social inclusion, and solidarity. Outcome information, which is generally determined by factors other than solidarity of relationship, simply does not have similar purity of relational information when it comes to revealing whether a relationship is healthy and reliable. This said, however, it should be remembered that outcome information can carry very important relationship information, as Greenberg (1993) has noted. If a person is denied a promotion or a raise while others receive desired outcomes of this sort, the implication is that the deprived person is not held in as high esteem nor deemed as important to the organization as are those who receive the positive outcomes. Employers often forget this aspect of organizational outcomes and allocate pay increases on the basis of what an employee would receive in the open market or on the basis of some idea of objective need (such as lowering the percentage raise of high-salary employees). The potential downside to this approach to reward is that such pay or promotion policies can send an unintentional message of exclusion or disapprobation to the very employees who are most loyal and most essential to the organization. The perceived unfairness that accompanies these outcomes can shift these valuable employees from group mode to individual mode and have disastrous effects on organizational functioning.

What Is the Relationship between Distributive and Procedural Justice?

The theory produces some rather radical notions about the relationships among distributive, interactional, and procedural justice. First, it suggests that instead of seeking some general conclusion about which type of justice judgment experience has the most influence on a particular organizational attitude or behavior, we should view the various categories of justice experience as more or less fungible. The earlier comments about the "relationality" of procedural and process justice experiences notwithstanding, the general thrust of the theory is that a perceiver "grabs" any justice-relevant information that is handy, forms a quick general fairness judgment, and then gets out of the business of processing fairness experiences. The practical implication is that instead of trying to discover empirical relationships of the form "procedural justice promotes acceptance of authority" or "distributive justice decreases turnover," we should be focusing on how to teach people to provide all the positive justice experiences they can early on in a person's experience with an organization, supervisor, or co-worker.

In more theoretical terms, the theory suggests that the reason the three categories of justice judgment are correlated is that each can be profoundly influenced by the others via the substitutability effect. This means that which type of justice predominates, in the sense of having the greatest influence on the others, may depend not on some structural or cognitive characteristic of one type of justice or another but may instead be an "accident" of the timing of justice experiences. In line with the arguments presented in the preceding paragraph, this means that we should be less preoccupied with differentiating between various types of justice and more concerned with understanding the consequences of patterns of justice experience, whatever their classification in the distributive-procedural-interactional categories.

Does Procedural Justice Matter More When Outcomes Are Negative?

I noted earlier that Brockner and Wiesenfeld (1996) have argued that procedural justice effects become stronger when outcomes are negative; I also noted that this statement seemed to me to be too general in light of a substantial number of research studies that fail to show this interactive effect. But although it is clear that there are many studies that do not show the Brockner and Wiesenfeld interaction, there are also many studies that do. The question posed earlier in this chapter asked when and how outcomes are related to the magnitude of procedural fairness effects.

From the perspective of the theory presented earlier, the real question should be how outcomes interact with all of the various forms of justice, and the answer is that outcomes can alter justice effects when the outcome, positive or negative, is radically divergent from expectations. When an outcome is experienced that is divergent enough from expectations to prompt a shift back into judgmental phase, the effect of any justice experience—procedural, interactional, or outcome—is magnified because the information is actively incorporated into the new general justice judgment that is being formed. This means that an unexpected negative outcome can indeed enhance the impact of procedural justice experiences as Brockner and Wiesenfeld predict, but then so could an unexpectedly positive outcome, and either could enhance the effects of distributive or interactional justice experiences as well. Similarly, unexpectedly positive or negative procedures or social process can enhance the effects of distributive, procedural, or interactional justice experiences. The key is that the outcome, procedure, or social process must be so unexpected that it prompts a phase shift and that the subsequent outcome, procedure, or social process experience follows in time to be processed during the judgmental phase. Brockner and Wiesenfeld did indeed anticipate this solution to some extent, but in my opinion they did not qualify their general statement sufficiently. The line of reasoning advanced here would say that the particular interaction they propose is a rather rare justice effect in the normal course of things.

Fairness as a Productive Social Dynamic

In presenting the mechanics of fairness heuristic theory earlier in this chapter, I argued that much of the logic of using fairness in this way turned on the one hand on the value of the heuristic in allowing people to get on with their relationships with the social and organizational entities to which they belong and on the other hand on the attractiveness of fairness as an indicator of safety from exclusion and exploitation. There is another implication of the theory that touches on a slightly different, but no less adaptive, function of fairness. The very fact that people use fairness to guide their behavior—and whether one accepts fairness heuristic theory or not, the research literature in organizational justice makes it clear that people do use fairness to a remarkable extent—implies that fair treatment can be as much a management heuristic as a compliance heuristic. That is to say, just as people who are treated fairly tend without much calculation to comply with requests from fair authorities, so too can authorities, without a great deal of calculation, count on fair treatment to produce favorable organizationally oriented responses. One of the standard lectures in classes on organizational behavior has to do with how one must be careful to "incent" only desired behaviors (i.e., to reward that which one wants to see more of and not to reward behaviors that are harmful to organizational goals). Many classical cases of management error involve instances in which one behavior was rewarded when another behavior altogether was what was sought.

But it is often very difficult to work through all the contingencies that connect what one can reward to what one wants. Indeed, sometimes—perhaps even oftentimes—the connections are so complex that it is impossible to forge a very close connection between reward and performance. In these circumstances, proxies for performance of specific desired actions are generally used. Thus, one might desire a service unit to resolve customer problems quickly and effectively, but not knowing quite how to measure the effectiveness of solutions in any but the most extreme negative cases, one might reward people in this unit on the basis of turnaround time and lack of complaints. Of course this reward system could be "gamed" by customer service representatives who found a quick way to stifle complaints, even if this approach did not benefit the company or accomplish the original goals.

Fairness heuristic theory suggests another way of dealing with this management dilemma. Given that one is already using a management heuristic (rewarding a *presumably* sensible proxy), why not use a tried and true one: fairness. There is a good argument to be made, I would suggest, that fair treatment—fair outcomes, procedures, and process—coupled with clear and convincing articulation of the goals of the unit could go a long way to producing exactly the results any good manager wants. Instead of trying to work out complicated contingencies, a wise manager can cut monitoring costs and eliminate layers of administration by being manifestly fair in how he or she treats subordinates, while at the same time clearly enunciating a vision and some concrete goals for the unit or organization. The earlier discussion suggests that this must be a policy that encompasses both outcomes and process. No possibility for fair treatment—where that means both equitable outcomes and respectful open process—should be missed, especially early on in the worker's tenure or at times of organizational turmoil, and it is crucial that what is asked of the employees is clearly in the interest of the organization or workgroup.

If this is done, the theory suggests, high levels of performance and compliance can be pretty much counted on. To be sure, just as the individual level fairness heuristic can be both wrong and abused, so too will some employees take advantage of the use of fairness as a management heuristic. Even so, the overall payoff seems likely to be well in the positive range, and the "process cost" savings might be substantial. If favorable reactions to fair treatment are as ubiquitous as the organizational justice literature suggests them to be, abuses will be infrequent and may well be self-limiting, as co-workers who have invested identity in the organization exert influence over those who have not.

Of course, this proposal needs a good bit of field testing before those of us who work in organizational justice can advance it with more than theoretical confidence. It is quite reasonable to suppose, however, that a "rule of thumb" of fair treatment on the part of management will be met with a "rule of thumb" of personal investment and acquiescence to the greater good on the part of employees to produce a favorable dynamic in fairness-oriented firms. The theory I have set forth in this chapter certainly argues that there is a productive dynamic that can be born of this combination of heuristics.

NOTES

1. The theory arose from my work with Tom Tyler on the psychology of procedural justice (e.g., Lind & Tyler, 1988, chapter 10; Tyler & Lind, 1990,

1992), and it has evolved in my work with Kees Van den Bos, Riël Vermunt, and Henk Wilke (Van den Bos, Lind, Vermunt, & Wilke, 1997; Van den Bos, Wilke, & Lind, 1998; Van den Bos, Wilke, Lind, & Vermunt, 1998).

2. Kelley and Thibaut (1978) recognize that shortcuts are often used; see their discussion of "transformations." In interdependence theory terms, I am in fact suggesting that fairness judgments are the basis of a ubiquitous simplifying transformation.

3. We justice researchers need to refine our measures of justice judgments if this idea is in fact correct (and the research literature I review suggests that it is). The general justice judgment I posit is probably best measured with items that ask things such as "in general how fairly are you treated . . ." or "in general how fair is your relationship with . . ." The "how fairly are you treated" formulation has in the past often been used to measure process or procedural justice, but the theory suggests that this is probably not wise. It makes a great deal more sense to direct measurements of particular types of justice at the relevant referent—"how fair is the outcome/procedure/process"—rather than risk misinterpreting ratings as showing one sort of fairness when in fact they tap another.

4. The values shown in the figure are taken from conditions in which a prior group-identity-inducing manipulation had been enacted. As predicted by the theory, primacy effects were stronger when the subjects identified with the group.

5. Of course, unexpectedly poor outcomes, experiences, and process at the hands of one who in past treated you fairly can prompt a reassessment of that prior judgment, and if the negative experiences continue a negative, individual-mode relationship can be forged. Witness the bitter battles that often accompany divorces in the personal sphere and the extremely negative reactions to betrayal by friends in virtually all spheres of life.

REFERENCES

Adams, J. S. (1965). Inequity in social exchange. In L. Berkowitz (Ed.), *Advances in Experimental Social Psychology* (Vol. 2, pp. 267–299). New York: Academic Press.

Bies, R. J., & Moag, J. S. (1986). Interactional justice: Communication criteria of fairness. In R. J. Lewicki, B. H. Sheppard, & M. H. Bazerman (Eds.), *Research on negotiation in organizations* (pp. 43–55). Greenwich, CT: JAI Press.

Brewer, M. B., & Kramer, R. M. (1986). Choice behavior in social dilemmas: Effects of social identity, group size, and decision framing. *Journal of Personality and Social Psychology, 50*, 543–549.

Brockner, J., & Greenberg, J. (1990). The impact of layoffs on survivors: An organizational justice perspective. In J. Carroll (Ed.), *Applied social psychology and organizational settings* (pp. 45–75). Hillsdale, NJ: Lawrence Erlbaum.

Brockner, J., Konovsky, M., Cooper-Schneider, R., Folger, R., Martin, C., & Bies, R. J. (1994). Interactive effects of procedural justice and outcome negativity on victims and survivors of job loss. *Academy of Management Journal, 37,* 397–409.

Brockner, J., & Wiesenfeld, B. M. (1996). An integrative framework for explaining reactions to decisions: Interactive effects of outcomes and procedures. *Psychological Bulletin, 120,* 189–208.

Daly, J. P., & Tripp, T. M. (1996). Is outcome fairness used to make procedural fairness judgments when procedural information is inaccessible? *Social Justice Research, 9,* 327–349.

Folger, R., Robinson, S. L., Dietz, J., McLean-Parks, J., & Baron, R. A. (1998, August). When colleagues become violent: Employee threats and assaults as a function of societal violence and organizational injustice. Paper presented at the 1998 meeting of the Academy of Management, Cincinnati, OH.

Greenberg, J. (1987). A taxonomy of organizational justice theories. *Academy of Management Review, 12,* 9–22.

Greenberg, J. (1993). The social side of fairness: Interpersonal and informational classes of organizational justice. In R. Cropanzano (Ed.), *Justice in the workplace* (pp. 79–103). Hillsdale, NJ: Erlbaum.

Greenberg, J. (1994). Using socially fair treatment to promote acceptance of a work site smoking ban. *Journal of Applied Psychology, 79,* 288–297.

Greenberg, J., & Scott, K. S. (1996). Why do employees bite the hands that feed them? Employee theft as a social exchange process. In B. M. Staw & L. L. Cummings (Eds.), *Research in organizational behavior* (Vol. 18, pp. 111–156). Greenwich, CT: JAI Press.

Huo, Y. J., Smith, H., Tyler, T. R., & Lind, E. A. (1996). Superordinate identification, subgroup identification, and justice concerns: Is separatism the problem? Is assimilation the answer? *Psychological Science, 7,* 40–45.

Kanfer, R., Sawyer, J., Earley, P. C., & Lind, E. A. (1987). Fairness and participation in task evaluation procedures: Effects on attitudes and performance. *Social Justice Research, 1,* 235–249.

Kanouse, D. E., & Hanson, L. R., Jr. (1972). Negativity in evaluations. In E. E. Jones, D. E. Kanouse, H. H. Kelley, R. E. Nisbett, S. Valins, & B. Weiner (Eds.), *Attribution: Perceiving the causes of behavior* (pp. 47–62). Morristown, NJ: General Learning Press.

Kelley, H. H., & Thibaut, J. (1978). *The psychology of interdependence.* New York: Wiley.

Konovsky, M., & Folger, R. (1991, August). The effects of procedural and distributive justice on organizational citizenship behavior. Paper presented at the 1991 meeting of the Academy of Management, Miami Beach, FL.

Lind, E. A. (1990). *Arbitrating high-stakes cases: An evaluation of court-annexed arbitration in a United States district court*. Santa Monica, CA: Rand Corporation.

Lind, E. A. (1994). Procedural justice and culture: Evidence for ubiquitous process concerns. *Zeitschrift für Rechtssoziologie, 15*, 24–36.

Lind, E. A. (1995a). Justice and authority in organizations. In R. Cropanzano and K. M. Kacmar (Eds.), *Politics, justice, and support: Managing the social climate of work organizations* (pp. 83–96). Westport, CT: Quorum.

Lind, E. A. (1995b). *Social conflict and social justice: Some lessons from the social psychology of justice*. Leiden, the Netherlands: Leiden University Press.

Lind, E. A., Greenberg, J., Scott, K. S., & Welchans, T. D. (2000). The winding road from employee to complainant: Situational and psychological determinants of wrongful termination lawsuits. Administrative Science Quarterly.

Lind, E. A., Kanfer, R., & Earley, P. C. (1990). Voice, control, and procedural justice: Instrumental and noninstrumental concerns in fairness judgments. *Journal of Personality and Social Psychology, 59*, 952–959.

Lind, E. A., Kray, L. J., & Thompson, L. (1999). Primacy effects in justice judgments: Testing predictions from fairness heuristic theory. Unpublished manuscript, Duke University.

Lind, E. A., Kulik, C., Ambrose, M., & Park, M. (1993). Individual and corporate dispute resolution: Using procedural fairness as a decision heuristic. *Administrative Science Quarterly, 38*, 224–251.

Lind, E. A., Kurtz, S., Musante, L., Walker, L., & Thibaut, J. W. (1980). Procedure and outcome effects on reactions to adjudicated resolution of conflicts of interests. *Journal of Personality and Social Psychology, 39*, 643–653.

Lind, E. A., and Lissak, R. I. (1985). Apparent impropriety and procedural fairness judgments. *Journal of Experimental Social Psychology, 21*, 19–29.

Lind, E. A., Lissak, R. I., & Conlon, D. E. (1983). Decision control and process control effects on procedural fairness judgments. *Journal of Applied Social Psychology, 4*, 338–350.

Lind, E. A., & MacCoun, R. J. (1992, March). The fairness heuristic: Rationality and relationality in procedural choice. Paper presented at the 1992 annual meeting of the Society for the Advancement of Socioeconomics, Irvine, CA.

Lind, E. A., & Tyler, T. R. (1988). *The social psychology of procedural justice*. New York: Plenum Press.

Podsakoff, P. M., & MacKenzie, S. B. (1993). Citizenship behavior and fairness in organizations: Issues and directions for future research. *Employee Responsibilities and Rights Journal, 6*, 235–247.

Smith, H. J., Tyler, T. R., Huo, Y. J., Ortiz, D. J., & Lind, E. A. (1998). The self-relevant implications of the group-value model: Group membership, self-worth, and treatment quality. *Journal of Experimental Social Psychology, 34,* 470–493.

Thibaut, J., & Kelley, H. H. (1959). *The social psychology of groups.* New York: Wiley.

Thibaut, J., & Walker, L. (1975). *Procedural justice: A psychological analysis.* Hillsdale, NJ: Erlbaum.

Thibaut, J., & Walker, L. (1978). A theory of procedure. *California Law Review, 66,* 541–566.

Tyler, T. R. (1994). Psychological models of the justice motive. *Journal of Personality and Social Psychology, 67,* 850–863.

Tyler, T. R., & Lind, E. A. (1990). Intrinsic versus community-based justice models: When does group membership matter? *Journal of Social Issues, 46,* 83–94.

Tyler, T. R., & Lind, E. A. (1992). A relational model of authority in groups. In M. Zanna (Ed.), *Advances in experimental social psychology* (Vol. 24, pp. 115–192). New York: Academic Press.

Tyler, T. R., & Smith, H. (1997). Social justice and social movements. In D. Gilbert, S. Fiske, G. Lindzey (Eds.), *Handbook of Social Psychology* (4th edition, vol. 2, pp. 595–629). New York: McGraw-Hill.

Van den Bos, K., Lind, E. A., Vermunt, R., & Wilke, H. (1997). How do I judge my outcome when I don't know the outcomes of others? The psychology of the fair process effect. *Journal of Personality and Social Psychology, 73,* 1034–1046.

Van den Bos, K., Lind, E. A., & Wilke, H. (in press). The psychology of procedural justice and distributive justice viewed from the perspective of fairness heuristic theory. In R. Cropanzano (Ed.), *Justice in the workplace: Volume II From theory to practice.* Hillsdale, NJ: Lawrence Erlbaum & Associates.

Van den Bos, K., Vermunt, R., & Wilke, H. A. M. (1997). Procedural and distributive justice: What is fair depends more on what comes first than on what comes next. *Journal of Personality and Social Psychology, 72,* 95–104.

Van den Bos, K., Wilke, H. A. M., & Lind, E. A. (1998). When do we need procedural fairness? The role of trust in authority. *Journal of Personality and Social Psychology, 75,* 1449–1458.

Van den Bos, K., Wilke, H. A. M., Lind, E. A., & Vermunt, R. (1998). Evaluating outcomes by means of the fair process effect: Evidence for different processes in fairness and satisfaction judgments. *Journal of Personality and Social Psychology, 74,* 1493–1503.

Walker, L., LaTour, S., Lind, E. A., & Thibaut, J. (1974). Reactions of participants and observers to modes of adjudication. *Journal of Applied Social Psychology, 4,* 295–310.

Walker, L., Lind, E. A., & Thibaut, J. (1979). The relation between procedural and distributive justice. *Virginia Law Review, 65,* 1401–1420.

3

Interactional (In)Justice: The Sacred and the Profane

Robert J. Bies

HE TAKES GREAT PLEASURE *in belittling me and publicly ridiculing me. He blames me for his mistakes . . . accuses me of things I never did nor was responsible for. He takes great pride that he treats everybody equally . . . that is, cruelly. I have my dignity . . . I am a human being, for God's sakes. And, if I experience one more indignity from him, he no longer will be a human being!*

—Product Manager of telecommunications company

EVERY MAN IS TO BE RESPECTED *as an absolute end in himself; and it is a crime against the dignity that belongs to him as a human being, to use him as a mere means for some external purpose.*

—Immanuel Kant

OVER THE PAST 15 YEARS, I have interviewed and surveyed hundreds, if not thousands, of working people about their experiences of injustice. After analyzing the data, I have concluded that our models of organizational justice are incomplete and inadequate. As researchers, our efforts have been primarily dedicated to the precise measurement of "perceptions" and "judgments" of justice, as if we are "intuitive philosophers" attempting to define "objective" concepts of justice (Bies, 1987). I am not belittling those efforts, nor am I suggesting that those efforts have been misguided. To the contrary, we need better construct validity and measurement of organizational justice variables. For, as Greenberg (1990c) has correctly admonished us, the sloppy and ad hoc measurement of our theoretical constructs has imposed serious limitations on our understanding of organizational justice.

At the same time, there is clearly more to justice than cognitive perceptions and judgments (Bies, 1987; Cahn, 1949; Solomon, 1990). The truth is that, as illustrated in the introductory quotation, when people talk about justice, their narratives are in terms of the injustices they experience (Shreve & Shreve, 1997) and, in particular, in terms of mistreatment they receive from another person—concerns that I have referred to as *interactional justice* (Bies, 1987; Bies & Moag, 1986). In these stories, interactional injustice is described as a "hot and burning" experience (Bies & Tripp, 2000; Mikula, 1986). The intense and personal pain associated with interactional injustice is experienced as a profound harm to one's psyche and identity (Bies & Tripp, 1996)—that is, one's sense of self. It is the human and existential dimensions to this harm that are underemphasized and underappreciated in organizational justice theory.

In this chapter I reexamine the construct of interactional justice and its development from the moment of "birth" to its current "adolescent" stage. I outline the controversy surrounding its conceptual status and identity. In addition, I review the empirical evidence assessing the distinction between interactional justice and procedural justice.

From this analysis, two conclusions emerge. First, *people can and do distinguish interactional justice from procedural justice.* A growing number of studies demonstrate that interactional justice and procedural justice are associated with different organizational behavior variables. The evidence for this conclusion is consistent and supportive.

Second, *people possess a view of the self as "sacred," and a violation of that sacred self arouses the sense of injustice.* I will argue that researchers can gain a deeper insight into justice by listening to and analyzing people's narratives of injustice (Shreve & Shreve, 1997). More specifically, if we begin our analysis by examining the events or incidents arousing the sense

Although I take full responsibility for the ideas in this chapter, justice requires that I acknowledge the constructive criticisms and suggestions of Tom Tripp, Dan McAllister, Susan Bies—and, of course, the two editors of this volume.

of *in*justice, then we can generate a more complete understanding of justice dynamics. Therefore, I find it useful to refer to concerns about interpersonal treatment as interactional (in)justice.

I conclude the chapter with a discussion of the movement of organizational justice theory into its "adulthood" stage. Evidence of this intellectual growth is found in the growing scholarly appreciation of the complexities and paradoxes of organizational justice. I argue that this intellectual growth also carries moral responsibilities for us as researchers, responsibilities that require us to be more "critical" of our research objectives.

The Birth of a Construct: The Search for Identity

Just a decade ago, I went forth boldly to proclaim that procedural justice theory and research did not capture the breadth of people's concerns about a "fair process" (Bies & Moag, 1986). In particular, I argued that, while people are clearly concerned about the formal procedures used in a decision-making process (Thibaut & Walker, 1975), they are also concerned about the interpersonal treatment they receive from another person. I referred to these concerns as *interactional justice*.

This justice construct, however, did not come from out of the blue—it had its roots in my basement office located in the Graduate School of Business at Stanford University. Almost two decades ago, I wrote a dissertation proposal entitled, "Injustice: A Valuation Framework." That proposal began with the sentence: "Through a variety of mediums, organizations convey how much they 'value their members.'" Of particular importance, I continued, are those mediums that are "interpersonal in nature," and "the undervaluing or unjust treatment of an interpersonal nature may be the primary target of an individual's anger and discontent in an organizational setting." Although I had great passion for that proposal and the ideas embedded in it, I could not persuade my dissertation committee (Joanne Martin, Gene Webb, and Hal Leavitt) or other faculty I respected greatly (for example, Jeff Pfeffer) of the "value-added" nature of my ideas. Thus, like many Ph.D. students, I watched my dissertation proposal go down in flames—and it was the proper fate at the time.

Even though my initial dissertation proposal "died," my passion for the ideas in the proposal did not. Five years later, the core ideas in my initial proposal were resurrected and found new life in a paper that I presented in 1985 at the Research in Negotiation in Organizations Conference held at Duke University. Now armed with data and a little more intellectual maturity, I introduced the topic of "interactional justice" to a collegial group of skeptical scholars. Although the conference participants were relatively open-minded about my ideas, I found little groundswell of support for *another* type of justice. In fact, most people tried to persuade me that I was just articulating another facet of procedural justice. (This paper was published in 1986 in the *Research on Negotiation in Organizations* series; Bies & Moag, 1986.)

Despite this initial lukewarm response to the construct of interactional justice, I persevered. Through the encouragement and support of Larry Cummings, I was provided another opportunity to "showcase" interactional justice in my chapter, "The Predicament of Injustice: The Management of Moral Outrage," which was published in 1987 in the *Research in Organizational Behavior* series. In this chapter I focused on the importance of social accounts, or explanations, as an interpersonal strategy to manage perceptions of organizational justice. This chapter generated more conceptual interest in the study of social accounts and organizational justice (for example, Greenberg, 1990b).

With these two publications, interest in, and empirical research on, interactional justice took off. Interactional justice has been found to be an important variable for understanding a variety of worker attitudes and behaviors in response to job layoffs (Bies, Martin, & Brockner, 1993; Bennett, Martin, Bies, & Brockner, 1995), budget decisions (Bies & Shapiro, 1987; Bies, Shapiro, & Cummings, 1988), purchase decisions (Bies & Shapiro, 1987), negotiation tactics (Daly, 1991; Shapiro & Bies, 1994), corporate recruitment practices (Bies & Moag, 1986; Bies & Shapiro, 1988), customer service practices (Clemmer, 1993), market exploitation practices (Bies, Tripp, & Neale, 1993), and abusive bosses (Bies & Tripp, 1995, in press; Hornstein, 1996).

In addition, interactional justice has been an important variable for understanding organizational citizenship behaviors (Moorman, 1991), trust in management and organizational commitment (Barling & Phillips, 1993), supervisor legitimacy (Masterson, Lewis-McClear, Goldman, & Taylor, 1997), acceptance of a worksite smoking ban (Greenberg, 1994), revenge (Bies & Tripp, 1996; McLean Parks, 1997; Tripp & Bies, 1997), employee theft (Greenberg, 1990a, 1997), employee litigation behavior (Bies & Tyler, 1993), consumer complaint behavior (Blodgett, Hill, & Tax, 1997), citizen encounters with the police and courts (Tyler, 1988), and workplace privacy concerns (Bies, 1993, 1996).

After the "coming out" of interactional justice, there emerged related theory-building efforts that also highlighted the importance of interpersonal treatment in an analysis of justice. For example, in the group-value model of procedural justice (Lind & Tyler, 1988) and the relational model of authority (Huo & Tyler, Chapter 7; Tyler & Lind, 1992), a key variable is *standing*, which shares conceptual properties with my construct, interactional justice. Indeed, when one examines the operationalization of standing by researchers (e.g., Tyler, 1990), standing is equivalent to my construct of interactional justice. Similarly, in an underappreciated conceptual analysis, Greenberg (1993b) proposed a conceptual framework for analyzing justice, one that explicitly recognized the importance of interpersonal determinants of organizational justice.

In these parallel efforts, however, Lind, Tyler, and Greenberg view interactional justice not as a separate construct but rather as an interpersonal or social dimension of procedural justice. Therein lie the seeds of controversy. Specifically, the controversy is over whether interactional justice is a separate form of justice (Bies & Moag, 1986; Bies, 1987), or an interpersonal component of procedural justice (Cropanzano & Randall, 1993; Folger & Bies, 1989; Greenberg, 1990c; Lind & Tyler, 1988; Sheppard, Lewicki, & Minton, 1992; Tyler & Bies, 1990; Tyler & Lind, 1992), or a social dimension of both distributive and procedural justice (Greenberg, 1993b).

If we are to advance our understanding of justice processes and dynamics and build a unified theory of organizational justice, then we must, as Greenberg (1990c, 1996) wisely reminds us, bring some clarity to this conceptual confusion. In the next section, I examine the conceptual controversy surrounding interactional justice. In addition, I review the relevant empirical evidence assessing the distinction between interactional justice and procedural justice.

"Ball of Confusion": Striving for Conceptual Clarity

In my initial theorizing (Bies, 1987; Bies & Moag, 1986), I conceptualized interactional justice as a third form of justice, separate from distributive and procedural justice. More specifically, I argued that interactional justice referred to people's concerns about "the quality of interpersonal treatment they receive during the enactment of organizational procedures" (Bies & Moag, 1986, p. 44). Clearly, my focus was on interpersonal treatment, thus making it separate from procedural justice as then defined in the literature. But because I embedded the analysis of interactional justice in the context of a decision-making process, one could view interactional concerns as another component of procedural justice—thus, the beginning of the confusion.

The fundamental debate in the controversy is over the relationship between interactional justice and procedural justice. The conventional wisdom that has emerged from the debate is best articulated by Greenberg and colleagues (1993b; Cropanzano & Greenberg, 1997). Although noting the importance of interpersonal determinants of justice, Cropanzano and Greenberg (1997) argue that interactional justice "became increasingly difficult to distinguish from structural procedural justice. For one thing, both the formal procedures and the interpersonal interactions jointly comprise the process that leads to an allocation decision. Additionally, interactional and structural procedural justice had similar consequences and correlates . . . (and were) highly related to one another" (p. 330).

But let us take another look at the three studies cited by Cropanzano and Greenberg (1997), which was their evidence to support the argument that we should view interactional justice as a social dimension of procedural justice. There were Clemmer (1993), Konovsky and Cropanzano (1991), and Koper, Van Knippenberg, Bouhuijs, Vermunt, and Wilke (1993). In Clemmer's (1993) study of fairness and customer satisfaction with services, she found similar correlates and consequences for procedural justice and interactional justice, as suggested by Cropanzano and Greenberg (1997). But Clemmer also found that procedural justice and interactional justice "each contributed uniquely to customers' satisfaction" (p. 202). Further, she reported that "the sorting process in the qualitative phase also supports separating the two constructs" (p. 202).

In their study of drug testing fairness, Konovsky and Cropanzano (1991) report a .62 correlation between procedural justice and interactional justice. Although that is a high correlation, they also reported a .53 correlation between procedural justice and distributive justice—and there was no call for integrating procedural justice and distributive justice. Further, the operationalization of interactional justice by Konovsky and Cropanzano, in the form of explanations, is a narrow and limited view of interactional justice. Finally, even with the problems with their narrow operationalization of interactional justice, the explanation variable was significantly related to affective commitment, along with procedural justice—but interactional justice was uniquely related to job satisfaction, whereas there was no significant relationship for procedural justice.

In two experiments designed to examine the relationship between procedural fairness and self-esteem, Koper et al. (1993) found a significant correlation between interactional justice and procedural justice ($r = .77$ in Study 1, $r = .56$ in Study 2), as suggested by Cropanzano and Greenberg. But, as in the Konovsky and Cropanzano study, procedural justice and distributive justice were also significantly correlated ($r = .58$ in Study 1, $r = .19$, $n.s.$ in Study 2). Importantly, interactional justice was significantly related to self-esteem in both experiments, whereas procedural justice was significantly related to self-esteem only in Study 1.

Although the findings from these three investigations may not be conclusive with respect to the distinctiveness of interactional justice, they do not necessarily support a view of integrating interactional justice with procedural justice. To assess the distinctiveness of interactional justice, we need to move beyond debating alternative interpretations of empirical findings. For guidance in how to proceed analytically, I turn to Greenberg's (1990c) important conceptual analysis of organizational justice.

Greenberg (1990c) outlined a two-stage analysis for determining whether there is a meaningful distinction between different justice constructs. In the first stage, following Greenberg's logic, we need to examine studies that have empirically differentiated procedural justice and interactional justice. In the second stage, we must determine whether there are different classes of dependent variables associated with procedural justice and interactional justice.

Assessing the Distinction between Procedural Justice and Interactional Justice

Following Greenberg (1990c), we need to establish that the distinction between procedural justice and interactional justice "is not simply a theoretical heuristic but rather a real one from the perspective of the worker's phenomenology" (p. 404) and "to determine whether employees are intuitively aware of the distinction" (p. 405). As mentioned earlier, Clemmer (1993) reported evidence supporting the separation of interactional justice and procedural justice in her study of customer service. Four additional investigations have addressed this issue (Bies & Tripp, 1996; Messick Bloom, Boldizar, & Samuelson, 1985; Mikula, 1986; Mikula, Petri, & Tanzer, 1990).

EMPIRICALLY ESTABLISHING THE BASIS FOR THE DISTINCTION
Mikula (1986) asked subjects to describe an unjust event that they had actually experienced as a victim. The social settings in which the unjust events occurred varied (e.g., school, family, friends, dealing with authorities). Many of the events identified were consistent with concepts of distributive injustice (e.g., unfair grade) and procedural injustice (e.g., ruthless use of one's high status and power). But, there were also injustice-arousing events identified that were neither distributive or procedural but interactional in nature. These events centered around the fairness of

everyday interactions and encounters (e.g., unjustified accusation and blaming, betrayal of confidence).

Messick et al. (1985) found a pattern of findings similar to Mikula (1986). Messick et al. asked their subjects to write lists of fair and unfair things that they or others did. The examples collected were of just and unjust events in general without specifying any social setting. Again, there were clear distributive and procedural events identified, but also identified was a separate category that dealt specifically with the quality of inter-personal treatment independent of procedure and outcome.

Mikula et al. (1990) collected 280 descriptions of unjust events from various student samples using different methodologies. As with Mikula (1986) and Messick et al. (1985), Mikula et al. reported a proportion of events that did not focus on distributive or procedural issues; indeed, sev-eral of the events identified focused on the quality of interpersonal treat-ment people received in a variety of interactions and encounters. Examples of such interpersonal treatment include disregarding the feelings and needs of others, reproach or accusation, and abusive or aggressive treatment.

Finally, in a study of revenge in organizations, Bies and Tripp (1996) surveyed 90 MBA students, who had significant work experience, about events that provoked thoughts and feelings of revenge. Consistent with the studies reviewed earlier, respondents in this study reported revenge-provoking events that were clearly distributive (e.g., shirking job respon-sibilities, stealing credit for ideas from others) and procedural (e.g., viola-tion of the formal rules, changing the rules "after the fact") in nature. But, again, events that centered on the quality of interpersonal treatment were identified (for example, disclosure of private confidences and secrets, and wrong or unfair accusations).

Taken together, the findings from these four studies, along with the results from Clemmer (1993), strongly indicate that people are aware of both procedural and interactional elements of fairness. The ability of peo-ple to distinguish between the different elements, although important, is insufficient evidence to make the case for the distinctiveness of interac-tional justice. In addition, we must demonstrate that procedural justice and interactional justice relate to different organizational variables.

JUSTICE-BASED PREDICTORS OF ORGANIZATIONAL VARIABLES   Fol-lowing Greenberg's logic (1990c), the next stage of analysis is to consider how procedural justice and interactional justice relate to a variety of orga-nizational variables. Five investigations address this issue (Barling & Phillips, 1993; Blodgett et al., 1997; Malatesta & Byrne, 1997; Masterson et al., 1997; Moorman, 1991; Skarlicki & Folger, 1997).

In a survey study of employees in two medium-sized companies, Moorman (1991) examined the relationship between perceptions of three types of justice (distributive, procedural, and interactional) and organizational citizenship behaviors. Empirical support was found for a causal relationship between perceptions of organizational justice and organizational citizenship behaviors. However, in a closer examination of the justice to citizenship behaviors relationship, Moorman found differential effects due to distributive justice, procedural justice, and interactional justice. Specifically, it was *only* interactional justice that was significantly related to citizenship behavior.

In a vignette study, Barling and Phillips (1993) investigated the different effects of the three types of justice (distributive, procedural, and interactional) on three outcomes associated with reactions to pay cuts (e.g., withdrawal, trust in management, affective commitment). The results of the data analysis uncovered significant main effects of interactional justice on all three outcomes, whereas procedural justice had a main effect only on the trust in management, and distributive justice had no significant effect on any of the variables.

In two survey studies, Masterson et al. (1997) examined the differential effects of procedural justice and interactional justice on work relationships and outcomes. In Study 1, Masterson et al. surveyed 153 administrative and staff employees during the pilot-testing of a new performance-management system at a large public university in the northeastern United States. Three organizational outcomes were measured (performance appraisal satisfaction, turnover intentions, and organizational commitment), and two supervisory-focused outcomes were measured (supervisor legitimacy and supervisor satisfaction). Consistent with their predictions, Masterson et al. found employees' procedural justice perceptions were significantly related to each of the three organizational outcomes but not related significantly to either of the supervisory-focused outcomes; in addition, interactional justice was significantly related to only one of the organizational outcomes (turnover intentions) but significantly related to both of the supervisory-focused outcomes.

In Study 2, Masterson et al. surveyed 651 employees and supervisors during the full-scale implementation of the new performance-management system at the same large public university in the northeastern United States. Masterson et al. introduced a new supervisory-focused variable, leader–member exchange, and a new organization-focused variable, perceived organizational support. As in Study 1, Masterson et al. found differential effects of interactional justice and procedural justice. Specifically, interactional justice affected directly and positively the perceived quality of the leader–member exchange, while procedural justice affected directly and positively employees' perceived organizational support.

In a field study, Malatesta and Byrne (1997) examined the differential impact of formal procedures and interactional justice on organizational commitment, supervisory commitment, and organizational citizenship behaviors. In this study, structural equations modeling was used to analyze data provided by 172 employee–supervisor dyads in a large, Midwestern university in the United States. Malatesta and Byrne found that the perception of fair formal procedures was related only to organizational commitment, whereas interactional justice was related to supervisory commitment and organizational citizenship behaviors.

In a field survey of 240 manufacturing employees, Skarlicki and Folger (1997) investigated the relationship between organizational justice and organizational retaliation behavior. In this study, they measured employee perceptions of distributive justice, procedural justice, and interactional justice, each of which was used to predict organizational retaliation behavior. In a noteworthy methodological improvement, the assessment of organizational retaliation behavior was done by peers of the employees, not the employees themselves. Skarlicki and Folger found that retaliation was predicted by the three-way interaction among distributive justice, procedural justice, and interactional justice. Based on this finding, Skarlicki and Folger argue that "a statistical model allowing only for the test of main effects and two-way interactions (Distributive Justice × Procedural Justice or Distributive Justice × Interactional Justice) might run the risk of being misspecified" (p. 439). Indeed, they add "that cues about interpersonal sensitivity provide *unique* (emphasis added) information to individuals when deciding whether to get even for low outcomes" (p. 439).

In a scenario study, Blodgett et al. (1997) investigated the effects of different levels of distributive justice, procedural justice, and interactional justice on consumer complaint behavior. The scenario involved a consumer attempting to return a product to a retail store. Blodgett et al. found that consumers who experienced higher levels of either distributive justice or interactional justice were predicted to be more likely to repatronize the retailer and less likely to "badmouth" the retailer. Procedural justice had no effect on postcomplaint behavior. As a key finding, interactional justice explained a significantly greater percentage of the variance of postcomplaint behavior than did distributive justice.

Taken together, these studies make a strong case for the relative roles of procedural justice and interactional justice. One emerging finding is that interactional justice perceptions tend to be associated with *direct supervisor evaluations* whereas procedural justice perceptions tend to be associated with *organizational system evaluations*. In addition to that finding, there is consistent evidence that interactional justice and procedural justice affect organizational behavior variables differently.

Summary and Punctuation

A variety of empirical studies demonstrate that (a) people can and do distinguish the fairness of formal procedures from the fairness of interpersonal treatment; and (b) interactional justice and procedural justice affect different worker attitudes and behaviors. As such, researchers have much to gain by maintaining the conceptual distinction, for that is what the people do as they experience their work life.

To hold on to an "umbrella" concept of procedural justice—one that covers both structural and interpersonal concerns—not only muddies the conceptual waters but it also lacks parsimony. If we are to advance our understanding of justice processes and dynamics, then parsimony is clearly an important conceptual objective (Greenberg, 1990c, 1996). Thus, given the empirical evidence, it makes theoretical and analytical sense to maintain the distinction between interactional justice and procedural justice.

Maintaining this important and parsimonious conceptual distinction carries important implications for research on interactional justice and procedural justice. For example, at a minimum, we need to be more precise in measuring interactional justice and procedural justice (Greenberg, 1990c). Specifically, interactional justice should include only items that focus on interpersonal treatment, while evaluations of formal procedures and their enactment should be the focus of procedural justice (for example, Folger & Konovsky, 1989). Further, an operationalization of interactional justice should not be limited to one aspect, such as social accounts (for example, Konovsky & Cropanzano, 1991), but should also include a broader range of items reflecting the richness of the construct (for example, Moorman, 1991).

To continue this line of reasoning, the evidence reviewed suggests strongly that current models of organizational justice that incorporate both interpersonal and formal procedure variables, as part of an umbrella procedural justice construct (for example, Lind & Tyler, 1988; Tyler & Lind, 1992), should separate, at least for analytical purposes, the potential differential effects due to the interpersonal and formal procedure variables. Indeed, it may be that the procedural justice findings in previous studies are due more to concerns about interpersonal treatment than to the characteristics of formal procedures. To that extent, we should reexamine procedural justice studies to pinpoint what accounted for the significance of the findings reported.

In all fairness, I am not the first justice researcher to advance this argument. A similar argument was articulated by Mikula et al. (1990) when they analyzed the controversy over status of interactional justice relative to procedural justice. Because their work may not be familiar to all of us, their words bear repeating. Specifically, Mikula et al. (1990) wrote:

> Bies and Moag (1986) proposed analysing the quality of interpersonal treatment as an independent form of justice in addition to justice of distributions and procedures. Lind and Tyler (1988), on the other hand, suggested regarding as a component of procedural justice. It strikes us that both viewpoints are equally reasonable as long as one focuses exclusively on social situations of judgement and decision-making (e.g. allocation decisions, conflict management, performance appraisal, corporate recruiting activities, etc.)—as the majority of justice research has done in the past. In these cases, interpersonal treatment relates mostly to the enactment of procedures. However, the results of the present and the Messick et al (1985) studies suggest a broader concept of interpersonal treatment which goes beyond situations of judgement and decision-making and includes all kinds of interactions and encounters. If one agrees to such a broad concept, it seems better to regard the manner of interpersonal treatment as an independent subject of justice evaluations rather than to subsume it under the concept of procedure. Otherwise, this latter concept, which usually denotes processes of judgment and decision-making, would be inflated and therefore lose its usefulness. In addition, it would be difficult and even impossible to distinguish between processes of decision-making and the interpersonal treatment by decision makers, both of which can become subjects of justice judgements independent of each other. (p. 143)

As a punctuation to this section, let me state what the evidence makes clear: *interactional (in)justice matters to people.* People are concerned about the interpersonal treatment they receive from others. Further, these interactional concerns are distinguishable from procedural concerns.

But, if the debate over the distinctiveness of interactional justice continues, even as the empirical evidence demonstrating its distinctiveness grows, one will be left to ponder why. Could it be that the continuing debate is the result of "normal scientists" trying to make sense of anomalous findings that do not neatly fit within the procedural justice paradigm? Or could it be the "politics of the paradigm," where those with vested interests are motivated to preserve the procedural justice paradigm? Even though determining which of those answers is more "true" will not be "easy," it is absolutely critical to determine which one is a more valid explanation if we are to build a unified theory of organizational justice. In the spirit of advancing our understanding of organizational justice, I now turn my attention to a more fine-grained analysis of specific interactional justice concerns.

Interactional (In)Justice: From the Profane to the Sacred

From my own research and the other evidence reviewed in this chapter, it is becoming clearer to me that, to fully appreciate the richness of justice dynamics in organizations, one must understand the events that arouse the sense of injustice (Bies, 1987; Bies, Tripp, & Kramer, 1997). The influential legal theorist, Edmond Cahn (1949), articulates this perspective more eloquently in his seminal book, *The Sense of Injustice*. In the book, Cahn poses the question: "Why do we speak of the 'sense of injustice' rather than the 'sense of justice'?" (p. 13). He responds with the answer: "Because 'justice' has been so beclouded by natural-law writings that it almost inevitably brings to mind some ideal relation or static condition or set of perceptual standards, while we are concerned, on the contrary, with what is active, vital, and experiential in the reactions of human beings" (p. 13). Cahn (1949) defines the sense of injustice as "the sympathetic reaction of outrage, horror, shock, resentment, and anger, those affections of the viscera and abnormal secretions of the adrenals that prepare the human animal to resist attack. Nature has thus equipped all men to regard injustice to another as personal aggression" (p. 24).

Embedded in Cahn's analysis is the assumption that people view the self as sacred. In particular, this sense of sacredness assumes an "inviolate personality . . . (and) the individual's independence, dignity and integrity" (Bloustein, 1964, p. 971). Following Cahn, to define the boundaries of the sacred self, we must examine the profanities that violate it.

My own research (for example, Bies & Moag, 1986, and Bies & Tripp, 1996) and that of others (for example, Mikula, 1986; Mikula et al. 1990) identify a variety of interpersonal profanities that can shed light on the boundaries of the sacred self. As one important category of profanities, people are concerned about *derogatory judgments* made about themselves by others, which in a justice context refers to the truthfulness and accuracy of statements and judgments about a person. A second and related category of profanities involves *deception,* which in a justice context refers to the correspondence between one's words and actions. As a third category of profanities, people are concerned with the *invasion of privacy,* which in a justice context refers to the legitimacy of disclosing of personal information about one person to another. A fourth category of profanities involves *disrespect,* which in a justice context refers to the signs and symbols conveying respect for the intrinsic value or worth of the individual.

Derogatory Judgments

The integrity of one's self-identity, particularly as it is communicated to other audiences, is a central aspect of the self-system (Steele, 1988). As a result, a wrongful accusation or a false and derogatory statement about a person should arouse the sense of injustice (Bies & Tripp, 1993). Several studies support this line of reasoning.

One frequently mentioned profanity is a *wrongful or unfair accusation* about one's work performance (Bies & Tripp, 1996, in press; Mikula, 1986; Mikula et al, 1990). In the Bies and Tripp (1996) study, one person recounted being accused of stealing ideas by a boss, yet it was the boss who had stolen the ideas! An unfair accusation is similar to a wrongful accusation in that both accusations are not true. But for many people, an unfair accusation typically reflected a "gross misrepresentation of the facts," rather than "I did not do it," as in the case of a wrongful accusation. An example of an unfair accusation involved a boss who blamed her team for failure even though the team had done its best despite some "questionable" decisions by the boss (Bies & Tripp, 1996). With either accusation, there was a feeling by the victim of being "discredited" and that these accusations "did not do justice" to them (Bies & Tripp, 1996).

Unfair attacks on one's identity also occur when one engages in *"bad-mouthing"* another. For example, a peer who "talks behind one's back," thus creating an unfavorable image of another, is perceived as wrong and unjust (Mikula et al., 1990). Similarly, people report an interactional injustice when a boss *uses pejorative labels* (for example, a "troublemaker" or a "traitor") to stigmatize a subordinate (Bies & Tripp, in press).

Deception

Expectations of honesty and fulfilled promises in dealings with others is a foundation of trust in a relationship (Lewicki, McAllister, & Bies, 1997). Trusting another person leaves one vulnerable in the relationship (Mayer, Davis, & Schoorman, 1995), as it exposes the sacred self. If that vulnerability is misused, as when people are deceived, it should arouse the sense of injustice (Bies & Tripp, 1996). Several studies support this line of reasoning.

Bies and Moag (1986) found job candidates angry and resentful at recruiters who *lied* to them. Bies and Tripp (1996) also found evidence that lying triggered feelings of outrage. One example of lying involved a boss stating that a subordinate would receive a raise when, in fact, no raise was forthcoming. In the face of being lied to, the typical reaction by people is that they have been "duped" and "manipulated" (Bies & Tripp, 1996; Mikula et al., 1990) and are unable to trust the perpetrator again.

As another form of deception, a *broken promise* can make people angry and resentful (Bies & Tripp, 1996, in press; Mikula, 1986; Mikula et al, 1990; Tripp & Bies, 1997). Respondents in the Bies and Tripp (1996) study identified broken promises as evoking feelings of outrage. As one example, a person received a promise from a co-worker friend to "help out" at a difficult client meeting, yet the co-worker "backed out" at the last minute with no explanation. In another example from Bies and Tripp (1996), a boss made explicit promises to support a subordinate's candidacy for a promotion in a management meeting determining such moves but did not do so. In response to that broken promise, the subordinate stated, "My boss's word means nothing, absolutely. I'll never trust him again" (p. 250).

Invasion of Privacy

Research on privacy (Stone & Stone, 1990) and self-disclosure (Derlega & Berg, 1987; Jourard, 1966) make it clear that people have a part of themselves that they want kept hidden or private from others. When the "hidden self" (Bies, 1996) is invaded, the violation should arouse the sense of injustice. Several studies have support this line of reasoning.

The *disclosure of confidences and secrets* is a common form of invasion of privacy in organizations (Bies & Tripp, 1996) and everyday life (Mikula, 1986; Mikula et al, 1990). Bies and Tripp (1996) report that regardless of whether it be disclosing a subordinate's private matter that was supposed to be held in confidence by the boss or a co-worker who received secret information disclosed by another but used it to his own advantage—such an action was viewed as a "fundamental betrayal" and "a knife in the back," resulting in what one person described as "not just a splintering, but a shattering of trust" (p. 251).

Research on privacy suggests a similar response to the unwarranted disclosure of personal information (Bies, 1993, 1996). For example, Woodman, Ganster, Adams, McCuddy, Tolchinsky, and Fromkin (1982) and Tolchinsky, McCuddy, Adams, Ganster, Woodman and Fromkin (1981) found that employees were much more concerned about the disclosure of personal information to parties outside the organization than about disclosure of the same information for internal uses of the organization. However, when people give permission for disclosure of information, then the sense of injustice is less likely aroused (Fusiler & Hoyer, 1980; Tolchinsky et al, 1981).

The *asking of improper questions* is also viewed as an invasion of privacy. For example, in a study of corporate recruiting practices, Bies and Moag (1986) found that respondents were very upset with questions about marital status or whether the job candidate was thinking about having children.

Finally, the *use of "spies"* is also viewed as invasion of privacy and unfair. For example, in a study of abusive bosses, Bies and Tripp (in press) found that people were particularly concerned about bosses who, in almost *1984*-like fashion, demanded that employees act as "snitches" to bring gossip and rumors about other employees. In addition, respondents were particularly appalled by bosses who would use secretaries as "spies" to ferret out the disloyal.

Disrespect

At a fundamental level, the quality of the interpersonal treatment accorded by one person to another can have an impact on one's self-identity (Steele, 1988). When that interpersonal treatment conveys disrespect, it should arouse the sense of injustice (Bies & Moag, 1986; Lind & Tyler, 1988; Tyler & Lind, 1992). Several studies support this line of reasoning and identify a variety of forms of disrespect: *inconsiderate actions, abusive words or actions,* and *coercion.*

INCONSIDERATE ACTIONS   On a fundamental level, people have minimal expectations for considerate treatment as core to their concerns of interactional justice (Bies & Moag, 1986; Tyler & Bies, 1990). In a work setting, one important sign of respect to the dignity of the person is *timely feedback* (Bies & Moag, 1986). When people have to wait for a response an undue amount of time, they feel unfairly treated. Similarly, people expect to *receive an explanation or account* of decisions made that affect them, and, when they fail to receive such information, they feel unfairly treated (Bies, 1987; Bies & Moag, 1986).

ABUSIVE WORDS OR ACTIONS   What people say or do and the manner in which they do it (e.g., abusively) can signal disrespect, thus arousing the sense of injustice (Bies & Tripp, 1996, in press; Mikula et al., 1990). One example of such disrespect is *rudeness* (Bies & Moag, 1986; Katz, Gutek, Kahn & Barton, 1975; Mikula et al., 1990). For example, Bies and Moag (1986) found job candidates angry and resentful at interviewers who would interrupt their answers to questions or take phone calls in the middle of the interview. Similarly, in a study of service agency clients, Katz et al. (1975) found that clients were angry and resentful at bureaucratic officials who were impolite and rude.

The practice of *publicly criticizing and berating people in public* has also been identified as a form of using abusive words and actions in a manner that can arouse the sense of injustice (Baron, 1988; Bies & Tripp, 1996, in press; Hornstein, 1996). This is particularly true in the case of the boss-subordinate relationship. For example, in a study of abusive bosses (Bies & Tripp, in press), one manager reported that his boss had a "Dr. Jeckyll and Mr. Hyde" personality. This meant that in one moment the boss could be very calm, peaceful, and satisfied, but then, without any warning, the boss would erupt into a loud, angry, temper tantrum, a public tirade directed at one or all employees. Indeed, these tirades occurred for no apparent reason.

Bies and Tripp (in press) also report that these tirades are not limited to emotional outbursts but often include the destruction of physical property (e.g., throwing telephones at the wall) or threatening, and occasionally even using, physical violence (e.g., shoving an employee). Finally, what makes the mood swings even more difficult to endure is that they are often uncorrelated with subordinate behavior, meaning that both trivial and serious events may trigger the same emotional outburst.

Related to public criticism and beratement, abusive treatment may take the form of *actions intended to embarrass and humiliate a person publicly* (Bies & Tripp, 1996, in press; Glass & Singer, 1972; Mikula et al., 1990). For example, Glass and Singer (1972) reported the results of a laboratory study in which people felt unfairly treated when they were unduly embarrassed or humiliated by a "bureaucratic administrator" who acted in an arrogant manner. Bies and Tripp (in press) report about one boss who brought the whole department together and singled out one employee for poor performance in "harsh" and "angry" terms, even making "fun" of the employee's lack of skills and abilities. According to the employee, he felt he had "lost face" and felt "belittled and degraded" and "emotionally scarred" as a result of this attack.

Prejudicial statements, as in racist and sexist statements, convey disrespect, arousing the sense of injustice (Bies & Moag, 1986). Similarly, being the target of *insults* can arouse the sense of injustice (Bies & Tripp, 1996, in press). Insults on a personal level typically involved "name-calling," as in questioning the person's intellectual capacities by referring to the employee as a "moron" or in challenging a male employee's lack of assertiveness by stating that he was a "wimp, probably had no balls." Insults to the collective involved sexist and racist remarks that were targeted at women and African-Americans (Bies & Tripp, 1996).

COERCION   Research suggests that when management practices impose undue psychological or physical pain, such actions are viewed as unjust. For example, job candidates in the Bies and Moag (1986) study viewed *"stress interviews"* as unfair because of the psychological pain and physiological stress they experienced during those types of interactions with recruiters.

Bies and Tripp (in press) report examples of *duress* as interactional injustices. For example, one employee was told that he had to fire one of his own subordinates, even though that subordinate was a good performer. The boss, however, did not personally like that subordinate and implied that if the employee did not fire his subordinate, it might reflect adversely on his managerial capabilities and limit his future at the company. This employee—young and recently married with a newborn, thus feeling quite vulnerable—submitted and terminated the employee under duress, even though he knew it was wrong.

Summary and Punctuation

Taken together, these studies suggest that people are concerned about a variety of interpersonal profanities and indignities. Moreover, consistent with the conclusion of Mikula et al. (1990), interactional justice concerns are not limited to *exchange* contexts, such as resource allocation and decision making; in addition, people are concerned about interpersonal treatment in their *everyday encounters* in organizations. The fact that interactional concerns transcend formal decision-making contexts is an important reason we should maintain the distinctiveness of interactional (in)justice.

But the evidence reviewed in this section suggests even another reason for maintaining the distinctiveness of interactional (in)justice. To wit, there are examples of injustice that I reviewed that are not easily captured by the current distributive-procedural distinction. For example, the injustice of coercion does not fit with distributive justice or procedural justice frameworks, yet it fits quite nicely within the interactional justice framework. In addition, concerns about invasion of privacy highlight the psychological importance of freedom (as does coercion, for that matter), and freedom as a justice concern has not been the focus of distributive justice or procedural justice theories.

To punctuate this line of reasoning, interactional (in)justice matters to people, and *it matters in ways that are not parsimoniously explained by a simple distributive-procedural distinction.* If we take this body of evidence about interactional (in)justice seriously, as we should, then our theorizing about organizational justice must leave its "adolescence" stage of development (Greenberg, 1993a) and embark on the journey into intellectual "adulthood." Navigating such an intellectual journey is the focus of the next section.

As Organizational Justice Comes of Age: Moving from Adolescence to Adulthood

Greenberg (1993a) noted that our understanding of organizational justice was in its formative stage, which he referred to as intellectual adolescence. Although I agree with this assessment, there is also growing evidence of an intellectual "growth spurt" in our understanding of organizational justice. For example, we are currently witnessing a growing appreciation by scholars of the *complexities and paradoxes of organizational justice.* Recent conceptual analyses exploring the multidimensional nature of justice (Greenberg, 1993b; Cropanzano & Ambrose, Chapter 4) highlight new complexities and paradoxes in the dynamics of justice.

The move into intellectual adulthood also carries important responsibilities. Specifically, we must *begin a moral discourse* about our research and its managerial implications. We, as justice researchers, must reflect on our responsibilities to conduct research that achieves not only "statistical" significance but also "moral" significance. To these issues I now turn my attention.

The Complexities and Paradoxes of Justice

As one enters adulthood, one becomes more aware of life's complexities and paradoxes. Such understanding is also relevant to analysis of organizational justice. For example, as the essays in this volume demonstrate, simple explanations of organizational justice are giving way to more textured and nuanced analyses. In addition, we are becoming more aware of how the pursuit of organizational justice can create injustice for people (Bies & Sitkin, 1993; Sitkin & Bies, 1993)—which may be the *fundamental* justice paradox.

As another sign of the move into intellectual adulthood for organizational justice, there is increasing scholarly activity dedicated to making conceptual sense of the interrelationships among the different facets of organizational justice (distributive, procedural, and interactional). One noteworthy analysis is provided by Greenberg (1993b), who proposes a taxonomy of justice classes by highlighting the distinction between structural and social determinants of justice and their relationship to the two different categories of justice—distributive and procedural. In this taxonomy, Greenberg presents an insightful and creative framework for incorporating the important interpersonal determinants of organizational justice, while highlighting new classes of organizational justice concerns (for example, configural justice).

Another noteworthy example of conceptual creativity is provided by Cropanzano and Ambrose (this volume), who argue that the distinction between procedure and outcomes may not be fundamental and that procedural justice and distributive justice are different components of a more global concept, social justice. In taking this "monistic" perspective, Cropanzano and Ambrose demonstrate how an event can be a procedure in one setting and an outcome in another setting. Further, and of relevance to the study of interactional justice, they highlight how both procedures and outcomes can affect human dignity.

Although the analyses of Greenberg, Cropanzano, and Ambrose are quite insightful, there is another approach for exploring the complexities and paradoxes of organizational justice. In this approach, we begin with examining the fundamental meaning of justice. What justice fundamentally means is to give a person *his or her due*. But how that due is determined may vary. Feinberg (1974) argues that "in some cases one's due is determined independently of that of other people, while in other cases, a person's due is determinable *only* by reference to his relations to other persons . . . the contexts, criteria, and principles of the former kind (are referred to) as *noncomparative*, and those of the latter sort as *comparative*" (p. 297). This distinction between comparative and noncomparative principles represents an alternative, yet potentially useful, approach for exploring organizational justice and appreciating the interrelationships between its distributive, procedural, and interactional facets.

Take the case of comparative justice. Feinberg identifies "some typical occasions for comparative justice: (i) when competitive prizes are to be awarded, (ii) when burdens and benefits are to be distributed, and (iii) when general rules are to be made, administered, or enforced" (p. 280). "All comparative justice involves, in one way or another, equality in the treatment accorded all the members of a class; but whether that equality be absolute or 'proportional,' whether it be equality of share, equality of opportunity, or equality of consideration, depends on the nature of the goods and evils awarded or distributed, and the nature of the class in which the assignments and allocations take place. Comparative injustice consists in arbitrary and invidious discrimination of one kind or another: a departure from the requisite form or equal treatment without good reason . . . And where the occasion for justice is the application or enforcement of general rules, comparative justice requires that the judge or administrator give precisely the same treatment to each person who falls within a class specified by the rule" (p. 281).

Principles of comparative justice underlie the research on distributive justice. For example, research inspired by equity theory (e.g., Adams, 1965; Walster, Walster, & Berscheid, 1978) and relative deprivation theory (e.g., Crosby, 1976; Martin, 1981) explicitly assumes that justice is determined through comparison with others. Comparative principles also underlie our models of procedural justice. Whether it be the opportunity for voice or process control (Thibaut & Walker, 1975) or the consistent application of different procedural rules (Leventhal, 1980) or the neutrality of the decision maker (Lind & Tyler, 1988), any deviation from equality of opportunity or the equality of administration of the rules forms the basis for claims of procedural injustice.

However, as Feinberg (1974) demonstrates, there is another class of principles, those that are noncomparative in nature, that can form and shape perceptions of justice and injustice. As Feinberg notes, "When our problem is to make assignments, ascriptions, or awards in accordance with noncomparative justice, what is 'due' the other person is not a share or portion of some divisible benefit or burden; hence it is not necessary for us to know what is due the other in order to know what is due the person with whom we are dealing. *His* rights-or-deserts alone determine what is due him; and once we have come to a judgment of *his* due, that judgment cannot be logically affected by subsequent knowledge of the condition of other parties. . . . When our task is to do noncomparative justice to each of a large number of individuals, we do not compare them with each other, but rather we compare each in turn with an objective standard and judge each (as we say) 'on his merits' " (p. 282). Examples of such objective and absolute standards might include truth, freedom, and human dignity, concerns that are highlighted by my conceptualization of interactional (in)justice and related models of procedural justice (Tyler & Lind, 1992).

To further illustrate the difference between comparative and noncomparative principles, consider the following example taken from Bies

(1987). Let us assume there is a "rude and abusive" journal reviewer who makes caustic and derogatory remarks about five different manuscripts reviewed. Let us further assume that each manuscript was of equal quality. Given that the manuscript "inputs" were the same and the outcomes were the same, applying principles of comparative justice would suggest there should be no sense of injustice aroused as the result of this process.

Yet, for most of us, there would be some residual resentment or anger as the target of such treatment. The principles that would explain our sense of injustice would be noncomparative in nature. For example, we might have some conception that we have a *right* to be treated with respect and that no one deserves to be the target of such mean-spirited comments or insults. Further, if the reviewer made derogatory and false accusations about the work, one would feel unjustly treated because one had not been "done justice." Regardless of the fact that everyone else was treated in the same manner, it would not totally mitigate the sense of injustice aroused by the violation of noncomparative principles.

The focus on interactional (in)justice highlights the importance of noncomparative principles of justice, which are largely overlooked in our conceptualization of organizational justice. Moreover, as Feinberg (1974) demonstrates, any event or outcome may be evaluated by comparative and noncomparative principles. As a result, people may invoke both sets of justice principles, which provides a plausible and powerful explanation of another justice paradox. That is, people want to be treated "equally, but uniquely" (Bies, 1987; Folger, 1994).

The purpose of my discussion of comparative and noncomparative principles is not to suggest that Greenberg, Cropanzano, or Ambrose are "wrong" and that I am "right." To the contrary, my purpose is to highlight the multiple approaches for developing a more sophisticated understanding of organizational justice and its dynamics. Such sophistication, I believe, is more evidence of our move into intellectual adulthood. But that move also carries some new responsibilities, which I now address.

Beginning a Moral Discourse

Bill Scott is a friend and scholar who has played a formative role in my thinking about justice. From the first moment I met him, Bill reminded me of the larger social and political context of justice. More specifically, justice is a concept invoked to legitimate existing governance structures (Scott, 1988). Moreover, Bill reminds me, justice researchers may be (un)wittingly supplying ideological support to management practices that destroy individual freedom and dignity (Scott & Hart, 1979). As a result, Bill argues that we need to create a forum for moral discourse in which we critically examine our research and its use by managers (Scott & Hart, 1989).

In the spirit of Bill Scott, such a moral discourse must begin with an acknowledgment that our justice research has a decidedly *promanagement bias* (Bies & Tripp, 1998; Treviño & Bies, 1997). There is an instrumental orientation and ideology that permeates so much of justice theory and research, which has put us, as scholars, in the role of apologists for management. Indeed, we cry for "joy" when our justice variables can legitimate promanagement interests such as organizational commitment, organizational citizenship behaviors, and trust in management (Treviño & Bies, 1997).

This is not to suggest that an examination of such relationships is misguided or morally wrong. To the contrary, for what I am suggesting is that, as we conduct such research, we live up to our *moral* responsibility as scholars to question how our efforts may unwittingly contribute to dehumanizing or exploitative—that is, unjust—management practices. Indeed, I would hope most, if not all, of us would be horrified that our research findings would be used to legitimate management practices that perpetuate, rather than ameliorate, injustice in the workplace.

Linda Treviño and I have "nailed" a normative manifesto to the doors of the Academy (Treviño & Bies, 1997). In this manifesto, we describe—and decry—the instrumental orientation and ideology that permeate so much of theory and research that has put us, as justice scholars, in the role of apologists and excuse-makers for management. In particular, we argue that our research has silenced or excluded the voices of a large group of people in organizations—those who are relatively powerless.

The suppression of these voices follows from prevailing ideology of management theory and practice: the *organizational imperative* (Scott & Hart, 1979), which is based on a primary and absolute proposition: "Whatever is good for the individual can only come from the modern organization" (p. 43), and the related secondary proposition: "Therefore, all behavior must enhance the health of such organizations" (p. 43). Indeed, as Scott and Hart conclude, "the organizational imperative is the sine qua non of management theory and practice . . . the metaphysic of management: absolute and immutable" (p. 46). In other words, the core assumptions of modern management theory are totalitarian.

To counteract the ideological bias of the organizational imperative, Treviño and I endorse *the individual imperative* proposed by Scott and Hart (1979). According to Scott and Hart, "the primary proposition of the individual imperative is: All individuals have the natural *right* (emphasis added) to realize their potentials through the stages of their lives. It thus follows that the primary purpose of any organization, public or private, is to allow for the realization of individual potentials" (p. 53).

If we take the individual imperative seriously, research on organizational justice should not only focus on advancing the interests of the managerial elite in organizations. In addition, our research should advance the interests of freedom and the dignity of individuals in organizations. If we adopt the latter agenda, it will not be "safe travels" at all times, particularly for those of us in business schools. For, if we assume that individuals possess certain innate and inalienable rights that we ascribe to them because they are human beings, such a perspective would be, indeed, quite "radical." Indeed, for those of us who adopt this radical view, our role will be that of a social critic: on the margin, not in the mainstream, motivated by what Beaney (1966) calls "a never-ending quest to increase the respect of all . . . for the essential values of human life" (p. 271). It is to this quest that I invite one and all.

REFERENCES

Adams, J. S. (1965). Inequity in social exchange. In L. Berkowitz (Ed.), *Advances in experimental social psychology* (Vol. 2, pp. 267–299). New York: Academic Press.

Barling, J., & Phillips, M. (1993). Interactional, formal, and distributive justice in the workplace: An exploratory study. *Journal of Psychology, 127,* 649–656.

Baron, R. A. (1988). Negative effects of destructive criticism: Impact on conflict, self-efficacy, and task performance. *Journal of Applied Psychology, 73,* 199–207.

Beaney, W. M. (1966). The right to privacy and American law. *Law and Contemporary Problems, 31,* 253–271.

Bennett, N., Martin, C. L., Bies, R. J., & Brockner, J. (1995). Coping with a layoff: A longitudinal study of victims. *Journal of Management, 21,* 1025–1040.

Bies, R. J. (1987). The predicament of injustice: The management of moral outrage. In L. L. Cummings & B. M. Staw (Eds.), *Research in organizational behavior* (Vol. 9, pp. 289–319). Greenwich, CT: JAI Press.

Bies, R. J. (1993). Privacy and procedural justice in organizations. *Social Justice Research, 6,* 69–86.

Bies, R. J. (1996). Beyond the hidden self: Psychological and ethical aspects of privacy in organizations. In D. Messick & A.Tenbrunsel (Eds.), *Codes of con-*

duct: Behavioral research into business ethics (pp. 104–116). New York: Russell Sage Foundation.

Bies, R. J., Martin, C. L., & Brockner, J. (1993). Just laid off, but still a "good citizen"? Only if the process is fair. *Employee Responsibilities and Rights Journal, 6*, 227–238.

Bies, R. J., & Moag, J. S. (1986). Interactional justice: Communication criteria of fairness. In R. J. Lewicki, B. H. Sheppard, & M. H. Bazerman (Eds.), *Research on negotiation in organizations* (pp. 43–55). Greenwich, CT: JAI Press.

Bies, R. J., & Shapiro, D. L. (1987). Interactional fairness judgments: The influence of causal accounts. *Social Justice Research, 1*, 199–218.

Bies, R. J., & Shapiro, D. L. (1988). Voice and justification: Their influence on procedural fairness judgments. *Academy of Management Journal, 31*, 676–685.

Bies, R. J., Shapiro, D. L., & Cummings, L. L. (1988). Causal accounts and managing organizational conflict: Is it enough to say it's not my fault? *Communication Research, 15*, 381–399.

Bies, R. J., & Sitkin, S. B. (1993). Law without justice: The dilemmas of formalization and fairness in the legalistic organization. *Employee Responsibilities Rights Journal, 6*, 271–275.

Bies, R. J., & Tripp, T. M. (1993). Employee-initiated defamation lawsuits: Organizational responses and dilemmas. *Employee Responsibilities and Rights Journal, 6*, 313–324.

Bies, R. J., & Tripp, T. M. (1995). The use and abuse of power: Justice as social control. In R. Cropanzano & M. Kacmar (Eds.), *Organizational politics, justice, and support: Managing social climate at work* (pp. 131–145). New York: Quorum Press.

Bies, R. J., & Tripp, T. M. (1996). Beyond distrust: "Getting even" and the need for revenge. In R. M. Kramer & T. Tyler (Eds.), *Trust in organizations* (pp. 246–260). Newbury Park, CA: Sage Publications.

Bies, R. J., & Tripp, T. M. (1998). Revenge in organizations: The good, the bad, and the ugly. In R. W. Griffin, A. O'Leary-Kelly, & J. Collins (Eds.), *Dysfunctional behavior in organizations, Vol. 1: Violent behaviors in organizations* (pp. 49–68). Greenwich, CT: JAI Press.

Bies, R. J., & Tripp, T. M. (2000). A passion for justice: The rationality and morality of revenge. In R. Cropanzano (Ed.), *Justice in the workplace, Volume II: From theory to practice.* Mahwah, NJ: Lawrence Erlbaum Associates.

Bies, R. J., & Tripp, T. M. (in press). Two faces of the powerless: Coping with tyranny. In R. M. Kramer & M. A. Neale (Eds.), *Power and influence in organizations.* Thousand Oaks, CA: Sage Publications.

Bies, R. J., Tripp, T. M., & Kramer, R. M. (1997). At the breaking point: Cognitive and social dynamics of revenge in organizations. In R. A. Giacalone &

J. Greenberg (Eds.), *Antisocial behavior in organizations* (pp. 18–36). Thousand Oaks, CA: Sage Publications.

Bies, R. J., Tripp, T. M., & Neale, M. A. (1993). Procedural fairness and profit seeking: The perceived legitimacy of market exploitation. *Journal of Behavioral Decision Making, 6,* 243–256.

Bies, R. J., & Tyler, T. (1993). The "litigation mentality" in organizations: A test of alternative psychological explanations. *Organization Science, 4,* 352–366.

Blodgett, J. G., Hill, D. J., & Tax, S. S. (1997). The effects of distributive, procedural, and interactional justice on postcomplaint behavior. *Journal of Retailing, 73,* 185–210.

Bloustein, E. J. (1964). Privacy as an aspect of human dignity: An answer to Dean Prosser. *New York University Law Review, 39,* 962–1007.

Cahn, E. (1949). *The sense of injustice.* New York: New York University Press.

Clemmer, E. C. (1993). An investigation into the relationship of fairness and customer satisfaction with services. In R. Cropanzano (Ed.), *Justice in the workplace: Approaching fairness in human resource management* (pp. 193–207). Hillsdale, NJ: Lawrence Erlbaum Associates.

Cropanzano, R., & Greenberg, J. (1997). Progress in organizational justice: Tunneling through the maze. In C. L. Cooper & I. T. Robertson (Eds.), *International review of industrial and organizational psychology: 1997* (pp. 317–372). New York: Wiley & Sons.

Cropanzano, R., & Randall, M. L. (1993). Injustice and work behavior: A historical review. In R. Cropanzano (Ed.), *Justice in the workplace: Approaching fairness in human resource management* (pp. 1–20). Hillsdale, NJ: Lawrence Erlbaum Associates.

Crosby, F. (1976). A model of egoistic relative deprivation. *Psychological Review, 83,* 85–113.

Daly, J. P. (1991). The effects of anger on negotiation in mergers and acquisitions. *Negotiation Journal, 7,* 31–39.

Derlega, V. J., & Berg, J. H. (Eds.) (1987). *Self-disclosure: Theory, research, and therapy.* New York: Plenum Press.

Feinberg, J. (1974). Noncomparative justice. *The Philosophical Review, 83,* 297–338.

Folger, R. (1994). Workplace justice and employee worth. *Social Justice Research, 7,* 225–241.

Folger, R., & Bies, R. J. (1989). Managerial responsibilities and procedural justice. *Employee Responsibilities and Rights Journal, 2,* 79–90.

Folger, R., & Konovsky, M. A. (1989). Effects of procedural and distributive justice on reactions to pay raise decisions. *Academy of Management Journal, 32,* 115–130.

Fusilier, M. R., & Hoyer, W. D. (1980). Variables affecting perceptions of invasion of privacy in a personnel selection situation. *Journal of Applied Psychology, 65,* 623–626.

Glass, D. C., & Singer, J. E. (1972). *Urban stress.* New York: Academic Press.

Greenberg, J. (1990a). Employee theft as a reaction to underpayment inequity: The hidden costs of pay cuts. *Journal of Applied Psychology, 75,* 561–568.

Greenberg, J. (1990b). Looking fair vs. being fair: Managing impressions of organizational justice. In B. M. Staw & L. L. Cummings (Eds.), *Research in Organizational Behavior* (Vol. 12, 111–157). Greenwich, CT: JAI Press.

Greenberg, J. (1990c). Organizational justice: Yesterday, today, and tomorrow. *Journal of Management, 16,* 399–432.

Greenberg, J. (1993a). The intellectual adolescence of organizational justice: You've come a long way, maybe. *Social Justice Research, 6,* 135–147.

Greenberg, J. (1993b). The social side of fairness: Interpersonal and informational classes of organizational justice. In R. Cropanzano (Ed.), *Justice in the workplace: Approaching fairness in human resource management* (pp. 79–103). Hillsdale, NJ: Lawrence Erlbaum Associates.

Greenberg, J. (1994). Using socially fair treatment to promote acceptance of a work site smoking ban. *Journal of Applied Psychology, 79,* 288–297.

Greenberg, J. (1996). *The quest for justice on the job: Essays and experiments.* Thousand Oaks, CA: Sage.

Greenberg, J. (1997). A social influence model of employee theft: Beyond the fraud triangle. In R. J. Lewicki, R. J. Bies, & B. H. Sheppard (Eds.), *Research on negotiation in organizations* (Vol. 6, pp. 29–51). Greenwich, CT: JAI Press.

Hornstein, H. A. (1996). *Brutal bosses and their prey.* New York: Riverhead Books.

Jourard, S. M. (1966). Some psychological aspects of privacy. *Law and Contemporary Problems, 31,* 307–318.

Katz, D., Gutek, B. A., Kahn, R. L., & Barton, E. (1975). *Bureaucratic encounters.* Ann Arbor, MI: Institute for Social Research.

Konovsky, M. A., & Cropanzano, R. (1991). The perceived fairness of employee drug testing as a predictor of employee attitudes and job performance. *Journal of Applied Psychology, 76,* 698–707.

Koper, G., Van Knipperberg, D., Bouhuijs, F., Vermunt, R., & Wilke, H. (1993). Procedural fairness and self-esteem. *European Journal of Social Psychology, 23,* 313–325.

Lane, R. E. (1988). Procedural goods in a democracy: How one is treated versus what one gets. *Social Justice Research, 2,* 177–192.

Leventhal, G. S. (1980). What should be done with equity theory? New approaches to the study of fairness in social relationships. In K. Gergen,

M. Greenberg, & R. Willis (Eds.), *Social exchange: New advances in theory and research* (pp. 27–55). New York: Plenum Press.

Lewicki, R. J., McAllister, D. M., & Bies, R. J. (1997). *Trust and distrust: New relationships and realities.* Manuscript under review.

Lind, E. A., & Tyler, T. R. (1988). *The social psychology of procedural justice.* New York: Plenum.

McLean Parks, J. (1997). The fourth arm of justice: The art and science of revenge. In R. J. Lewicki, R. J. Bies, & B. H. Sheppard (Eds.), *Research on negotiation in organizations* (Vol. 6, pp. 113–144). Greenwich, CT: JAI Press.

Maletesta, R. M., & Byrne, Z. S. (1997, April). *The impact of formal and interactional justice on organizational outcomes.* Paper presented at the annual conference of the Society for Industrial and Organizational Psychology, St. Louis, MO.

Martin, J. (1981). Relative deprivation: A theory of distributive injustice for an era of shrinking resources. In L. L. Cummings & B. M. Staw (Eds.), *Research in organizational behavior* (Vol. 3, pp. 53–107). Greenwich, CT: JAI Press.

Masterson, S. S., Lewis-McClear, K., Goldman, B. M., & Taylor, M. S. (1997). *Interactional justice revisited: The differential effects of treatment and procedures on work relationships and outcomes.* Manuscript under review.

Mayer, R. C., Davis, J. H., & Schoorman, F. D. (1995). An integrative model of organizational trust. *Academy of Management Review, 20,* 709–734.

Messick, D. M., Bloom, S., Boldizar, J. P., Samuelson, C. D. (1985). Why we are fairer than others. *Journal of Experimental Social Psychology, 21,* 480–500.

Mikula, G. (1986). The experience of injustice: Toward a better understanding of its phenomenology. In H. W. Bierhoff, R. L. Cohen, & J. Greenberg (Eds.), *Justice in interpersonal relations* (pp. 103–123). New York: Plenum Press.

Mikula, G., Petri, B., & Tanzer, N. (1990). What people regard as just and unjust: Types and structures of everyday experiences of injustice. *European Journal of Social Psychology, 20,* 133–149.

Moorman, R. H. (1991). Relationship between organizational justice and organizational citizenship behaviors: Do fairness perceptions influence employee citizenship? *Journal of Applied Psychology, 76,* 845–855.

Scott, W. G. (1988). Management governance theories of justice and liberty. *Journal of Management, 14,* 277–298.

Scott, W. G., & Hart, D. K. (1971). The moral nature of man in organizations: A comparative analysis. *Academy of Management Journal, 14,* 241–255.

Scott, W. G., & Hart, D. K. (1979). *Organizational America: Can individual freedom survive within the security it promises?* Boston: Houghton Mifflin.

Scott, W. G., & Hart, D. K. (1989). *Organizational values in America.* New Brunswick, NJ: Transaction Publishers.

Shapiro, D. L., & Bies, R. J. (1994). Threats, bluffs, and disclaimers in negotiations. *Organizational Behavior and Human Decision Processes, 60,* 14–35.

Sheppard, B. H, Lewicki, R. J., & Minton, J. W. (1992). *Organizational justice: The search for fairness in the workplace.* New York: Lexington Books.

Shreve, S. R., & Shreve, P. (Eds.) (1997). *Outside the law: Narratives on justice in America.* Boston: Beacon Press.

Sitkin, S. B, & Bies, R. J. (1993). The legalistic organization: Definitions, dimensions, and dilemmas. *Organization Science, 4,* 345–351.

Skarlicki, D. P., & Folger, R. (1997). Retaliation in the workplace: The roles of distributive, procedural, and interactional justice. *Journal of Applied Psychology, 82,* 434–443.

Solomon, R. C. (1990). *A passion for justice: Emotions and the origins of the social contract.* Reading, MA: Addison-Wesley.

Steele, C. M. (1988). The psychology of self-affirmation: Sustaining the integrity of the self. In L. Berkowitz (Ed.), *Advances in experimental social psychology* (Vol. 21, pp. 261–302). New York: Academic Press.

Stone, E. F., & Stone, D. L. (1990). Privacy in organizations: Theoretical issues, research findings, and protection mechanisms. In K. M. Rowland & G. R. Ferris (Eds.), *Research in personnel and human resources management,* (Vol. 8, pp. 349–411). Greenwich, CT: JAI Press.

Thibaut, J., & Walker, L. (1975). *Procedural justice: A psychological analysis.* Hillsdale, NJ: Lawrence Erlbaum Associates.

Tolchinsky, P. D., McCuddy, M., Adams, J., Ganster, D. C., Woodman, R., & Fromkin, H. L. (1981). Employee perceptions of invasion of privacy: A field simulation experiment. *Journal of Applied Psychology, 66,* 308–313.

Treviño, L. K., & Bies, R. J. (1997). Through the looking glass: A normative manifesto for organizational behavior. In C. L. Cooper and S. E. Jackson (Eds.), *Creating tomorrow's organizations: A handbook for future research in organizational behavior* (pp. 439–452). London: John Wiley & Sons Ltd.

Tripp, T. M., & Bies, R. J. (1997). What's good about revenge? The avenger's perspective. In R. J. Lewicki, R. J. Bies, & B. H. Sheppard (Eds.), *Research on negotiation in organizations* (Vol. 6, pp. 145–160). Greenwich, CT: JAI Press.

Tyler, T. R. (1988). What is procedural justice? *Law and Society Review, 22,* 301–335.

Tyler, T. R. (1990). *Why people obey the law: Procedural justice, legitimacy, and compliance.* New Haven, CT: Yale University Press.

Tyler, T. R., & Bies, R. J. (1990). Beyond formal procedures: The interpersonal context of procedural justice. In J. S. Carroll (Ed.), *Applied social psychology and organizational settings* (pp. 77–98). Hillsdale, NJ: Lawrence Erlbaum Associates.

Tyler, T. R., & Lind, E. A. (1992). A relational model of authority in groups. In M. P. Zanna (Ed.), *Advances in experimental social psychology* (Vol. 25, pp. 115–191). New York: Academic Press.

Walster, E., Walster, G., & Berscheid, E. (1978). *Equity: Theory and research.* Boston: Allyn & Bacon.

Woodman, R. W., Ganster, D. C., Adams, J., McCuddy, M. C., Tolchinsky, P. D., & Fromkin, H. (1982). A survey of employee perceptions of information privacy in organizations. *Academy of Management Journal, 25,* 647–663.

4

Procedural and Distributive Justice Are More Similar Than You Think: A Monistic Perspective and a Research Agenda

Russell Cropanzano
and
Maureen L. Ambrose

TRADITIONAL ORGANIZATIONAL JUSTICE RESEARCH distinguishes between distributive justice and procedural justice, assuming them to be distinct constructs (Folger, 1986). However, there is some evidence to suggest these constructs may overlap. For example, in a recent meta-analysis of justice research, Hauenstein, McGonigle, and Finder (1997) report a population relationship of .64 between the constructs. Research also demonstrates that procedural justice and distributive justice can affect one another. Individuals make inferences about procedural justice from distributive justice information (Lind & Lissak, 1985; Van den Bos, Vermunt, & Wilke, 1997) and make inferences about distributive justice from procedural justice perceptions (Van den Bos, Lind, Vermunt, & Wilke, 1997). In this

The authors would like to thank Robert Folger, Carol Kulik, Marshall Schminke, and Kees Van den Bos for their helpful comments in the preparation of this chapter.

chapter we suggest that procedural justice and distributive justice are more similar than is generally believed. We suggest that both procedural justice perceptions and distributive justice perceptions are, in some sense, derived from individuals' expectations about outcomes, which at times tend to be economic and at other times socioemotional. Regardless of whether events are labeled "processes" or "distributions," they both have to do with the allocation of these two types of outcomes. We call this the "monistic" view of organizational justice. We suggest that by explicitly considering socioemotional and economic outcomes, the similarity between procedural and distributive justice becomes more apparent. Finally, we suggest that thinking about distributive justice and procedural justice in this way can be useful because it highlights possible avenues for future research that might otherwise be ignored.

We begin this chapter by discussing why fairness matters to individuals and briefly review the basis for distributive and procedural justice. Next we discuss two models of procedural justice and how each would address the role of outcomes in perceptions of procedural fairness. We then consider how the interaction between procedural and distributive justice influences our analysis. Finally, we outline a research agenda that stems from considering procedures and outcomes as more similar than different.

Why Do People Care about Fairness?

It is axiomatic that humans lead social lives. Much of our day-to-day existence is lived within social institutions, such as schools, courtrooms, town meeting halls, and businesses (Coleman, 1993). In order to function effectively in these institutions, some measure of interpersonal affiliation and cooperation is required. As such, participants pay a certain price in their time, effort, and taxes. In return, social institutions allow us to obtain various benefits. Broadly speaking, researchers have organized these benefits into two loose categories: economic and socioemotional (cf. Cropanzano, Howes, Grandey, & Toth, 1997; Cropanzano & Schminke, in press; Foa & Foa, 1974; Folger & Cropanzano, Chapter 1). Economic, sometimes called "instrumental," benefits are those that have to do with material well-being, comfort, and standard of living. They tend to be easily monetizable and relatively concrete. Socioemotional benefits are those that refer to one's standing in and identification with a group. Socioemotional benefits are often called "symbolic" because they provide an indication of one's status and value within the context of some social group. Of course, economic and socioemotional goods are closely related. For example, individuals seek far more profit than is necessary for material well-being (Schor, 1991); the acquisition of surplus material goods often suggests something positive about one's social status and personal worth.

Social institutions are prolific sources of economic and socioemotional benefits. How these goods are distributed is of major importance to individuals. People's responses to what they get and what they give comprise the content matter for social justice research. The manner in which these distributions are made, as well as the distributions themselves, are evaluated by the individuals who participate in these social institutions. People form perceptions as to whether these methods and distributions are "fair" or "unfair." These fairness perceptions allow individuals to make assessments about the likelihood of their outcomes and treatment in the future. If an organization distributes rewards unfairly, the individual is likely to believe similarly unfair distributions will occur in the future. If a manager solicits and considers an individual's concerns, the individual is likely to believe he or she will be similarly included in the future. These assessments allow individuals to make decisions about how to allocate their resources within the organization and how likely it is that their affiliation with the organization will allow them to obtain valued economic and socioemotional benefits. When the good and the bad of social life is meted out in a fair manner, individuals are more committed and more willing to sacrifice on behalf of the social collective (Lind & Tyler, 1988; Tyler & Lind, 1992). On the other hand, when events are seen as unfair, individuals are less loyal and less willing to exert effort on behalf of the institution. They may choose not to affiliate and may even engage in acts of theft, aggression, or revolution (Crosby, 1976; Greenberg & Scott, 1996; Neuman, Baron, & Geddes, 1997). In the past few decades, researchers have identified two categories of justice judgments.

What Is Distributive Justice?

Distributive justice refers to the perceived fairness of resources received. For example, in courtrooms people receive favorable and unfavorable verdicts (e.g., Tyler, 1984). Distributive justice addresses the perceived fairness of those verdicts. Generally speaking, individuals judge the fairness of their outcomes with respect to some referent standard (Kulik & Ambrose, 1992; Stepina & Perrewe, 1991). People do not always divide things the same way. For this reason, allocations can be judged against the outcomes produced by certain allocation rules. Three rules in particular have received a great deal of attention: equality, need, and equity (see Deutsch, 1985; Kabanoff, 1991; Skitka & Tetlock, 1992). When using an equality rule, distributive fairness occurs when every member of a given social group receives the same outcomes. When using a need rule, distributive fairness occurs when the most needy receive the most compensation. When using an equity rule, fair compensation is based on individuals' contributions or inputs.

Although a variety of distribution rules exist, within organizational justice the equity rule has garnered the most attention (Greenberg, 1982). Indeed, when procedural justice researchers have also examined distributive fairness, they have often operationalized distributive injustice as a negative departure from the equity rule (e.g., Ambrose, Harland, & Kulik, 1991; Cropanzano & Folger, 1989; Cropanzano & Randall, 1995; Flinder & Hauenstein, 1994; Greenberg, 1987; Taylor, Moghaddam, Gamble, & Zellerer, 1987). In fact, early work on procedural justice was sometimes treated as an explicit extension of equity theory (e.g., Folger, 1986; Cropanzano & Folger, 1989; Folger & Greenberg, 1985). Equality and need distributions have not been as fully integrated into the procedural justice literature, although as we shall see, the perspective suggested here may help remedy this.

There is one other significant issue here. Many presentations of distributive justice have emphasized the economic or instrumental aspects of outcome fairness. For example, in research on performance appraisal, distributive justice is operationalized as people's reactions to their formal rating or to their pay raise (cf., Folger & Cropanzano, 1998). In research on organizational selection, distributive justice is operationalized as the presence or absence of a job offer (cf. Gilliland, 1993), and in layoffs, distributive justice is operationalized as whether or not people retain their jobs. All of these are outcomes with an economic or quasi-economic value. None of them is directly socioemotional, although, as we discuss later, all may have indirect socioemotional implications.

Even though nothing is inherently wrong with treating distributive justice as "reactions to economic allocations," it is potentially limited. In fact, distributive justice researchers have explicitly maintained that outcomes can have either economic or socioemotional consequences (cf. Deutsch, 1985; Foa & Foa, 1974; Markovsky, 1985). Organizations also distribute benefits with much less economic but much more symbolic value. In one important study, Greenberg (1988) found that working people can experience a sense of inequity at not being assigned a prestigious office. Likewise, Martin and Harder (1994) and Chen (1995) found that individuals actively distribute some socioemotional benefits, such as invitations to social functions. These events signal one's standing and status within the work group.

Of course, many of the most important benefits we receive from work have both economic and socioemotional benefits. For example, research has investigated why people value pay (often viewed as the quintessential economic outcome). Pay is valued because it provides individuals the means to achieve social status, a sense of self-worth or esteem, and material comfort. This same analysis can be applied to promotion opportunities. Markham, Harlan, and Hackett (1987) suggest that this is because promotions convey such benefits as heightened status as well as greater economic rewards.

Regardless, the larger point remains. In the organizational sciences, distributive justice has been somewhat narrowly equated with people's reactions to economic allocations. Other research, however, suggests that individuals evaluate the fairness of both economic and socioemotional benefits. As we shall see, broadening our perspective on distributive justice so that it includes socioemotional allocations brings it much closer to the concept of process fairness.

What Is Procedural Justice?

As the term is used within justice research, a procedure is a series of sequential steps used to guide allocation behaviors or judgments. As individuals participate in these procedures, they form opinions about their fairness. Thus, *procedural justice* can be defined as the fairness of the means by which an allocation decision is made. According to Leventhal (1976, 1980), procedures are apt to be considered fair if they conform to six rules. Just procedures must be consistent, free from bias, accurate, correctable, representative of all concerns (this is often equated with "voice"; see Van den Bos, 1996), and based on prevailing ethical standards. Although these rules have been modified somewhat in order to make them applicable to particular settings, they have proven to be generally useful (Cropanzano & Greenberg, 1997). However, by themselves Leventhal's rules do not tell us why individuals are desirous of procedural fairness. This is an important question for our purposes because a closer look suggests some underlying similarities between procedural and distributive justice. For this reason, we need to take up the issue of fairness perceptions in more detail. In general, two frameworks have been proposed: an instrumental (or self-interest) model and a relational (or group-value) model. Although neither approach precludes the other, and both can be true simultaneously, for pedagogical purposes we will consider each separately.

The Instrumental Model of Procedural Justice

According to the instrumental (or self-interested) view of procedural justice, people do not attend exclusively to their short-term outcomes.

Rather, they are also concerned with how they are likely to do in future transactions. The decision-making procedure is critical because it can divulge information about one's future prospects. From this information, individuals are able to estimate whether their future opportunities appear promising or bleak. According to the instrumental model, those procedures that offer the most attractive future outcomes are the ones that are judged to be the most fair (Greenberg, 1990; Lind & Tyler, 1988; Shapiro, 1993). There is a good deal of evidence consistent with the instrumental point of view (Conlon, 1993; Lind, Kanfer, & Earley, 1990; Shapiro, 1993). Procedural justice is more profitable than procedural injustice. Put differently, one prefers fair processes to unfair ones because fair processes ultimately serve an economic benefit.

To the extent that the instrumental model is correct, when people make judgments of procedural justice, they are actually attending to their possible long-range economic or instrumental consequences. Under this view, procedural fairness can be viewed as a type of enlightened outcome fairness; procedures are evaluated relative to the (economic) consequences that they may produce.

The Relational Model of Procedural Justice

A second perspective is offered by the relational or group-value model, which has been described in a series of papers by Lind and Tyler (Lind, 1995; Lind & Tyler, 1988; Tyler, 1990; Tyler & Lind, 1992). The relational model argues that social groups are useful means of obtaining socioemotional benefits. For example, they can supply a sense of self-worth and offer us personal dignity. Consequently, people spend a good deal of energy worrying about and trying to improve social relationships—even those who live in individualistic cultures (Lind & Earley, 1992).

According to the relational model, procedures are judged to be fair to the extent that they indicate the group's (or at least an authority figure's) esteem. Procedures that suggest a lack of respect from the group are judged to be unfair. The relational model further specifies that people evaluate procedures with respect to three relational concerns: neutrality, benevolence, and status recognition (Lind, 1995). A procedure will likely be perceived as fair if it is free from bias (neutral), if the decision maker is concerned with the perceiver's interests (benevolence), and if the procedure confers status on the individual (status recognition). The relational model has amassed considerable support (for reviews see Lind, 1995; Lind & Tyler, 1988; Tyler, 1990; Tyler & Dawes, 1993; Tyler & Lind, 1992). Interestingly, under the relational model, processes can be seen as a type of socioemotional benefit. Fair procedures are those that indicate one's standing and value to the group. Unfair procedures are those that indicate a lack of standing or value. That is, certain procedural attributes give one a feeling of self-worth, dignity, and status. As a result, these procedures are judged to be fair.[1]

It is interesting to consider research on the relational model side-by-side with organizational research on distributive justice. As we observed earlier, within the organizational sciences many scholars have often operationalized distributive justice as individuals' reactions to economic or quasi-economic allocations. Relational theorists, on the other hand, have tended to treat procedural justice as individuals' reactions to the allocation of socioemotional benefits. To overstate somewhat for the sake of clarity, distributive justice has been loosely equated with economic benefits, whereas procedural justice has been loosely equated with socioemotional benefits. Because of this rough one-to-one correspondence between type of fairness and type of benefit, some researchers may have seen procedural and distributive justice as more different than is actually the case.

Summary

Procedural justice refers to fairness judgments made about the means by which some benefit is assigned. The instrumental model says that if a procedure acts as an economic benefit (e.g., indicates long-term profits), then that procedure is likely to be seen as fair. The relational model says that if a procedure acts as a socioemotional outcome (e.g., it conveys a sense of status), then that procedure is likely to be seen as fair. In both cases, the fairness of the procedure is determined by whether a person ultimately receives some economic or socioemotional benefit. In both the instrumental and relational models, procedures derive their meaning because they help to ensure important outcomes. Thus, it is the two sorts of outcomes (economic and socioemotional) that drive justice perceptions. If this is so, then procedural justice and distributive justice could be conceptualized as functionally similar.

Interactional Justice: Part Procedure and Part Outcome

So far we have maintained that individuals base their justice judgments on the outcomes they are granted or on the procedures they experience. However, people also infer fairness from the interpersonal treatment that they receive. This phenomenon has been examined under the rubric of "interactional justice." The term was first coined by Bies and Moag (1986), who argued that interactional justice was a third type of fairness that was conceptually distinct from distributive and procedural. In particular, procedural justice refers to the means by which a decision is made, whereas interactional justice refers to the social enactment of that procedure. Individuals respond to the quality of their interpersonal treatment as well as to structural aspects of the process (Bies & Sitkin, 1992; Bobocel, McCline, & Folger, 1997; Tyler & Bies, 1990).

Although considerable evidence suggests that interactional justice is important (see Tyler & Bies, 1990, for a review), it is not entirely clear what precisely this construct entails. Separating procedural justice from interactional justice involves an especially fine distinction between the procedure and how the procedure is manifested. As a result of this ambiguity, many researchers have tended to conceptualize interactional justice as a social "aspect" of procedural justice (e.g., Tyler & Bies, 1990; Brockner & Wiesenfeld, 1996; Cropanzano & Greenberg, 1997; Folger & Bies, 1989; Greenberg, 1990; Lind & Tyler, 1988).

However, some work suggests a problem with this approach (e.g., Bies, this volume; Cropanzano & Prehar, 1999; Greenberg, 1993; Masterson, Lewis-McClear, Goldman, & Taylor, in press). To take but one example, research by Mikula, Petrik, and Tanzer (1990) suggests that interactional justice has some distributive aspects. Consider the case of an insult. To belittle someone definitely involves a social interaction and hence is the domain of interactional justice. But an insult need not figure into the means by which a resource allocation is made. By definition, therefore, this type of insult is not necessarily procedural. If this is true, then it follows that the same kind of interpersonal event could sometimes be seen as an outcome and sometimes as a procedure, depending upon whether it is used to allocate resources.

Let us consider this point in detail. Suppose that an individual is denied input into his or her performance review. This is perceived as an unfair procedure. The means is the (lack of) voice and the outcome is the decision. Now let us consider a second example. Suppose an individual and her manager are talking in a social setting. No economic allocation decisions are being made. In the course of this conversation, the manager treats the employee impolitely, perhaps ignoring or interrupting her. All would agree that such behavior is certainly insensitive and impolite. One could say that the employee's "voice" is being ignored, at least in the sense that her statements are not being considered. So is the manager's disrespectful behavior procedurally unfair or distributively unfair? As we have seen, some justice writings classify interpersonal (in)sensitivity as a procedure (e.g., Tyler & Bies, 1990). However, only in the "no voice" performance evaluation is the insensitivity used to assign something. In the second case, the impoliteness is not a means for assigning a concrete outcome. Insensitivity becomes important for itself. Thus, it can act as an outcome in its own right, behaving as a socioemotional reward (Lind, 1995, see his footnote 4; Greenberg, 1993).

Greenberg (1993) deals most directly with this theoretical issue. He proposes a new justice taxonomy that crosses structural and social aspects with procedural and distributive justice. Thus, Greenberg proposes four categories of justice: systemic (structural/procedure), informational (social/procedure), configural (structural/distributive), and interpersonal (social/distributive). Greenberg considers the social sensitivity aspects of interactional justice to be a type of distributive justice. As the reader will observe, Greenberg's (1993) framework bears much in common with the monistic view proposed here.

Previous research has treated interactional justice as independent, a type of procedural justice, or as a type of both procedural and distributive justice. Under our new model, most of these distinctions could be swept away. If all justice is derived from outcomes, then the term *interactional fairness* refers to one's evaluation of certain socioemotional allocations. We have suggested that procedural and distributive justice are more similar than previously believed, in that both derive from outcomes—socioemotional and economic. However, as we argue for the value of considering the similarity of procedural and distributive justice, we are implicitly arguing for the value of considering different types of outcomes. Thus, one could envision two "families" of justice, one based on economic outcomes and the other based on socioemotional outcomes. It is to this possibility that we now turn.

But Is There Any Distinction Worth Making?

Throughout this chapter we have noted that outcomes can be categorized into two broad classes: economic and socioemotional. Based on these two groups of outcomes, one could envision one family of justice perceptions that is based on economic allocations and another type that is based on the socioemotional allocations. The first type would be more closely related to concrete allocations; the latter would be more closely related to interpersonal treatment (for a related model, see Greenberg, 1993). Curiously, if research supports the utility of the economic/socioemotional dichotomy, then it will imply that our monistic view is not monistic at all! In effect, there will be two new "types" of justice.

The theoretical utility of the economic/socioemotional distinction is still an open question. At the present time there is insufficient research for us to make this claim with certainty. Nonetheless, this is a promising avenue for future research. Based on our analysis so far, our expectation would be that people divide their outcomes into those that are economic and those that are not. However, we should caution the reader not to infer that this is a repackaging of the procedural/distributive dichotomy. In fact, as Greenberg (1993) shows, both procedures and outcomes have social and nonsocial aspects.

When a Procedure Becomes an Outcome and an Outcome Becomes a Procedure: A Justice Paradox

Even leaving aside the issue of interactional justice, there remains some overlap between events classified as procedures and those classified as outcomes. Let us discuss this issue in two different ways. First, we will consider point-of-view effects. Next we shall consider the conceptual status of procedural consistency.

Procedural Justice and Point-of-View Effects

When justice researchers use the terms *process* or *procedure*, they are referring to something that is a method, manner, technique, or means by which something else is accomplished. The outcome results from the process and is simply the consequence, end, or result that is assigned by way of the procedure. When considered in this light, we shall see that under certain circumstances, the same event can be either a process or an outcome. The difference depends largely on the point of view of the observer. Let us consider the case of desirable policy changes.

The study of policy changes raises some interesting implications for our purposes. When people are seeking some policy change, then what is normally thought of as a procedure can become—from the seekers' perspective—an outcome. For example, labor unions sometimes lobby for grievance systems that offer due process protection (cf. Ury, Brett, & Goldberg, 1989). When doing so, the grievance system is the outcome they are pursuing. Presumably there must be some other procedure or means by which this goal is pursued. The union may be granted voice through worker–management planning groups. Let us say that a desirable grievance policy is implemented. This might well constitute distributive justice (i.e., the union obtained the new policy) though a fair procedure (i.e., they were allowed to participate in the procedure). However, suppose a worker later used that grievance policy to appeal a fine. Let us say that during the course of this procedure the worker was not allowed voice (e.g., Shapiro & Brett, 1993). At this new juncture the grievance system would produce a procedural injustice. In short, the policy caused a distributive justice at one time and a procedural injustice at another. We call this a point-of-view effect. Observers who evaluate the grievance policy could be describing either distributive or procedural justice; this depends upon their point of view.

We can understand these ideas better by considering a political psychology study conducted by Azzi (1992), who had subjects pretend that they were citizens of a fictitious nation. In this nation there were two ethnic groups of varying sizes—one was large and the other was small. Among other things, the participants' task was to divide up seats for a hypothetical constitution-drafting committee. To keep things simple, let us simply say that some subjects divided these seats equally between the two ethnic groups, whereas others divided up the seats proportionally. This committee would later write a constitution that would allocate resources among the citizens in the nation. The citizens' opinions (actually, the subject's ratings) were used to select the drafting committee. The committee, in turn, divided up resources.

Notice the implications of this example. Whether an event *is* a procedure changes with the perspective of the observer. In Azzi's (1992) study, the constitution-drafting committee was an outcome in the first step and a process in the second. Subject voice is the procedure through which committee seats are acquired. However, in the second step, committee seats are critical to the means through which resources are allocated. Azzi (1992) suggests that in this case the committee seats have the flavor of both procedures and outcomes.

If an event can be both a procedure and an outcome, then this would suggest that the two "types" of justice are not fundamentally distinct. There is, at the very least, considerable overlap between the idea of process and the idea of distribution. This does not argue that the procedural justice/distributive justice perspective lacks utility, of course. However, the observation that an outcome can be a procedure does suggest that a monistic view is reasonable under some circumstances and may have utility as well.

The Conceptual Status of Procedural Consistency

As we have seen, Leventhal (1976, 1980) argued that a procedure is more likely to be seen as fair if it treats everyone consistently. Later procedural justice researchers have tended to maintain Leventhal's (1976, 1980) view (e.g., Cropanzano & Greenberg, 1997; Van den Bos, Vermunt, & Wilke, 1996). In some circumstances, this would seem reasonable, while in others it may not. An experimental study by Smith and Spears (1996) provides one example. Briefly, Smith and Spears required student subjects to achieve a certain performance level to earn $10. The personally advantaged subjects could earn the money by working on an easy task, whereas the personally disadvantaged subjects could earn the money only by working on a difficult task.

The Smith and Spears manipulation could be seen either as a procedural injustice or as a distributive injustice. Procedurally, it is unfair because the two groups were treated inconsistently, in the sense that they were being appraised on different performance criteria. This would be a clear violation of Leventhal's (1976, 1980) consistency rule. However, the Smith and Spears manipulation is also important because it violates the distributive justice rule of equity. Recall that according to equity allocation rules, individuals are compensated in accordance with their contributions or inputs (Markovsky, 1985). However, in the Smith and Spears study, personally disadvantaged participants needed to do *more* work (i.e., successfully complete a more difficult task) in order to earn the *same* pay. Consequently, the inconsistency creates a distributive injustice as well. In the Smith and Spears study, a violation of the equity distribution rule is also a violation of Leventhal's consistency rule. We shall have more to say about the consistency rule later in this chapter. For now, it should suffice to note that consistency or equal treatment is an important aspect of both procedural and distributive justice (cf. Rutte & Messick, 1995). It does not clearly belong to one or the other.

Why the Term "Procedural Justice" Is Still Useful

When we present point-of-view effects and the consistency rule to our colleagues, we often get the following questions: Who's right? Is it a procedure or an outcome? The answer, though not as simple and elegant as we might like, is that the event is both. A thing is no less a process if it can also be thought of as an outcome. For this reason, the events we have been describing can reasonably be thought of as either processes or as distributions. Because scholars have a logical option to treat these events in one of two different ways, researchers can ask which perspective is the most useful means of pursuing different scholarly and practical goals. For some purposes it is more useful to think about these events as procedures, but for other purposes it is more useful to think about them as outcomes.

When, for analytic purposes, processes "become" outcomes, we may gain some theoretical insights that were not previously available.

This analysis implies that the term *procedural justice* could be maintained, so long as researchers define it with respect to a well-delineated interpersonal transaction. By selecting one particular interaction and then isolating it for other transactions and from the individual's broader, personal goals, one could distinguish identifiable procedures and outcomes. This is because the transaction is segregated based upon some outcome that catches a researcher's interest, such as judicial decisions or pay allocations. For example, a researcher may be interested in how students evaluate their professors. As such, the researcher could reasonably isolate teacher evaluations from the broader academic context by simply designating the favorability of the rating as the "outcome" of importance. Once this decision is made, then events such as class participation and interpersonal sensitivity become procedures by definition. By selecting one particular interaction, then temporarily isolating it from other transactions, one could distinguish identifiable procedures and outcomes. We term this process *bracketing* because the transaction of interest is segregated based upon some outcome that is important to a researcher, practitioner, or society at large. Clearly, under our monistic view, the idea of "procedure" remains sound, so long as individuals define it with respect to a well-delineated interpersonal transaction. Bracketing allows justice scholars to retain the term *procedural justice* as a kind of heuristic shorthand that allows researchers to conveniently discuss certain specific allocation decisions.

The Monistic Perspective and the Interaction between Procedures and Outcomes

A potential problem with the monistic view is that procedures and outcomes do not always operate independently. Instead, the two may interact to predict individual reactions (Brockner & Wiesenfeld, 1996; Cropanzano & Greenberg, 1997). As Brockner and Wiesenfeld (1996) note, this procedure by outcome interaction can be described in multiple ways. For simplicity we will focus on one, although others are consistent with our analysis here. (For a more detailed treatment, the reader may wish to refer to Brockner and Wiesenfeld, 1996.) One frequently used model argues that procedures obviate the potential ill effects of unfavorable outcomes (e.g., Cropanzano & Folger, 1991). Disadvantageous outcomes tend to produce anger and resentment. However, if the procedures by which these outcomes are assigned contain various safeguards (e.g., Leventhal's [1980] criteria), then the ill effects of these unfavorable outcomes are at least somewhat mitigated (Cropanzano & Folger, 1991). This raises an interesting possibility: Might outcomes qualify the effects of procedures? The monistic view would imply that the effect that processes have on outcome reactions is mirrored by the effect that outcomes have on process reactions.

The data to address this possibility are quite limited. Nevertheless, the existing research is promising. Van den Bos, Vermunt, and Wilke (1997) investigated these ideas in two experiments. One experiment used a role-playing approach (Study 1), and the other used a "real life" manipulation (Study 2). Supportive results were found in both of these experiments. For ease of explanation, however, we emphasize the role-playing study. Van den Bos and his colleagues argue that procedures and outcomes can interact with one another in a symmetrical fashion. According to Van den Bos et al., events that occur first in a sequence are apt to have the most powerful influence. The reason that procedures seem to qualify outcomes, but not the reverse, is because most studies have been conducted in settings where the participant knew the procedure before he or she knew the outcome. Thus, procedures tended to color subsequent judgments, thereby producing the effects that Cropanzano and Folger (1991) observed. On the other hand, Van den Bos et al. maintained that when the outcome is known in advance of the procedure, then it will drive subsequent evaluations. That is, it will mitigate the effects of inappropriate procedures.

In the role-playing study (Van den Bos, et al., 1997, Study 1), subjects read an experimental vignette informing them that they were job applicants for a position in an organization. As part of the application process, subjects had to go through a screening procedure. There were three independent variables: whether individuals were hired (favorable) or not hired (unfavorable), whether the procedure was accurate (in support of one of Leventhal's [1980] rules) or inaccurate, and whether process information preceded outcome information or outcome information preceded process information (this is the critical manipulation for our analysis here).

Let us first consider the case where process information comes before outcome information. In Figure 4.1, we have graphed Van den Bos et al.'s (1997, Study 1) findings for perceptions of procedural fairness. For effect, we have done so in two different ways. In the left panel the x-axis shows the accuracy of the procedure; it was either high or low. Inside the graph is the favorability of the outcome. In the right panel the x-axis shows outcome favorability. Procedural accuracy is inside the graph. As the reader can see, Van den Bos et al.'s (Study 1) data replicated previous work in that procedural justice perceptions are high whenever accuracy is high. Thus, accuracy mitigated the ill effects of an unfavorable outcome. It

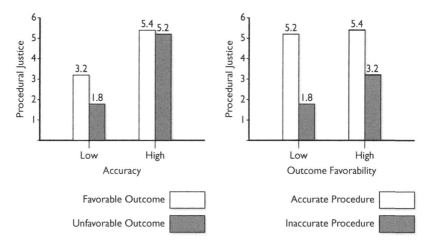

Figure 4.1   The Interaction of Procedures and Distributions When Predicting Procedural Justice Perceptions. The procedural information was presented in advance of the outcome information (adapted from data reported by Van den Bos et al., 1997, Study 1).

should be noted that Van den Bos et al. obtained the same findings for perceptions of distributive fairness.

Now let us consider the case where outcome information comes first and process information comes last. The results are shown in Figure 4.2. The reader should compare Figures 4.1 and 4.2. As will be noted, the results mirror one another. In Study 2, when the outcome was favorable, individuals perceived high procedural justice. Put another way, a favorable outcome mitigated the effects of a disadvantageous procedure.

In another experiment (Van den Bos et al., 1997, Study 2) replicated and extended these findings. Most important, subjects in these two studies actually experienced the manipulation (no role playing). In addition, Van den Bos et al. (Study 2) used a wider range of outcomes. In particular, procedures and outcomes showed the same interaction(s) when predicting satisfaction and intention to protest. Van den Bos et al.'s findings are especially interesting because they suggest that procedure and outcomes behave in a similar fashion. Each can mitigate the effect of the other. If procedures and allocations act with such consistency, then this suggests that they could reasonably be thought of as a single phenomenon.

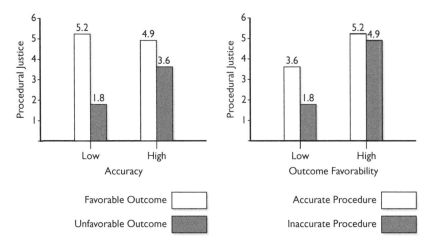

Figure 4.2 The Interaction of Procedures and Distributions When Predicting Procedural Justice Perceptions. The outcome information was presented in advance of the procedural information (adapted from data reported by Van den Bos et al., 1997, Study 1).

Implications of the Monistic View: A Research Agenda

This chapter has raised the possibility that it may be useful to think of procedural and distributive justice as representing a monistic form of outcome fairness. However, our analysis still has a critical limitation. We have not addressed *why* anyone would want to rethink organizational justice in the first place. After all, we have already noted that the justice literature has made many conceptual and practical contributions. If the process/outcome dichotomy has shown so much utility, then why add another perspective?

Our response is not to say that the traditional procedural justice/ distributive justice view is wrong. Indeed, our view is entirely the opposite. The procedural/distributive dichotomy has been an exceedingly useful perspective for both research and practice. However, we maintain that a monistic view is important to consider because it can lead scholars to think about justice phenomenon in new ways. One could envision a variety of conceptual and practical issues that could become salient once the similarities between procedural justice and distributive justice have been observed. Most basically, our monistic view would imply that research on outcome allocations could be applied directly to research on procedures.

In the remainder of the chapter, we consider five new research directions suggested by our monistic perspective.

Violated Expectations and Judgment of Procedural Fairness

To determine whether an allocation is fair, individuals need a standard of comparison. One widely used reference point is the individual's expectations. Considerable evidence suggests that individuals compare what they receive to what they expect. When these expectations are achieved or exceeded, people feel that the outcome was fair. However, when the reality falls short of what was anticipated, then individuals experience a sense of distributive injustice (Crosby, 1976; Greenberg, 1982; Van den Bos, 1996).

If procedures and outcomes are similar, then judgments of procedural fairness should be made relative to one's expectations—not relative to some absolute standard. Thus, perceived procedural injustice should occur when people expect a certain type of favorable treatment and this expectation is violated. Conversely, when these expectations are met, then individuals should judge themselves to be fairly treated. Very little research has tested this proposition. Fortunately, the available data seem to support this reasoning somewhat.

These ideas were put to the test in a vignette study by Greenberg, Eskew, and Miles (1991). Their experimental scenario described a departmental policy regarding student input into course grades. There were three possible departmental policies: a) students receive input (voice is expected), b) department is indifferent (ambiguous expectations), and c) students receive no voice (muteness is expected). The course instructor then decided to either grant or deny student voice. Thus, sometimes student voice was in accordance with expectations and other times it was not. Likewise, sometimes student muteness was in accordance with expectations and other times it was not. Greenberg et al.'s findings were generally consistent with the perspective presented here. When research participants expected voice and then subsequently had it denied, they reported more injustice than when they did not expect voice. Likewise, when the students expected muteness, they reported similar levels of fairness—regardless of whether voice was actually denied by the instructor. Thus, denying voice produced more pernicious effects when students expected to be allowed input and fewer pernicious effects when students did not expect to be allowed input. Received voice affected fairness differently, depending upon individuals' initial expectations.

Even stronger results were presented by Van den Bos et al. (1996, Studies 1 and 2). Using both role-playing (Study 1) and experimental (Study 2) methodologies, Van den Bos and his colleagues found that individuals who were told that they would not be allowed voice reported *less* procedural justice when voice was unexpectedly inserted into the procedure. Conversely, when participants were initially promised voice, they reported less procedural justice when voice was unexpectedly omitted. In short, violated expectations lowered judgments of procedure fairness even when this violation allowed individuals more input into the procedures. Clearly more research is needed in this area. Nevertheless, based on our monistic model and on the data obtained so far, we would propose that prior expectations affect judgments of procedural fairness in that procedures that meet expectations are evaluated more positively than those that do not meet expectations.

Social Comparison and Procedural Justice

As mentioned earlier, it is well known that judgments of distributive fairness are made relative to the outcomes of some referent (Crosby, 1976; Folger, 1986; Kulik & Ambrose, 1992). Often, though not necessarily, this referent is another person (Crosby, 1984; Martin, 1981). Indeed, the impact of social comparison information for judgments of distributive justice has been well known for some time (Pettigrew, 1967). Therefore, distributive justice perceptions do not result from the objective worth (if such a thing exists) of a stimulus. Rather, they result from the worth of one outcome relative to another. For instance, when average Americans are compared to major league baseball players, the players seem to make princely sums. However, the players often feel inequitably treated (Harder, 1992). Presumably, this is because their referents are other major league baseball players and not "average" Americans.

It is interesting to compare this social comparison perspective to current research on procedural justice. In practice, much of this work has been strongly influenced by Leventhal's (1976, 1980) justice criteria. Operationally, procedural fairness is presumed to result from the incorporation of Leventhal's justice criteria. So, for example, with voice, correctability, ethicality, and so on, procedural justice is served. In practice, this suggests that procedural fairness is inferred relative to a theoretical standard, whereas distributive justice is inferred relative to a referent standard. Thus, the fairness of procedures is evaluated against a different type of standard than is the fairness of outcomes.

Note, of course, that this difference is implicit in the way the variables have been operationalized. It is not explicit in theories of procedural justice. However, if it could be shown that procedures are evaluated against abstract moral standards, whereas outcomes are evaluated against concrete social referents, then this would argue for maintaining the distinction between procedures and outcomes. On the other hand, if procedures are really a type of outcome, as we have maintained here, then it follows that people should also use referent standards to make appraisals of procedural justice. In other words, just as individuals perceive distributive unfairness relative to some referent, they may also utilize some (at least implicit) social standard by which to gauge the fairness of procedures (cf. Van den Bos, 1996). It could be that procedures, like outcomes, are not absolute. Instead, people expect different kinds of treatment based upon the comparisons they make in a particular situation. This idea makes some intuitive sense. A worker may be less indignant at his or her lack of voice if the same lack of voice exists for everyone.

Unfortunately, very little research has examined the role of social comparison in judgments of procedural justice. We were able to locate only four experiments that tested the matter directly. Two of these were reported by Folger, Rosenfield, Grove, and Corkran (1979). In both studies Folger and his collaborators exposed undergraduate subjects to unfavorable resource allocations. These allocations came as a result of procedures that either allowed voice or did not. In the absence of any other experimental treatment, research participants perceived the voice procedures to be more fair. However, when the subjects heard a co-worker (actually an experimental accomplice) disparage the allocation decision, then they reported no difference between the voice and no voice conditions. Folger et al. concluded that social information could affect one's evaluation of procedural justice.

In another study, Ambrose, Harland, and Kulik (1991) examined the influence of social comparisons on procedural justice perceptions. They argued that an individual who had no choice in a task would rate such treatment as more unfair to the extent that the individual knew of others who were able to exercise choice. These ideas were tested in a laboratory experiment. Unfortunately, they were not supported. Instead, procedural justice ratings were largely determined by the favorability of the outcomes that the subjects obtained. Although this is compatible with our general view that procedural justice ratings can be thought of as a form of outcome fairness, it is certainly not consistent with our expectation that social comparisons can influence perceptions of procedural justice.

A fourth experiment recently was conducted by Grienberger, Rutte, and van Knippenberg (1997). These researchers suggest that Ambrose et al.'s conclusions were premature. Rather, they suggest that Ambrose and her colleagues had the right idea but the wrong operationalization. In the Ambrose et al. study, participants were told the assignments to the low-control or high-control condition were determined randomly by the computer. Grienberger and her colleagues argue that the low-control condition was still perceived as fair because random assignment is generally considered fair. Grienberger et al. replicated the study using a purer operationalization: Some participants were allowed to participate in task selection whereas others were not. Grienberger et al. found that lacking the ability to influence the procedure was not enough to trigger perceptions of injustice. Rather, these perceptions were most evident when voice was lacking for the subject and when a bogus co-worker was allowed to participate. Thus, procedural (in)justice was defined relative to a social standard.

These experiments suggest that social comparisons are important for determining perceptions of procedural fairness. This supports our monistic view, but more research is needed. We expect that future research will demonstrate that individuals make their judgments of procedural justice, at least in part, by comparing the treatment they receive to the treatment that others receive.

Integrating Procedural Justice with the Three Allocation Rules

Our monistic view also suggests that procedures can be "allocated" in a manner analogous to outcomes. Let us consider the traditional viewpoint first. As we have noted, Leventhal (1976, 1980) maintains that people should be treated consistently. For example, it would be unfair to give voice to some but not to others. Procedures that treat people differently are likely to be seen as unjust. However, this is often not the case for distributive outcomes. The fairest way to allocate outcomes depends upon the rule in force. Equity, equality, and need are all rules by which outcomes, but not procedures, can fairly be assigned (Deutsch, 1985). Because circumstances change across different situations, then what is perceived to be distributively fair will tend to change as well (Elliott & Meeker, 1986; Sinclair & Mark, 1991). Decision makers will want to be equitable in some situations but egalitarian in others (Chen, 1995; Kabanoff, 1991; Leung & Bond, 1984; Leung & Park, 1986).

The procedural/distributive justice perspective on justice seems to suggest that outcomes can be differentially apportioned but that procedures should be assigned via a common rule. However, this view is strongest to the extent that procedures and outcomes are fundamentally different "things." If, as we have maintained here, procedures and outcomes are not fundamentally different, then the rules by which outcomes can be assigned may also be used to assign what researchers have been calling procedures. In fact, the monistic perspective would suggest that there are many situations when firms should *not* treat everyone the same procedurally. There is some indirect evidence that procedures can also be fairly assigned in accordance with equity and need rules.

An equity rule would suggest that individuals receive more favorable procedures based upon certain relevant inputs. At times it may be considered just to treat people differently before the "law." Consider, for example, the case of managerial decision making. If a manager is going to consult with an employee, he or she is likely to consult with someone who has the necessary information (Vroom & Jago, 1988) or someone who is trusted (cf., Dansereau, Graen, Haga, 1975; Duchon, Green, & Taber, 1986; Dienesch & Liden, 1986). The net result of this is that some individuals get more voice than others. This violates a strict consistency rule, but it would probably not be considered fair to offer equal amounts of voice to individuals who lack information or who are not trusted. When people provide certain important inputs, such as information or trust, they may be seen as more deserving of favorable procedural outcomes. These ideas should certainly be investigated in future research.

Need distributions might also be reasonable in some situations. Suppose a business manager has an employee who is diffident and shy. It would be reasonable for the manager to develop this individual's self-confidence. One effective means of developing employees is by involving them in participation (Vroom & Jago, 1988). If circumstances do not allow the manager to involve every other employee in the same fashion, and they often will not, then the manager is faced with a dilemma. To develop this reserved individual, the manager must violate both the equality and equity rules of social justice. Instead, the manager is abiding by a need rule: The worker gets extra voice because of his or her lack of skills. Would this be seen as unfair by others? Perhaps not always; it would likely depend somewhat on the nature of the participation. It is also noteworthy that in the context of performance evaluation, managers will give special consideration to needy subordinates (Longnecker, Sims, & Gioia, 1987). The bottom line is that by thinking of the things that procedures and outcomes share in common, one can examine them in light of the three major rules for resource allocation.

Fraternal versus Egoistical Procedural Justice

So far we have considered only the case in which an individual makes some kind of comparison and decides that he or she—as an individual— is being treated unfairly. This has been termed *egoistical deprivation* (Crosby, 1976). In the distributive justice literature there is another important idea. An individual could be receiving personal outcomes that are quite just. However, the individual may be a member of a group that is not being treated favorably. For example, in the United States a middle-class African American could in principle have pay and status equal to that of middle-class Whites. However, in general, African Americans suffer relative economic and social disadvantages (i.e., racism). Consequently, a middle-class African American might feel a sense of moral outrage, not for him-or herself, but for African Americans as a community. This group-level sense of injustice is called *fraternal deprivation* (Crosby, 1976; James, 1993; James & Cropanzano, 1994). If "procedures" and outcomes are similar, then there should be such a thing as "fraternal-procedural injustice." Individuals may experience a sense of moral outrage, not because they are personally treated unfairly, but because others like them live and work under unfair procedures.

A few studies do offer some indirect evidence. None of the research we could locate examined fraternal-procedural deprivation per se. However, some evidence indicates that observers are at least sympathetic to the victims of procedural injustice, although even this is limited. For example, in one role-playing experiment, Leung, Chiu, and Au (1993) found that observers were sympathetic to various sorts of industrial actions (e.g., strikes, slowdowns) following a procedural impropriety. However, this type of research only demonstrates that people can become supportive if they witness an injustice. It does not show that they are more sympathetic to the treatment of some groups than to others. Nonetheless, based on the fraternal-distributive justice literature, we predict that observers tend to be more affected when the victim of a procedural impropriety is a member of their own social group and less affected when the victim is from another group.

Process Failure: Practical Criteria for Procedural Justice

According to our monistic view, procedures are valuable because they act as economic and socioemotional benefits. Another way of stating this is to say that we value fair procedures because they convey material comfort, self-worth, and dignity. If this is the case, then it suggests another commonality that procedures have with outcomes. Procedures are not inherently fair or unfair but rather that they are judged to be fair based on what they allow individuals to obtain. Thus, procedural attributes—such as those listed by Leventhal (1980)—do not necessarily lead one to view the procedures as just. Rather, under most conditions these safeguards make it more likely that people will obtain some economic and socioemotional benefits. To the extent that this is (or is likely to be) realized, then the procedures will be judged to be fair. Conversely, to the extent that these procedural attributes do not act as economic and socioemotional benefits, then the process will be seen as less fair.

What follows from this is a proposition that is counterintuitive in theory but common sense in practice. Regardless of the objective characteristics of the process, if the procedures do not act as some kind of benefit, then these procedures will be seen as unfair. In other words, even a procedure that includes voice, correctability, consistency, and so on can be unfair under certain conditions. We call this *process failure*.

What remains to make this proposition testable is to specify the conditions under which these effects may occur. The most obvious example of process failure refers to those circumstances when an organization is, loosely speaking, too fair. That is, there are times when a firm may try so hard to adhere to every principle of procedural fairness that it is left with a Byzantine snarl of rules, regulations, and policies. This sea of red tape, much of it enacted in the name of fairness, often produces a sense of injustice—despite ad nauseam opportunities of voice, appeals, and so on. As a result, the procedure stops serving its larger objectives. It becomes "legalistic" (Bies & Tripp, 1995; Cropanzano & Byrne, in press; Sitkin & Bies, 1993). In addition to work of Bies and his colleagues, some political science writings have also addressed the issue (e.g., Sykes, 1992). Unfortunately, the available evidence tends to be somewhat anecdotal.

Howard (1994) and Sowell (1995) discuss the example of American tort law. According to these authors, the process of tort law is often perceived as unfair partially because it has built in too many of Leventhal's procedural attributes. For example, everyone has an opportunity for voice, to the point where a important law suit can involve legal brief after legal brief. Likewise, the decision must be correctable. For this reason there can be many, many appeals before a case is finally settled. The system has become so complicated and costly that it is unworkable for many (Howard, 1994; Sowell, 1995).

When procedures become too elaborate, they can have the effect of stifling the very fairness they seek to obtain (Sitkin & Bies, 1993). They no longer act as economic and socioemotional benefits. Thus, for procedures to be seen as fair, it helps if they are also practical. If the notion of process failure proves to be a viable construct, it will provide evidence for our monistic perspective. Perhaps more important, however, it may also supply some cautions regarding our confidence in procedures. It may be that overzealous attempts to provide procedural justice could backfire, working against the very goals they seek to attain. Organizations may wish to proceed with prudence.

Summary and Conclusions

Historically, procedures have been seen as one type of phenomenon and outcomes as another. This distinction has been conceptually useful; considerable evidence now suggests that procedural justice predicts an assortment of work-relevant criteria (Cropanzano & Greenberg, 1997; Greenberg, 1990, 1996). However, certain issues remain. We have argued that these issues can be addressed by emphasizing the things that procedures and outcomes have in common—a perspective termed the monistic view. But what does it all mean? An analogy might help.

Suppose someone has a very long, very official-looking book. When the individual opens the book, she get an unpleasant surprise—she can't read it. Why? Because the text is written is in three different colors. The letters are bright red, green, and yellow. The three colors present the reader with a complicated piece of text, and her eyes can't make sense out of the ensuing jumble. After struggling for a while, she decides to purchase some special glasses. The lens of these glasses have a red tint. With these red-tinted glasses, the reader discovers that the red-colored letters are no longer visible. All she sees when she reads is the green and the yellow text. Freed of the red clutter, the green letters gradually begin to form words. These provide pithy sayings that give advice. The book is even more impressive than originally imagined!

Then one day, the individual realizes that she's read only one-third of the book—the green part. And she gets curious once again. What would happen if she read the red or the yellow part? So she goes back to the store and buys a new set of special glasses. These new spectacles have green lenses. Now the green letters are gone, and she can clearly read the yellow and red ones. What might she find?

This little story articulates the situation in organizational justice research. Our social world is like a complicated and jumbled book. When we open it, we cannot easily read it. So to guide us in our task, we view it through special lenses. These lenses are akin to our scientific paradigms. The scientific paradigm used in justice research is that of processes and outcomes. A paradigm works, in part, because it tells the researcher what is important and what is not. In essence, it "blots out" the "irrelevant" details and gives meaning to the remainder of the text. This is what the red lens did in our story. There is no scientific progress without the special viewpoint of our scientific paradigms (Kuhn, 1962). But they do have a cost—the missing "irrelevant" details may not be so "irrelevant" after all! We'll never know unless we find a way to take a closer look at them.

This is the crux of our chapter. How do we take that "closer look" when the lens of process and outcome is so strong? Might we be missing important information? *The only way to find out is to change the lens.* We are proposing that justice researchers keep two pairs of "glasses" in their intellectual tool kit. One process/outcome set for the everyday work that has made this research area so successful. But also keep another set handy—the monistic set. Let's see what happens when we change our glasses every now and then!

Let's finish this tiny parable by returning once more to the central question: Who's right and who's wrong? Well, both or neither, depending upon how you look at it. The traditional view is clearly "right" in the sense that it does three things: (a) explains vast amounts of empirical data, (b) helps design more humane work organizations, and (c) does the first two while also promoting business effectiveness. But the traditional view does not tell the full story because there are some phenomena left unaccounted for and it misdirects us away from certain practical problems (e.g., legalism, standards for procedural justice, and so on).

Now let's subject the monistic view to the same analysis. Because this perspective is new, having only been proposed in the present chapter, the monistic view is right only to the extent that (a) it helps account for events that have not been well explained within the traditional paradigm and (b) it points us to some neglected practical concerns. In this chapter, we believe that we've made this case. On the other hand, the monistic view remains less complete than the process/outcome paradigm. This is because there is probably a host of events that fall outside of the monistic view. For this reason, the monistic view is best seen as a complement to the procedural/distributive justice approach.

The bottom line is a simple one: Justice is a complicated social phenomenon. There is more than one way to look at it. In this chapter we have argued for retaining *both* perspectives. In fact, in our discussion of bracketing, we illustrated one mechanism by which the two viewpoints could be integrated. There are probably others. Thus, the monistic perspective and the traditional perspective are not even logical opposites. To say that procedural justice and distributive justice are similar does not make either of them any less important. Clearly, procedures matter a great deal to people. We hope our discussion highlights new avenues of research that stem from considering the similarities between two types of justice.

NOTE

1. Although most discussions of the relational model emphasize that groups are important for noneconomic reasons (e.g., Lind, 1995; Tyler & Lind, 1992), relational theorists are certainly not oblivious to economic considerations. For instance, Tyler (1989, p. 831) states that "groups are important sources of material resources." According to Tyler (1989), these "material resources" are one reason that relational concerns are important. In any case, excluding these economic considerations would not substantially change our present analysis.

REFERENCES

Ambrose, M. L., Harland, L. K., & Kulik, C. T. (1991). Influence of social comparisons on perceptions of organizational fairness. *Journal of Applied Psychology, 76,* 239–246.

Azzi, A. E. (1992). Procedural justice and the allocation of power in intergroup relations: Studies in the United States and South Africa. *Personality and Social Psychology Bulletin, 18,* 736–747.

Bies, R. J. (1987). The predicament of injustice: The management of moral outrage. In L. L. Cummings & B. M. Staw (Eds.), *Research in organizational behavior* (Vol. 9, pp. 289–319). Greenwich, CT: JAI Press.

Bies, R. J., & Moag, J. S. (1986). Interactional justice: Communication criteria for fairness. In R. J. Lewicki, B. H. Sheppard, & M. Bazerman (Eds.), *Research on negotiation in organizations* (Vol. 1, pp. 43–55). Greenwich, CT: JAI Press.

Bies, R. J., & Sitkin, S. B. (1992). Explanation as legitimation: Excuse-making in organizations. In M. L. McLaughlin, M. J. Cody, & S. J. Read (Eds.), *Explaining one's self to others: Reason-giving in a social context* (pp. 183–198). Hillsdale, NJ: Erlbaum.

Bies, R. J., & Tripp, T. M. (1995). The use and abuse of power: Justice as social control. In R. Cropanzano & M. K. Kacmar (Eds.), *Politics, justice, and support: Managing the social climate of work organizations* (pp. 131–145). Westport, CT: Quorum Books.

Bobocel, D. R., McCline, R. L., & Folger, R. (1997). Letting them down gently: Conceptual advances in explaining controversial organizational policies. In C. L. Cooper & D. M. Rousseau (Eds.), *Trends in organizational behavior* (Vol. 4, pp. 73–88). Sussex, England: John Wiley & Sons.

Brockner, J., & Wiesenfeld, B. M. (1996). An integrative framework for explaining reactions to decisions: The interactive effects of outcomes and procedures. *Psychological Bulletin, 120*, 189–208.

Chen, C. C. (1995). New trends in rewards allocation preferences: A Sino–U.S. comparison. *Academy of Management Journal, 38*, 408–428.

Coleman, J. S. (1993). The rational reconstruction of society. *American Sociological Review, 58*, 1–15.

Conlon, D. E. (1993). Some tests of the self-interest and group-value models of procedural justice: Evidence from an organizational appeal procedure. *Academy of Management Journal, 36*, 1109–1124.

Cropanzano, R., & Byrne, Z. S. (in press). When it's time to stop writing policies: A procedural justice perspective. *Human Resource Management Review*.

Cropanzano, R., & Folger, R. (1989). Referent cognitions and task decision autonomy: Beyond equity theory. *Journal of Applied Psychology, 74*, 293–299.

Cropanzano, R., & Folger, R. (1991). Procedural justice and worker motivation. In R. M. Steers & L. W. Porter (Eds.), *Motivation and Work Behavior* (5th Ed., pp. 131–143). New York: McGraw-Hill.

Cropanzano, R., & Greenberg, J. (1997). Progress in organizational justice: Tunneling through the maze. In I. T. Robertson & C. L. Cooper (Eds.), *International Review of Industrial and Organizational Psychology* (Vol. 12, pp. 317–372). New York: Wiley.

Cropanzano, R., Howes, J. C., Grandey, A. A., & Toth, P. (1997). The relationship of organizational politics and organizational support to work behavior, attitudes, and stress. *Journal of Organizational Behavior, 18*, 159–180.

Cropanzano, R., & Prehar, C. (1999, April). *Using social exchange theory to distinguish procedural and interactional justice*. Paper presented at the annual meeting of the Society for Industrial and Organizational Psychology. Atlanta, GA.

Cropanzano, R., & Randall, M. L. (1995). Advance notice as a means of reducing relative deprivation. *Social Justice Research, 8*, 217–238.

Cropanzano, R., & Schminke, M. (in press). Justice as the mortar of social cohesion. In M. Turner (Ed.), *Groups at work: Advances in theory and research*. Hillsdale, NJ: Erlbaum.

Crosby, F. (1976). A model of egoistical relative deprivation. *Psychological Review, 83*, 85–113.

Crosby, F. (1984). Relative deprivation in organizational settings. In B. M. Staw & L. L. Cummings (Eds.), *Research in organizational behavior* (Vol. 6, pp. 51–93). Greenwich, CT: JAI Press.

Dansereau, F., Jr., Graen, G., & Haga, W. J. (1975). A vertical dyad linkage approach to leadership within formal organizations: A longitudinal investigation of the role making process. *Organizational Behavior and Human Performance, 13*, 46–78.

Deutsch, M. (1985). *Distributive justice.* New Haven, CT: Yale University Press.

Dienesch, R. M., & Liden, R. C. (1986). Leader-member exchange model of leadership: A critique and further development. *Academy of Management Review, 11,* 618–634.

Duchon, D., Green, S. G., & Taber, T. D. (1986). Vertical dyad linkage: A longitudinal assessment of antecedents, measures, and consequences. *Journal of Applied Psychology, 71,* 56–60.

Elliott, G. C., & Meeker, B. F. (1986). Achieving fairness in the face of competing concerns: The different effects of individual and group characteristics. *Journal of Personality and Social Psychology, 50,* 754–760.

Flinder, S. W., & Hauenstein, M. A. N. (1994). *Antecedents of distributive and procedural justice perceptions.* Unpublished manuscript, Virginia Polytechnic Institute and State University, Blacksburg, Virginia.

Foa, U. G., & Foa, E. B. (1974). *Societal structures of the mind.* Springfield, IL: C. C. Thomas.

Folger, R. (1986). Rethinking equity theory: A referent cognitions model. In H. W. Bierhoff, R. L. Cohen, & J. Greenberg (Eds.), *Justice in social relations* (pp. 145–162). New York: Plenum.

Folger, R. (1994). Workplace justice and employee worth. *Social Justice Research, 7,* 225–241.

Folger, R., & Bies, R. J. (1989). Managerial responsibilities and procedural justice. *Employee Responsibilities and Rights Journal, 2,* 79–90.

Folger, R., & Cropanzano, R. (1998). *Organizational justice and human resource management.* Beverly Hills, CA: Sage.

Folger, R., & Greenberg, J. (1985). Procedural justice: An interpretive analysis of personnel systems. In K. Rowland & G. Ferris (Eds.), *Research in personnel and human resources management* (Vol. 3, pp. 141–183). Greenwich, CT: JAI Press.

Folger, R., Rosenfield, D., Grove, J., & Corkran, L. (1979). Effects of "voice" and peer opinions on responses to inequity. *Journal of Personality and Social Psychology, 22,* 531–564.

Gilliland, S. W. (1993). The perceived fairness of selection systems: An organizational justice perspective. *Academy of Management Review, 18,* 694–734.

Greenberg, J. (1982). Approaching equity and avoiding inequity in groups and organizations. In J. Greenberg & R. L. Cohen (Eds.), *Equity and justice in social behavior* (pp. 389–435). New York: Academic Press.

Greenberg, J. (1987). Reactions to procedural injustice in payment decisions: Do the means justify the ends? *Journal of Applied Psychology, 72,* 55–61.

Greenberg, J. (1988). Equity and workplace status: A field experiment. *Journal of Applied Psychology, 73,* 606–613.

Greenberg, J. (1990). Organizational justice: Yesterday, today, and tomorrow. *Journal of Management, 16,* 606–613.

Greenberg, J. (1993). The social side of fairness: Interpersonal and informational classes of organizational justice. In R. Cropanzano (Ed.), *Justice in the workplace: Approaching fairness in human resource management* (pp. 79–103). Hillsdale, NJ: Erlbaum.

Greenberg, J. (1996). *The quest for justice on the job: Essays and experiments.* Thousand Oaks, CA: Sage.

Greenberg, J., Eskew, D. E., & Miles, J. A. (1991, August). *Adherence to participatory norms as a moderator of the fair process effect: When voice does not enhance procedural fairness.* Paper presented at the annual meeting of the Academy of Management. Miami Beach, FL.

Greenberg, J., & Scott, K. S. (1996). Why do workers bite the hands that feed them? Employee theft as a social exchange process. In B. M. Staw & L. L. Cummings (Eds.), *Research in organizational behavior* (Vol. 18, pp. 111–156). Greenwich, CT: JAI Press.

Grienberger, I. V., Rutte, C. G., & van Knippenberg, A. F. M. (1997). Influence of social comparisons of outcomes and procedures on fairness judgments. *Journal of Applied Psychology, 82,* 913–919

Harder, J. W. (1992). Play for pay: Effects of inequity in a pay-for-performance context. *Administrative Science Quarterly, 37,* 321–335.

Hauenstein, N. M. A., McGonigle, T., & Flinder, S. (1997). Meta-analysis of the relationship between procedural and distributive justice. Paper presented at the annual meeting of the Society of Industrial/Organizational Psychology. St. Louis, MO.

Howard, P. K. (1994). *The death of common sense: How law is suffocating America.* New York: Random House.

James, K. (1993). The social context of organizational justice: Cultural, intergroup, and structural effects on justice behaviors and perceptions. In R. Cropanzano (Ed.), *Justice in the workplace: Approaching fairness in human resource management* (pp. 21–50). Hillsdale, NJ: Erlbaum.

James, K., & Cropanzano, R. (1994). Dispositional group loyalty and individual action for the benefit of an ingroup: Experimental and correlational evidence. *Organizational Behavior and Human Decision Processes, 60,* 179–205.

Kabanoff, B. (1991). Equity, equality, power, and conflict. *Academy of Management Review, 16,* 416–441.

Kuhn, T. S. (1970). *The structure of scientific revolutions* (2nd ed). Chicago, IL: University of Chicago.

Kulik, C. T., & Ambrose, M. L. (1992). Personal and situational determinants of referent choice. *Academy of Management Review, 17,* 212–237.

Leung, K., & Bond, M. H. (1984). The impact of cultural collectivism in reward allocation. *Journal of Personality and Social Psychology, 47,* 793–804.

Leung, K., Chiu, W-H., & Au, Y-F. (1993). Sympathy and support for industrial actions: A justice analysis. *Journal of Applied Psychology, 78,* 781–787.

Leung, K., & Park, H. (1986). Effects of interactional goal on choice of allocation rule: A cross-national study. *Organizational Behavior and Human Decision Processes, 37,* 111–120.

Leventhal, G. S. (1976). The distribution of rewards and resources in groups and organizations. In L. Berkowitz & E. Walster (Eds.), *Advances in experimental social psychology* (Vol. 9, pp. 91–131). New York: Academic Press.

Leventhal, G. S. (1980). What should be done with equity theory? In K. J. Gergen, M. S. Greenberg, & R. H. Willis (Eds.), *Social exchange: Advances in theory and research* (pp. 27–55). New York: Plenum.

Lind, E. A. (1995). Justice and authority relations in organizations. In R. Cropanzano & M. K. Kacmar (Eds.), *Organizational politics, justice, and support: Managing the social climate of the workplace* (pp. 83–96). Westport, CT: Quorum Books.

Lind, E. A., & Earley, P. C. (1992). Procedural justice and culture. *International Journal of Psychology, 27,* 227–242.

Lind, E. A., Kanfer, R., & Earley, P. C. (1990). Voice, control, and procedural justice: Instrumental and noninstrumental concerns in fairness judgments. *Journal of Personality and Social Psychology, 59,* 952–959.

Lind, E. A., & Lissak, R. I. (1985). Apparent impropriety and procedural fairness judgments. *Journal of Experimental Social Psychology, 21,* 19–29.

Lind, E. A., & Tyler, T. (1988). *The social psychology of procedural justice.* New York: Plenum.

Longnecker, C. O., Sims, H. P., Jr., & Gioia, D. A. (1987). Behind the mask: The politics of employee appraisal. *Academy of Management Executive, 1,* 183–193.

Markhan, W. T., Harlan, S. L., & Hackett, E. J., (1987). Promotion opportunity in organizations: Causes and consequences. In K. M. Rowland & G. R. Ferris (eds.), *Research in personnel and human resource management* (Vol. 5, pp. 223–287). Greenwich, CT: JAI Press.

Markovsky, B. (1985). Toward a multilevel distributive justice theory. *American Sociological Review, 50,* 822–839.

Martin, J. (1981). Relative deprivation: A theory of distributive injustice for an era of shrinking resources. In B. M. Staw & L. L. Cummings (Eds.), *Research in organizational behavior* (Vol. 3, pp. 53–107). Greenwich, CT: JAI Press.

Martin, J., & Harder, J. W. (1994). Bread and roses: Justice and the distribution of financial and socioemotional rewards in organizations. *Social Justice Research, 7,* 241–264.

Masterson, S. S., Lewis-McClear, K., Goldman, B. M., & Taylor, M. S. (in press). Organizational justice and social exchange: An empirical study of the distinction between interactional and formal procedural justice. *Academy of Management Journal.*

McFarlin, D. B., & Sweeney, P. D. (1992). Distributive and procedural justice as predictors of satisfaction with personal and organizational outcomes. *Academy of Management Journal, 35,* 626–637.

Mikula, G., Petrik, B., & Tanzer, N. (1990). What people regard as unjust: Types and structures of everyday experiences of injustice. *European Journal of Social Psychology, 20,* 133–149.

Neuman, J. H., Baron, R. A., & Geddes, D. (1997). A three-factor model of workplace aggression: Predicting specific forms of aggression in organizational settings. Unpublished manuscript.

Pettigrew, T. (1967). Social evaluation theory. In D. Levine (Ed.), *Nebraska symposium on motivation* (Vol. 15). Lincoln, NB: University of Nebraska Press.

Rutte, C. G., & Messick, D. M. (1995). An integrated model of perceived unfairness in organizations. *Social Justice Research, 8,* 239–261.

Schor, J. B. (1991). *The overworked American: The unexpected decline of leisure.* New York: Basic Books.

Shapiro, D. L. (1993). Reconciling theoretical differences among procedural justice researchers by re-evaluating what it means to have one's view "considered": Implications for third-party managers. In R. Cropanzano (Ed.), *Justice in the workplace: Approaching fairness in human resource management* (pp. 51–78). Hillsdale, NJ: Erlbaum.

Shapiro, D. L., & Brett, J. M. (1993). Comparing three processes underlying judgments of procedural justice: A field study of mediation and arbitration. *Journal of Personality and Social Psychology, 65,* 1167–1177.

Sinclair, R. C., & Mark, M. M. (1991). Mood and the endorsement of egalitarian macrojustice versus equity-based microjustice principals. *Personality and Social Psychology Bulletin, 17,* 369–375.

Sitkin, S. B., & Bies, R. J. (1993). The legalistic organization: Definitions, dimensions, and dilemmas. *Organization Science, 4,* 345–351.

Skitka, L. J., & Tetlock, P. E. (1992). Allocating scarce resources: A contingency model of distributive justice. *Journal of Experimental Social Psychology, 28,* 491–522.

Smith, H. J., & Spears, R. (1996). Ability and outcome evaluations as a function of personal and collective (dis)advantage: A group escape from individual bias. *Personality and Social Psychology Bulletin, 22,* 6909–704.

Sowell, T. (1995). *The vision of the anointed: Self-congratulation as the basis for social policy.* New York: Basic Books.

Stepina, L. P., & Perrewe, P. L. (1991). The stability of comparative referent choice and feelings of inequity: A longitudinal field study. *Journal of Organizational Behavior, 12,* 185–200.

Sykes, C. J. (1992). *A nation of victims: The decay of the American character.* New York: St. Martin's Press.

Taylor, D. M., Moghaddam, F. M., Gamble, I., & Zellerer, E. (1987). Disadvantaged group responses to perceived inequity: From passive acceptance to collective action. *Journal of Social Psychology, 127,* 259–272.

Tyler, T. R. (1984). The role of perceived injustice in defendants' evaluations of their courtroom experience. *Law and Society Review, 18,* 51–74.

Tyler, T. R. (1989). The psychology of procedural justice: A test of the group-value model. *Journal of Personality and Social Psychology, 57,* 830–838.

Tyler, T. R. (1990). *Why people obey the law: Procedural justice, legitimacy, and compliance.* New Haven, CT: Yale University Press.

Tyler, T. R. (1991). Using procedures to justify outcomes: Testing the viability of a procedural justice strategy for managing conflict and allocating resources in work organizations. *Basic and Applied Social Psychology, 12,* 259–279.

Tyler, T. R., & Bies, R. J. (1990). Beyond formal procedures: The interpersonal context of procedural justice. In J. S. Carroll (Ed.), *Applied social psychology and organizational settings* (pp. 77–98). Hillsdale, NJ: Lawrence Erlbaum Associates.

Tyler, T. R., & Dawes, R. M. (1993). Fairness in groups: Comparing self-interest and social identity perspectives. In B. A. Mellers & J. Baron (Eds.), *Psychological perspectives on justice: Theory and applications* (pp. 87–108). New York: Cambridge University Press.

Tyler, T. R., & Lind, E. A. (1992). A relational model of authority in groups. In M. P. Zanna (Ed.), *Advances in experimental social psychology* (Vol. 25, pp. 115–191). San Diego: Academic Press.

Ury, W. L., Brett, J. M., & Goldberg, S. G. (1989). *Getting disputes resolved: Designing systems to cut the costs of conflict.* San Francisco: Jossey-Bass.

Van den Bos, K. (1996). *Procedural justice and conflict.* Unpublished doctoral dissertation. University of Leiden, the Netherlands.

Van den Bos, K., Lind, E. A.. Vermunt, R., & Wilke, H. A. M. (1997). How do I judge my outcome when I do not know the outcome of others? The psychology of the fair process effect. *Journal of Personality and Social Psychology, 72,* 1034–1046.

Van den Bos, K., Vermunt, R., & Wilke, H. A. M. (1996). The consistency rule and the voice effect: The influence of expectations on procedural fairness judgments and performance. *European Journal of Social Psychology, 26,* 411–428.

Van den Bos, K., Vermunt, R., & Wilke, H. A. M. (1997). Procedural and distributive justice: What is fair depends more on what comes first than on what
comes next. *Journal of Personality and Social Psychology, 72,* 95–104.

Vroom, V. H., & Jago, A. G. (1988). *The new leadership: Managing participation
in organizations.* Englewood Cliffs, NJ: Prentice-Hall.

5

Anticipatory Injustice: The Consequences of Expecting Injustice in the Workplace

---

Debra L. Shapiro
and
Bradley L. Kirkman

"Seek, and you will find."

—*Luke 11:9*

IF WE SUBSTITUTED the word "expect" for "seek" in the opening quote, the concluding words "and you will find" would remain unchanged. Numerous studies empirically support the "confirmatory bias" phenomenon, that is, our tendency to see things that we expect to see (Snyder & Swann, 1978a; 1978b). For example, performance appraisers expecting to see high levels of performance from those being appraised typically see this, and the reverse is also true—a phenomenon also referred to as a "halo effect" (Ilgen & Feldman, 1983; Kozlowski & Kirsch, 1987; Siegall, 1992; see reviews by Bretz, Milkovich, & Read, 1992; and Balzer & Sulsky, 1992). Similarly, job interviewers expecting to see a job candidate as weak, based on an initial impression, typically do (Dougherty, Turban, & Callender, 1994). As another example, Elaad, Ginton, and Ben-Shakhar (1994) found that polygraph examiners who expect their interviewee to be guilty rather than not guilty—based on case facts they receive prior to administrating a lie-detection test called the Control Question Technique (CQT)—typically see indicators of guilt in the test results. However, this expectation effect was *not* observed when the polygraph charts showed strong, objective (physiological) evidence that clearly contradicted examiners' expectations.

Taken together, these findings suggest that if employees expect to see injustice in their work situations, *unless they have unequivocal, objective evidence to indicate otherwise,* they will be likely to see it—or at least more likely than employees who lack this expectation. If this is so, then employees' perceptions of injustice, indeed anyone's perceived injustice—the primary dependent variable comprising the bulk of the justice literature (see reviews by Greenberg, 1990a; Lind & Tyler, 1988)—may be a result of *expected,* and not necessarily experienced, injustice. We refer to this phenomenon as *"anticipatory* injustice." The purpose of this chapter is fourfold: (1) to introduce this concept, (2) to make salient the likely prevalence of anticipatory injustice in the workplace, especially during times of organizational change, (3) to identify the likely consequences of anticipatory injustice, including (but not limited to) the perceptions and related behaviors of (distributive, procedural, and interactional) injustice, and (4) to discuss the theoretical and practical implications of noting that injustice is not only perceived but also *anticipated* and that this anticipation can bring about the perception, and possible reality, of injustice.

Anticipatory Justice

To "anticipate," according to *Webster's Dictionary,* is "to sense or realize beforehand; foresee; to look forward to as likely or certain; to expect." If the substance of these expectations regards the extent to which one will, or won't, see justice, then we have what we call *anticipatory (in)justice.* Anticipatory justice is similar to the concept of trust, as defined by Shaw (1997); thus conversely, anticipatory injustice is similar to the concept of distrust, or fear. We have reached this conclusion based on Shaw's defining trust as the "belief that those on whom we depend will meet our *expectations* of them" (p. 21, emphasis ours). Others have similarly defined trust as an expectation or probability assessment about another's behavior. For example, Brockner and Siegel (1996) say "Trust refers to a belief about a party's *future* behavior" (p. 401, emphasis ours). Tyler and Degoey (1996) define both a "calculative image of trust" and a "social conception of trust" as expectations about the favorability of a *future* interaction (in terms of its outcome or relational experience, respectively). When the expectation is that desirable behavior (e.g., cooperation, honesty, justice) is forthcoming, then it is called trust; when undesired behavior (e.g., noncooperation, dishonesty, injustice) is expected instead, this is called distrust (Deutsch, 1958; Kramer, 1995; Mayer, Davis, & Schoorman, 1995; Robinson, 1996). Trust-related judgments pertaining to acts of justice are thus another way of describing anticipatory justice.

Expressions of anticipatory injustice, or negative expectations—hence distrust—are illustrated by the following quotes, which were made by employees recently assigned to self-managing work teams.

> Quote 1: "I might work harder than other people on the same job."
>
> Quote 2: "Will I work more than others for the same money?"
>
> Quote 3: "How will I be appraised? Will it be fair? How can someone at another location know what I am doing?"
>
> Quote 4: [I'm concerned about] how to be fair when doing peer evaluations."
>
> Quote 5: "Bullies will ride rough-shod over divergent and valuable ideas."
>
> Quote 6: [I'm concerned about] cliques! One or two people making the decision for the team and doing a very good political job at it."
>
> Quote 7: "Management [will] say one thing and do another—inconsistency."
>
> Quote 8: "Management [will] not be able to stay out of the teams."

Kirkman, Shapiro, Novelli, and Brett (1996) collected these quotes, along with others. It is possible that these expressions of anticipatory injustice are unique to the participants of Kirkman et al.'s study. Or it is possible that they are unique to employees recently assigned to self-managing work teams. Or it is possible that anticipatory injustice is expressed or privately feared by employees who have recently experienced *any* change. Of all these possibilities, we believe the latter one is the most realistic, and we believe anticipatory injustice is prevalent.

The Likely Prevalence of Anticipatory Injustice in Organizations

Several researchers have noted that during times of uncertainty, people ask "why" questions (Wong & Weiner, 1981), or similarly, they engage in sense-making behavior (Dutton & Duncan, 1987; Louis, 1980; Thomas, Clark, & Gioia, 1993; Weick, 1995). The purpose of seeking sense or certainty, these researchers explain, is that this understanding then enables the sense makers to predict subsequent events and thereby feel a greater sense of control. People's need for control or certainty has been described as fundamental. Absent this, people are prone to experience uncomfortable cognitive (Festinger, 1954), as well as emotional, states including depression (Abramson, Seligman, & Teasdale, 1978).

Members of organizations characterized by uncertainty are therefore likely to be engaged in sense making, thus predictive, activity. Said differently, *anticipatory* activity is likely to characterize members of organizations whose environment is uncertain. In an age in which (1) products' price, quality, and accessibility are easily and quickly copied as a result of market globalization, (2) employees are transitory as a result of increased use of highly specialized contract personnel, and (3) intellectual (as opposed to physical) assets determine organizations' competitiveness, many theorists and commentators have noted that the speed of organizational change, and thus uncertainty, is greater than ever (Bennis & Mische, 1995; Petrini & Hultman, 1995); therefore, so too is the likelihood of anticipatory activity. Interestingly, this same logic leads Shaw (1997) to conclude that in organizations today, more than ever before, there is a need for trust. Shaw explains that trust is needed to operate the new organizational structures (e.g., self-managing individuals and teams, nearly totally autonomous business units, mergers and acquisitions, global alliances among firms) that have resulted from new business challenges, such as the increased pressure to reduce costs, meet or exceed customer expectations, and develop employees' capabilities and sense of ownership—all a result of an increasingly competitive global market. Given the tendency for sense making (predictive or anticipatory) activity to increase under circumstances of uncertainty (Dutton & Duncan, 1987) and the conceptual similarity between anticipatory and trust (probability) judgments, it is not surprising that we and Shaw (1997) reach the same conclusion: anticipatory justice judgments, a special case of trust-related judgments, "will become increasingly important as organizations struggle to adapt to today's turbulent business environment" (Shaw, p. 5).

But what, precisely, will be the behavioral focus of organizational members' anticipatory judgments? The quotes presented earlier suggest that much of organizational members' anticipations will regard the likely *un*fairness of future organizational outcomes (e.g., task-, reward-, or credit-related allocations as illustrated by Quotes #1 and #2), procedures (e.g., criteria for appraising performance, as illustrated by Quotes #3 and #4), and interpersonal (e.g., respect-related) exchanges, as illustrated by Quotes #5 and #6). Organizational members' justice-related anticipations are likely to focus on organizational authorities, too, as is illustrated by

Quotes #7 and #8, because—despite the increased use of *self*-management, or leaderless teams (Kirkman et al., 1996; Manz & Sims, 1993; Novelli, Kirkman, & Shapiro, 1995; Wellins et al., 1990)—authorities are still primarily the ones to take action (in the form of decisions, procedures, and/or exchanges) relating to individuals' hiring, overall compensation (including the possibility of temporary pay cuts), discipline, and (temporary or permanent) termination (Greenberg, 1990b).

The prevalence with which organizational members evaluate distributive, procedural, and interactional justice has already been noted (Greenberg, 1990a). The importance of these types of justice, along with evidence that potentially *losing* one or more of these forms of justice is anticipated by employees during times of change (Kirkman et al., 1996; Novelli et al., 1995) and the frequency of organizational change required to remain competitive today (Shaw, 1997; Bennis & Mische, 1995) leads us to suspect that *anticipatory* (distributive, procedural, and interactional) injustice may be prevalent in organizations. Next we discuss the consequences of anticipatory injustice.

Consequences of Anticipatory Injustice

Anticipating injustice means expecting unfairness, and therefore more specifically, expecting unfair outcomes or decisions (distributive injustice), unfair decision-making procedures (procedural injustice), and/or unfair interpersonal treatment (interactional injustice). The negative consequences of injustice anticipations are likely to be many.

GREATER LIKELIHOOD OF PERCEIVING INJUSTICE The confirmatory bias phenomenon (Snyder & Swann, 1978a) discussed previously, whereby people's perceptions generally match their expectations, suggests that one consequence of anticipatory injustice in the workplace is that those who *anticipate* injustice are more likely than those who don't to *see* injustice. Indirect support for this comes from Kramer's (1995) review of distrust- and paranoia-related consequences:

> [P]aranoid cognitions help individuals maintain their motivation to overcome perceived dangers and obstacles, even in situations where those dangers and obstacles, from the perspective of a more neutral observer, seem grossly exaggerated. In fact, precisely *because* they are so willing to expend considerable cognitive resources, including a willingness to maintain vigilance and to ruminate at length about others' intentions, motives, and plans, such individuals might actually be more

likely to detect patterns of threat that others fail to see. (p. 148, emphasis in original)

Similarly, Sanchez and Brock's (1996) finding suggests that minorities who expect workplace discrimination, based perhaps on having a history of this (or other negative work experiences), are more likely to detect discrimination than minorities who do not have this expectation. They found that, among Hispanic employees, more discrimination was generally perceived by those who grew up outside rather than in the United States, those who had relatively low salary and job rank, and those who had relatively little interaction with ethnic peers. Apparently, then, more discrimination was seen by those whose work experience had been generally more negative than positive.

Our speculation is consistent with others' finding that people's perceptions generally match their schemata, which is based on their prior experience (Markus & Zajonc, 1985). Additionally, it is consistent with Davidson and Friedman's (1998) finding of what they call a "persistent injustice effect," that is, a tendency for people who have experienced injustice to continually see it—*despite* receiving explanations, or "social accounts" (Bies, 1987) that in previous research have generally mitigated perceptions of injustice (Bies & Shapiro, 1987; Bies, Shapiro, & Cummings, 1988; Brockner et al., 1990; Shapiro, 1991; see reviews by Greenberg, 1990c, Davidson & Friedman, 1998, and Tyler & Bies, 1990).

More specifically, Davidson and Friedman (1998), in four sets of studies, gave study participants, all of whom were asked to assume the role of arbitrator, a case describing a manager who appeared to take credit for a subordinate's idea (i.e., a process innovation) and get a bonus as a result. They then obtained participants' perceptions of this incident's degree of justice and subsequently provided participants two brief reports containing other managers' observations of this incident. Only half of the participants received a third report that provided a social account, or excuse, for the manager's action—namely, that the manager had been advised that if the idea was to get any serious consideration, it must be presented as the manager's own. After receiving the supplemental materials, all participants were asked to report their perceptions of the incident's justice again. The race of the manager and the victim was varied in the experimental materials as well. In all but one of their studies,[1] the persistent injustice effect was found. That is, relative to white respondents, black respondents generally changed their initial perceptions of injustice less after receiving the social account. This was especially the case when the victim of injustice (i.e., the subordinate) was black, when there was higher racial identification with the victim, and when respondents reported higher levels of personal experience with injustice. Consistent with our interpretation of Sanchez and Brock's (1996) findings (discussed previously), Davidson and Friedman also found that, relative to white respondents, black respondents generally reported higher levels of past injustice, higher levels of expected future injustice, and greater mistrust of others.

Davidson and Friedman note that the pattern of their findings is consistent with (1) social psychologists' finding that prior experience, including previously formed attitudes, influence what information people will attend to and process and, as a result, the extent to which people's attitudes and perceptions will change (see Fiske & Taylor, 1991, for a review); and (2) the theorizing and observations of sociologists.

Jauss (1982), for example, argues that interpretation of literary works is affected by the reader's literary history, which creates a *"horizon of expectations" that shapes what the reader sees.* Griswold (1987) has documented this pattern, showing that when the same novels are described by book reviewers in the United States, Britain, and the West Indies, each sees concerns that are dominant within their own societies: American reviewers focus heavily on racial themes in these novels, whereas they are barely mentioned by British or West Indian reviewers (Davidson & Friedman, 1998, pp. 4–5, emphasis ours). Davidson and Friedman explain that the "horizon of expectations" with respect to justice held by minority group members (e.g., African Americans in the United States) versus majority group members (e.g., American white males) is likely to be different as a result of African Americans' more frequent experience with past injustice and consequently more expectations about future injustices. This different set of expectations may explain why, despite a justice-enhancing intervention, perceptions of injustice persisted among the black managers but not the white managers in Davidson and Friedman's sample.

This may explain, too, the field survey-based findings of Smolinski and Shapiro (2000), in which minorities (African Americans and white females), relative to majority members in the United States (white males), generally perceived more injustice in the workplace. Interestingly, these results were obtained despite the fact that, relative to white males, minorities reported feeling more benefited by their organization's affirmative action policy. Smolinski and Shapiro speculate that their pattern of findings may be due to the persistent injustice effect.

GREATER LIKELIHOOD OF PERCEIVING MULTIPLE TYPES OF INJUSTICE   Our discussion thus far has led us to conclude that perceiving injustice may be one consequence of anticipating injustice. Consistent with this are the findings of Lind, Kanfer and Earley (1990), who told half of their study participants that their views regarding a task goal *would* be, and the other half that their views would *not* be, "taken into account." The latter group perceived more procedural injustice. It seems likely that those who were, in essence, told that they *might* influence the experimenter's task-goal assignment anticipated a fairer outcome (i.e., task assignment). Thus, a possible explanation for Lind et al.'s finding may be that *anticipations* regarding one type of injustice (e.g., the allocation of unfair tasks or other examples of distributive injustice) affected perceptions of another (e.g., procedural injustice).

GREATER LIKELIHOOD OF SELF-DEFEATING ORGANIZATIONAL BEHAVIOR

Expecting (anticipating) injustice is a negative expectation and thus very similar to fear. More accurately, anticipatory injustice fits Shaw's (1997) description of *"unhealthy fear"* because this is:

> more often than not an unwarranted dread of change, growth, and the uncertainty of the future. It's an emotion that can cause uncertain individuals and organizations to react frantically in an attempt to establish control in the midst of perceived chaos. It triggers a response intended to freeze the organization at the present point in its development. (p. 18)

Shaw identifies unhealthy fear as the single root cause behind most self-defeating patterns of organizational behavior, including productivity loss, poor health, and employee turnover. Consistent with this, employees' resistance to change (and the productivity losses associated with this) has generally been found to be greater when employees fear that a change will result in undesired outcomes (Kotter & Schlesinger, 1979; Zaltman & Duncan, 1977). In a study that included almost 500 blue-collar manufacturing employees and white-collar service workers who had recently been assigned to self-managing work teams (SMWTs), Shapiro and Kirkman (1999) found that there was significantly greater resistance, fewer organizational citizenship behaviors (OCBs), less organizational commitment, and greater turnover intentions associated with high (rather than low) levels of anticipatory distributive injustice (i.e., concerns about losing valued work outcomes) as a result of the SMWT-related change.

Similarly, Shapiro, Lewicki, and Devine (1995) found, in a survey of 98 managers, that negative work behaviors (i.e., a willingness to use deceptive tactics) were significantly associated with managers' concerns about a proposed change in their organizations (that respondents described as one they personally opposed). More specifically, the greater managers' concerns were about the proposed change in their organization, the more willing they were to engage in deception (e.g., tell an authority that a majority of employees oppose the change when this is not true).

Related to the latter finding, organizational members who fear interactional injustice specifically (i.e., being treated insensitively or with little respect) have been found to be less likely to voice whatever true concerns or grievances (e.g., about change or other issues) they have (Ashford, Rothbard, Piderit, & Dutton, 1995; Saunders, 1987; Saunders, Sheppard, Knight, & Roth, 1992). For example, Saunders (1987) found that the reason individuals most often gave for why they would not voice their grievance was that "their manager does not listen." In a later study, Saunders et al. (1992) conducted an exploratory factor analysis and found that "supervisor approachability," which was significantly positively associated with employee voice, included this item: "I don't know how my boss will behave when I take a concern to him or her."

When employees fear confrontation with others in the workplace (who have previously harassed them), manifestations of this fear typically include psychological symptoms (e.g., nervousness, depression, humiliation, and embarrassment) and physical symptoms (e.g., headaches, nausea, chronic fatigue, and more frequent illnesses) in addition to work-related symptoms (discussed more elaborately in the next section because these affect the organization also), such as reduced productivity (Burstein, 1986), more negative feelings toward co-workers and supervisors (Gruber & Bjorn, 1982), and higher turnover (Loy & Stewart, 1984; see also Crull, 1982, and Sandroff, 1992, for reviews).

Thus, in summary, the self-defeating patterns of organizational behavior that Shaw identifies as consequences of unhealthy fear in the workplace have been seen when employees anticipate distributive injustice (e.g., likely undesirable outcomes of proposed organizational changes) and interactional injustice (e.g., harassment by previous harassers). Earlier we theorized that the anticipation of injustice is likely to raise the probability of perceiving injustice. The negative attitudes (e.g., reduced support for organizational leaders) and behaviors (e.g., reduced cooperation and extra-role behaviors, or OCBs, and increased stealing) that previous researchers have found to accompany injustice perceptions (see Greenberg, 1990a, for a review) are thus likely to be found in organizations whose members have high, rather than low, levels of anticipatory injustice. This logic returns us to our initial premise: Anticipatory injustice is likely to lead to self-defeating organizational attitudes and behavior—a premise thus far empirically supported with regard to anticipated distributive injustice (Shapiro & Kirkman, 1999).

GREATER LIKELIHOOD OF SELF-DEFEATING ORGANIZATIONS Hardy and Schwartz (1996) highlight that what makes an organization self-defeating is not just the presence of negative attitudes and behaviors (noted earlier) but the aggregate impact they have on the organization's core beliefs. They explain:

> The ongoing practice of self-defeating organizational behavior patterns leads ineluctably to the formation of what we call a *self-defeating organizational character*. As core beliefs are eroded, the organization's principles are superseded by a set of counter-beliefs: cynical, negative, or deluded visions of what the organization is, what it stands for, and *what its future holds*. (pp. 41–42, emphasis ours)

Kanter and Mirvis (1989) have similarly argued that an organization as a whole becomes an uncivil entity when a majority of its employees believe the organization *intends to harm or discount them*. A common message among these theorists thus is this: Fearing or anticipating negative events in organizations has not only individual-level, but also organization-level, effects. The organization-level effects occur because the cumulative effect of the negative anticipations (or fears) held by individuals ultimately changes the organization's culture, hence perceived values.

Numerous studies demonstrate how negative work attitudes, manifested by counterproductive individual behavior, ultimately become systemic (or aggregate) organizational characteristics. For example, Shapiro et al.'s (1995) finding that managers opposing an organizational change reported a greater willingness to use deceptive tactics to try to stop it was especially likely when the managers also reported that they expected the use of deception by others in their organization to be likely (and thus a normative act). More directly, several researchers have observed that the extent to which individuals are absent at work is significantly influenced by the extent to which they see others absent at work and they see this absence to be apparently tolerated or justifiable and thus a group norm (Harrison & Schaffer, 1994; Johns, 1994; Markham & McKee, 1995; Mathieu & Kohler, 1990). Additionally, Blau (1995, p. 1491) found that the frequency of employees' lateness to work was explained significantly more by the average frequency of prior lateness behavior on the part of— *not* oneself but—one's departmental members. Apparently, then, one's own lateness behavior ultimately creates more of this behavior from others who witness it, and once lateness appears to be an organization-wide norm, more of this behavior occurs on the part of many others. Thus, an "absence culture" ensues (Nicholson & Johns, 1985).

Similarly, in the negotiation literature, several researchers have observed that conflict-escalating communications (e.g., threats) generally get reciprocated, creating a "conflict spiral" (Schelling, 1960) or repeated feuding (Brett, Shapiro, & Lytle, 1998). Axelrod (1984) explains:

> For example, in Albania and the Middle East, a feud between families sometimes goes on for decades as one injury is repaid by another, and each retaliation is the start of the next cycle. The injuries can echo back and forth *until the original violation is lost in the distant past.* (p. 138, emphasis ours)

We have emphasized that the original violation gets lost once the cyclical nature of conflict spirals begins because this notion is similar to Hardy and Schwartz's (1996) observation that an organization's original core values get lost once unhealthy fear (and its associated behaviors, such as work absence and tardiness) in the workplace has caught and spread.

Thus far, the discussion has been focusing on the consequences (e.g., negative interpersonal reactions) of anticipated poor outcomes. Negative interpersonal behaviors may similarly accompany employees' anticipation of being treated disrespectfully or insensitively—that is, in an interpersonally (interactionally) unfair manner (Bies & Moag, 1986). An illustration of negative interpersonal behavior resulting from anticipated interactional injustice comes from Sitkin and Stickel's (1996) observation of professional workers' reaction to these researchers' monitoring their work for the purpose of obtaining precise measurement and standardizing task routines (as part of a total quality management [TQM] program). One worker explained to them that the fears aroused by the researchers' presence regarded the "*prospect* that what was nonroutine could become routine [if it were analyzed] . . . and then . . . [the professionals] wouldn't be so special anymore" (p. 209, emphasis ours). These fears about being less appreciated translated into unfriendly behaviors. Sitkin and Stickel (1996) note:

> [W]hen nearly all interviewees were told that the topic of the interview concerned the TQM program, they were usually visibly put off and suspicious. Their bodies sometimes physically drew back, their tone of voice changed, answers became more terse and were more carefully worded, and even their smiles disappeared. (p. 208)

Earlier we noted that another potential consequence of anticipating interactional injustice is that organizational members may be less likely to voice whatever concerns or grievances they may have. If anticipating interactional injustice stifles employees' willingness to express work-related concerns, and among these may be the extent to which proposed change matches the organization's core beliefs or competencies, then an absence of conversation relating to "healthy fear" (Shaw, 1997) will be yet another consequence. Shaw describes healthy fear as a procedural and cognitive assessment of how well current, or currently considered, measures or policies match the organization's system of core beliefs. If, collectively, organizations' members fear openly questioning these issues, then aggregate consequences similar to "groupthink" (Janis, 1972) and thus low levels of innovation are possible.

Finally, because perceptions of procedural injustice regard judgments about the fairness of the organizational *system,* anticipations about the system's unfairness (anticipatory procedural injustice) may be more likely than other forms of anticipatory injustice to influence organizational members to take system-level actions. Consistent with this, Tyler (1986) has observed that "procedural justice concerns continue to influence political actions (i.e., organizational actions), but they have less influence upon personal behavior, such as quitting one's job" (p. 11). As an example, Bies and Tyler (1993) found that employees were more likely to sue their organizations when they felt the procedures used to make an organizational decision were unfair rather than fair. Thus, when employees anticipate procedural injustice, as opposed to other types of injustice, more system-level actions (possibly in the form of class action lawsuits) to address potential injustice may take form.

Summary of Anticipatory Injustice Consequences for Organizations

We have theorized that the consequences for organizations when their members anticipate injustice are these: (1) an increased likelihood of organizational members perceiving injustice; (2) an increased likelihood of multiple types of perceived injustice; (3) an increased frequency of counterproductive, or self-defeating, behaviors among its members, such as increased tardiness, absenteeism, and resistance to change; and (4) an aggregate impact of these self-defeating behaviors that erodes the organization's initial core beliefs and thereby creates a new culture (e.g., an absence-culture), or what Shaw (1997) calls a self-defeating organizational character. Because people's expectations result, at least in part, from their prior experiences (Fiske & Taylor, 1991), anticipatory injustice is likely to be influenced by previous injustice; indeed, the findings of Davidson and Friedman (1998) support this.

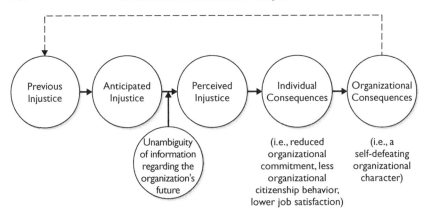

Figure 5.1. A Model of Anticipatory Justice.

The model in Figure 5.1 illustrates these relationships. Additionally, Figure 5.1 shows a causal link between the organizational consequences of anticipatory injustice and previous (experienced) injustice. This is because we believe members of self-defeating organizations—which are characterized by negative attitudes and behaviors *by a majority*—are likely to experience injustice. An important moderator shown in Figure 5.1 is the clarity of information pertaining to the organization's future. Extrapolating from the findings of Elaad et al. (1994), we theorize that perceptions of injustice will *not* match injustice-related anticipations (or expectations) if there is unambiguous, objective evidence that contradicts these. Next we discuss the theoretical and practical implications of our model.

Implications of Recognizing Anticipatory Injustice

Recognizing anticipatory justice has both theoretical and practical implications. We now discuss both.

Theoretical Implications

By introducing the term *anticipatory justice,* our model highlights something that previous justice theory has not: The potentially deleterious effects of organizational injustice may not occur only when injustice has occurred. Rather, negative work-related attitudes and behaviors are likely when employees anticipate that injustice may occur. Consequently, justice theories and management practices should be sensitive to conditions that are likely to give rise not only to the perception of injustice, but also to worries about the possibility of injustice.

We have highlighted the likelihood of anticipatory injustice occurring in situations of uncertainty, hence organizational change, when sense making is acute (Dutton & Duncan, 1987). Consequently, during organizational transitions, examining *anticipations* of (in)justice, in addition to perceptions of (in)justice as advised by Cobb, Wooten, & Folger (1995) and Novelli et al. (1995) are both likely to be important. The question of how to create perceptions of justice have long been the focus of justice researchers. The likely (individual and organization-wide) consequences of anticipatory injustice that we have identified—which are identical, in most cases, to the consequences of encountered injustice (Greenberg, 1990a)—suggest that it is equally, and perhaps more, important to understand how to create *anticipations* of justice in the workplace because the latter are likely to influence the justice organizational members actually see. Recognizing that anticipatory injustice reactions are similar to encountered injustice reactions points to the importance of managers and researchers assessing employee's concerns about injustice and hopes for justice (potential justice)—a measure that is woefully lacking from the justice literature (as argued by Shapiro [1993]). The latter point is essential in light of the *future*-oriented assessments of anticipatory injustice.

The importance of measuring people's hopes for justice has already been argued by Shapiro (1993), who introduced the importance of adding "*potential* decision control" to the model of procedural justice. More specifically, Shapiro noted that if researchers measured voicers' perceptions of *potential* influence over others' decisions, as opposed to actual decision control as most studies comprising the procedural justice literature have done (Lind & Tyler, 1988), a clearer answer may be found to the long-debated question of why having opportunities to voice typically enhances perceptions of procedural justice (i.e., is this due to value-expressive or instrumental motives?). The dynamics of anticipatory injustice, which we have articulated here, reinforce the importance of measuring the extent to which those perceiving injustice anticipated its potential, as well as the potential of their voiced concerns or discontent being considered or actually satisfied.

Numerous findings by justice researchers can be explained by the parsimonious relationships proposed by our model of anticipatory injustice. For example, findings regarding the mitigating effect of explanations when their substance is specific rather than vague (Shapiro, Buttner, & Barry, 1994), our model suggests, may be a result of such explanations providing the unambiguous evidence needed to curb the confirmatory bias of expectations. The inability of social accounts, or explanations, to significantly curb the perceived injustice of black (rather than white) managers (Davidson & Friedman, 1998) suggests that the degree of information's clarity or objectivity may need to be especially high for people expecting to perceive injustice.

As another example, our model explains justice researchers' consistent finding that people generally perceive less procedural injustice after they have, rather than have not, received (adequate) explanations for outcomes that are severely rather than trivially unfair—a phenomenon that Brockner and Siegel (1996) call the procedural justice-distributive justice interaction effect. Our model's explanation is this: The quality (e.g., clarity) of information people receive is generally of no interest (hence of no impact) to recipients who lack a need for it; conversely, when information is needed, its quality *is* of interest and thus creates an impact (Janis & Mann, 1977). People who have experienced a mildly unfair outcome probably need an explanation less than do people who have experienced unfair outcomes of great (or at least greater) severity.

Our model explains, too—with two different causal paths—why justice researchers have recently observed a positive relationship between procedural justice and trust. First, because anticipatory injustice is synonymous with expected injustice, and trust is an expectation (Brockner & Siegall, 1996), and expectations often lead to confirmatory perceptions (Snyder & Swann, 1978a), procedural justice may be a result of trust—that is, the expectation of procedurally just behavior. Consistent with this, employees who are more trusting of their supervisors tend to respond more favorably to the performance appraisal process (Fulk, Brief, & Barr, 1985; Nathan, Mohrman, & Milliman, 1991). Second, because expectations result from prior experience (Fiske & Taylor, 1991), the expectation of procedurally just behavior (or trust) in authorities may be a result of previous justice. The latter causal order has been suggested by Brockner and Siegel (1996) and observed by Davidson and Friedman (1998). Our model illustrates why both of these causal orderings of procedural justice and trust are likely to be accurate and the dynamics that heighten the likelihood of either one.

Additionally, our model offers an explanation for the "voice effect" (Folger, 1977) and its universality (Lind & Tyler, 1988)—that is, why people in many different cultures generally perceive more procedural justice when they have had, rather than lacked, an opportunity to express their views regarding *impending* decisions, such as court judges' decisions regarding traffic-related fines (Tyler, 1987), arbitrators' decisions regarding dispute resolution (Shapiro & Brett, 1993), and managers' decisions regarding performance appraisals (Greenberg & Folger, 1983). We highlight the word *impending* to point out that the voice opportunities typically studied by justice researchers regard future (not past) decisions. Because our model suggests that perceived justice results directly from an expectation (hence futuristic judgment) of this, another explanation for the voice effect is this: Giving or not giving people the chance to voice their views influences their expectation about receiving justice (hence potential justice), and this expectation determines how much justice they indeed see. Thus, the "voice effect" may really be an "expectation (confirmatory bias) effect," whose generalizability across a variety of contexts was noted earlier.

Any cultural differences that are found regarding voice effects may thus be due to differences in cultural expectations about the likely consequences of expressing oneself. Consistent with this, Welsh, Luthans, and Sommer (1993) attributed their finding to a decrease, rather than an increase, in Russian employees' performance following a participative management (employee voice-enhancing) initiative to be the result of a long history of management ignoring employee ideas. Apparently, the Russian employees did not expect their voiced opinions to management to have any effect. Welsh et al. speculate that this expectation—not necessarily the "voice initiative" (i.e., participative management) or the cultural differences—accounts for the performance decreases they observed. (See James, 1993, for an elaboration of justice issues across culture). Other voice effects reported in the justice literature may similarly be the result of the expectations held by those who have or have not been given the chance to voice.

Because our model highlights that individual consequences of perceived injustice are likely to ultimately have an aggregate impact on the organization's culture or character, our model also points to the importance of justice researchers measuring in subsequent studies organization-level (in addition to individual-level) perceptions. Doing so may assist us in answering questions such as how to create perceptions of justice in generally cynical organizations today (Kanter & Mirvis, 1989).

Practical Implications

Our model has several important practical implications, too. One obvious implication of our theory for managers is that it is important to manage not only employees' perceptions of injustice in the workplace (Cropanzano, 1993) but also their *anticipations* of injustice. Indeed, managing concerns about *potential injustice* may be more important if, as we have theorized, anticipated injustice heightens the probability that injustice will be perceived. Importantly, the link between anticipated and perceived injustice is not merely our theory; it has been observed directly by Davidson and Friedman (1998) and we think indirectly by Sanchez and Brock (1996).

It is also important to remember that the positive relationship between expected and perceived phenomena, and thus anticipated and perceived injustice, is less likely to occur *when there is unambiguous information to counter the injustice perception* (Elaad et al., 1994; Siegall, 1992). As noted earlier, this may explain why Shapiro et al. (1994) found that the specificity of information provided in social accounts, more so than the explainer's perceived sincerity, mitigated perceptions of injustice.

Taken together, our model (shown in Figure 5.1) leads us to advise managers or anyone needing to manage injustice to take two actions:

1. Assess organizational members' expectations regarding (distributive, procedural, and interactional) injustice, especially during organizational transitions when uncertainty, hence sensemaking needs and a desire for prediction, will be high; and

2. Make unambiguous information available to organizational members that relates to whatever assurances they receive regarding the organization's future.

ASSESSING PEOPLE'S (INJUSTICE-RELATED) ANTICIPATIONS With regard to the first action recommendation, one means of assessing employees' hopes and concerns about their future is to listen to the "wants" and concerns they express. Although this advice may seem self-evident, managers often fail to hear what their employees tell them. Or, perhaps more accurately, managers fail to recognize the message opportunities available to them. One of these message opportunities is rumors, which are the collective product of organizational members' musings and whose substance often reflects people's concerns (Rosnow, 1980; Shibutani, 1966).

Listening to rumors, or whatever other source of employees' concerns there may be, is not enough, however. Actively listening is key (Rogers, 1977). This means that managers ought to acknowledge the concerns or fears that employees express as valid because doing so will increase employees' willingness to listen to what managers subsequently say. The injustice-mitigating effect of explanations (see reviews by Bies, 1987; Greenberg, 1993, 1990c) may then be delivered. The utility of acknowledging employees' directly (or indirectly) expressed concerns is illustrated by the observations Sitkin and Stickel (1996) made of the professional workers they interviewed. Recall that these professionals' behavior became characteristic of incivility (e.g., smiles disappeared) when the researchers identified the topic of their interview to be the TQM program, as a result of the anticipatory injustice associated with this. Sitkin and Stickel go on to explain:

> Only after they were told that the project was aimed at "understanding both the value *and the limitations* of TQP" [intentionally stressing the italicized words] did their smiles return, their bodies relax and move closer, and their tone and language become less stilted and controlled. These observed shifts took place even in several instances where the individual being interviewed was a familiar colleague to the interviewer. Further, the shifts were sudden and very striking and they took place in less than a minute of elapsed time in otherwise routine and cordial interviews. (p. 208)

Apparently, Sitkin and Stickel's acknowledgement of the workers' concerns—that the TQM program may have limitations—enabled Sitkin and Stickel to ease tensions and, presumably thereby, obtain needed information from the interviewees. Similarly, managers who listen to and acknowledge employees' *anticipations* regarding (distributive, procedural, and interactional) injustice may ease employees' openness to proposed or newly implemented organizational change. Novelli et al. (1995) similarly argue that being sensitive to employees' perceptions of (in)justice during organizational transitions is key in facilitating support for change. Note here, however, that we are arguing that managers' effectiveness as change agents may be increased if they pay attention to the *potential,* hence anticipatory, injustice likely to preoccupy their employees.

One of the advantages of engaging in active listening that we noted earlier was that recipients of this may then be more open to hearing what the active listeners subsequently say. Although explanations and other types of social accounts can be effective in changing initial perceptions of injustice (Bies, 1987; Greenberg, 1993, 1990c), it is important to remember Davidson and Friedman's (1998) finding that injustice perceptions nevertheless sometimes persist. Friedman and Robinson (1993) found the persistent injustice effect, too. More specifically, injustice perceptions held by union representatives (rather than management representatives) in the Friedman and Robinson study, and injustice perceptions held by blacks (rather than whites) in the Davidson and Friedman (1998) study did not significantly lessen after they received explanations that in previous studies (e.g., Bies, Shapiro, & Cummings, 1988) had injustice-mitigating effects. Davidson and Friedman (1998) theorize that the persistence of perceived injustice seems to characterize members of relatively powerless groups. Thus, the utility of providing explanations even after first active listening may depend on recipients' feelings of powerlessness.

MAKING UNAMBIGUOUS (FUTURE-RELATED) INFORMATION AVAILABLE TO PEOPLE Other characteristics that influence the likelihood of explanations' adequacy, hence effectiveness in mitigating perceived injustice, have been noted as well (Greenberg, 1993; Shapiro, 1991; Shapiro et al., 1994). Among these is the specificity of an explanation's substance, and this returns us to the second action-recommendation we offered managers earlier: make *unambiguous* information available to organizational members that relates to whatever assurances they receive regarding the organization's future. This recommendation results from Elaad et al.'s (1994) finding that polygraph examiners expecting their lie-detection test takers to be guilty generally found evidence of guilt in the test results except when the evidence included unambiguous, physiological data that clearly contradicted their expectation. Findings supporting a "persistent injustice effect" (Davidson & Friedman, 1998; Friedman & Robinson, 1993) suggest that when recipients of bad-news givers' explanations *expect* injustice (and thus, possibly, manipulative [e.g., excuse-making] behavior), it is especially important to provide highly specific, hence unambiguous, data to support the explanation. The same conclusion holds, therefore, when *managers* are dealing with anticipatory injustice. Perhaps if managers view their employees as shareholders in the organization and therefore as people whose commitment (and investment) they need to gain for the long term, managers will be more likely to provide the specific data-based forecast regarding the organization's future that they generally provide shareholders and prospective shareholders.

The futuristic nature of our prescriptions thus far differentiates this work from previous justice-related prescriptions whose focus has been on how to effectively explain why past or current decisions have been made (Bies, 1987; Greenberg, 1990c, 1993). In addition to curbing perceptions of injustice, the futuristic nature of our prescriptions may assist, too, in curbing cynical or other self-defeating beliefs in organizations that, in the interest of remaining competitive, *must* be future-oriented (Hardy & Schwartz, 1996; Kanter & Mirvis, 1989).

Having noted the future orientation of our recommended actions up to this point, it is important to remind the reader that our model of anticipatory injustice also recognizes the importance of organizational members' past and current experience of injustice (for which there is a well-developed literature of strategies; Greenberg, 1993). Additionally, our model recognizes the likelihood that injustice experiences will be more frequent in an organization that has become self-defeating in character. This suggests that managers who are aware of anticipatory injustice in their organizations ought to remember that the likely consequence of ignoring it (e.g., allowing rumors to go unrefuted) is an increased probability of organization-wide anticipatory injustice and its associated negative behaviors.

Conclusion

In this chapter we have advanced the notion of "anticipatory injustice" because we believe this is a justice dynamic that is part of organizations experiencing change, and organizations experiencing change today are all of those who are either competitive or trying to be. Our model of anticipatory injustice explains numerous effects previously reported by justice researchers and thus may offer a more parsimonious set of variables to examine in future research. At a minimum, our model of anticipatory injustice points to the importance of measuring the *potential* injustice respondents foresee in the workplace. Doing so, we argued earlier, may help resolve the still-debated question of why voice generally universally enhances perceived justice (Shapiro, 1993).

Additionally, the model of anticipatory injustice suggests that the relationship between trust and procedural justice proposed recently by justice theorists (e.g., Brockner & Siegall, 1996) may be reversed, thus giving impetus to studying this dynamic from a new perspective. The increasing importance of trust in organizations today (Shaw, 1997; see the special issue on trust in *Academy of Management Review,* 1998) suggests that its study, thus new perspectives on it, can benefit managers as well as management scholars. We caution researchers and managers interested in anticipatory injustice dynamics to remember, however, the human tendency, and thus theirs, too, to see what we expect to see (see Alderfer & Smith, 1982, for a similar caution). If we are not careful to design studies and measures that allow us to capture objective, unambiguous evidence of injustice—which the bulk of perception-based justice studies lack—then in our attempt to seek new understanding, we too will find merely what we expect to find.

NOTE

1. The exception was when Davidson and Friedman's case materials described the manager as white and the subordinate as black, which apparently created

such initially high perceptions of injustice among the black respondents that no significant change after they received the supplemental material (containing the social account) was possible.

REFERENCES

Abramson, L. Y., Seligman, M. E. P., & Teasdale, J. P. (1978). Learned helplessness in humans: Critique and reformulation. *Journal of Abnormal Psychology, 87,* 49–74.

Alderfer, C. P., & Smith, K. K. (1982). Studying intergroup relations embedded in organizations. *Administrative Science Quarterly, 27,* 35–65.

Ashford, S. J., Rothbard, N. P., Piderit, S. K., & Dutton, J. E. (1995, August). *Out on a limb: The role of context and impression management in issue selling.* Paper presented at the national meeting of the Academy of Management, Vancouver, BC, Canada.

Axelrod, R. (1984). *The evolution of cooperation.* New York: Basic Books.

Balzer, W. K., & Sulsky, L. M. (1992). Halo and performance appraisal research: A critical examination. *Journal of Applied Psychology, 77,* 975–985.

Barry, B., & Shapiro, D. L. (1997). *Voice and procedural justice: Disentangling instrumental and non-instrumental explanations.* Unpublished manuscript, University of North Carolina.

Bennis, W., & Mische, M. (1995). *The 21st century organization: Reinventing through reengineering.* San Diego: Pfeiffer & Company.

Bies, R. J. (1987). The predicament of injustice: The management of moral outrage. In L. L. Cummings and B. M. Staw (Eds.), *Research in organizational behavior* (Vol. 9, pp. 289–319). Greenwich, CT: JAI Press.

Bies, R. J,. & Shapiro, D. L. (1987). Interactional fairness judgments: The influence of causal accounts. *Social Justice Research, 1,* 199–218.

Bies, R. J., Shapiro, D. L., & Cummings, L. L. (1988). Causal accounts and managing organizational conflict: Is it enough to say it's not my fault? *Communication Research, 15,* 381–399.

Bies, R. J., & Tyler, T. R. (1993). The "litigation mentality" in organizations: A test of alternative psychological explanations. *Organization Science, 4,* 352–366.

Blau, G. (1995). Influence of group lateness on individual lateness: A cross-level examination. *Academy of Management Journal, 38,* 1483–1496.

Brett, J. M., Shapiro, D. L., & Lytle, A. (1998). Breaking the bonds of reciprocity in negotiations. *Academy of Management Journal, 41,* 410–424.

Bretz, R. D., Jr., Milkovich, G. T., & Read, W. (1992). The current state of performance appraisal research and practice: Concerns, directions, and implications. *Journal of Management, 18,* 321–352.

Brockner, J., DeWitt, R. L., Grover, S., & Reed, T. (1990). When it is especially important to explain why: Factors affecting the relationship between managers' explanations of a layoff and survivors' reactions to the layoff. *Journal of Experimental Social Psychology, 26,* 389–407.

Brockner, J., Greenberg, J., Brockner, A., Bortz, J., Davy, J., & Carter, C. (1986). Layoffs, equity theory, and work performance: Further evidence of the impact of survivor guilt. *Academy of Management Journal, 29,* 373–384.

Brockner, J., & Siegel, P. (1996). Understanding the interaction between procedural and distributive justice: The role of trust. In R. M. Kramer & T. R. Tyler (Eds.), *Trust in organizations: Frontiers of theory and research* (pp. 390–413). Thousand Oaks, CA: Sage.

Burstein, B. (1986). Psychiatric injury in women's workplaces. *Bulletin of American Academy of Psychiatry Law, 14,* 245–251.

Cobb, A. T., Wooten, K. C., & Folger, R. (1995). Justice in the making: Toward understanding the theory and practice of justice in organizational change and development. *Research in Organizational Change and Development, 8,* 243–295.

Cropanzano, R. (Ed.) (1993). *Justice in the workplace: Approaching fairness in human resource management.* Hillsdale, NJ: Lawrence Erlbaum Associates.

Crull, P. (1982). Stress effects of sexual harassment on the job: Implications for counseling. *American Journal of Orthopsychiatry, 52,* 539–544.

Davidson, M., & Friedman, R. (1998). When excuses don't work: The persistent injustice effect among black managers. *Administrative Science Quarterly, 43,* 154–183.

Deutsch, M. (1958). Trust and suspicion. *Journal of Conflict Resolution, 2*(4), 265–279.

Dougherty, T. W., Turban, D. B., & Callender, J. C. (1994). Confirming first impressions in the employment interview: A field study of interviewer behavior. *Journal of Applied Psychology, 79,* 659–665.

Dutton, J. E., & Duncan, R. B. (1987). The creation of momentum for change through the process of strategic issue diagnosis. *Strategic Management Journal, 8,* 279–295.

Elaad, E., Ginton, A., & Ben-Shakhar, G. (1994). The effects of prior expectations and outcome knowledge on polygraph examiners' decisions. *Journal of Behavioral Decision Making, 7,* 279–292.

Festinger, L. (1954). A theory of social comparison processes. *Human Relations, 7,* 117–140.

Fiske, S., & Taylor, S. (1991). *Social cognition.* New York: McGraw-Hill.

Folger, R. (1977). Distributive and procedural justice: Combined impact of "voice" and improvement on experienced inequity. *Journal of Personality and Social Psychology, 35,* 108–119.

Friedman, R. A., & Robinson, R. (1993). Justice for all? Union versus management responses to unjust acts and social accounts. *International Journal of Conflict Management, 4,* 99–117.

Fulk, J., Brief, A. P., & Barr, S. H. (1985). Trust in supervisor and perceived fairness and accuracy of performance evaluations. *Journal of Business Research, 13,* 301–313.

Greenberg, J. (1990a). Organizational justice: Yesterday, today, and tomorrow. *Journal of Management, 16,* 399–432.

Greenberg, J. (1990b). Employee theft as a reaction to underpayment inequity: The hidden cost of paycuts. *Journal of Applied Psychology, 75,* 561–568.

Greenberg, J. (1990c). Looking fair vs. being fair: Managing impressions of organizational justice. In B. M. Staw & L. L. Cummings (Eds.), *Research in organizational behavior* (Vol. 12, pp. 111–157). Greenwich, CT, JAI Press.

Greenberg, J. (1993). The social side of fairness: Interpersonal and informational classes of organizational justice. In R. Cropanzano (Ed.), *Justice in the workplace: Approaching fairness in human resource management* (pp. 79–103). Hillsdale, NJ: Lawrence-Erlbaum Associates.

Griswold, W. (1987). The fabrication of meaning: Literary interpretation in the United States, Great Britain, and the West Indies. *American Journal of Sociology, 92,* 1077–1117.

Gruber, J. E., & Bjorn, L. (1982). Blue collar blues: The sexual harassment of women autoworkers. *Work and Occupations, 9,* 271–298.

Hardy, R. E., & Schwartz, R. (1996). *The self-defeating organization.* New York: Addison-Wesley Publishing Company.

Harrison, D., & Shaffer, M. (1994). Comparative examinations of self-reports and perceived absenteeism norms: Wading through Lake Wobegon. *Journal of Applied Psychology, 79,* 240–251.

Ilgen, D. R., & Feldman, J. M. (1983). Performance appraisal: A process focus. In L. L. Cummings & B. M. Staw (Eds.), *Research in organizational behavior* (Vol. 5, pp. 141–197). Greenwich, CT: JAI Press.

James, K. (1993). The social context of organizational justice: Cultural, intergroup, and structural effects on justice behaviors and perceptions. In R. Cropanzano (Ed.), *Justice in the workplace: Approaching fairness in human resource management.* Hillsdale, NJ: Lawrence Erlbaum Associates.

Janis, I. L. (1972). *Victims of groupthink.* Boston: Houghton-Mifflin.

Janis, I. L., & Mann, L. (1977). *Decision making: A psychological analysis of conflict, choice, and commitment.* New York: The Free Press.

Jauss, H. R. (1982). *Toward an aesthetic of reception.* Minneapolis University of Minnesota Press.

Johns, G. (1994). Absenteeism estimates by employees and managers: Divergent perspectives and self-serving perceptions. *Journal of Applied Psychology, 79,* 229–239.

Kanter, D. H., & Mirvis, P. H. (1989). *The cynical Americans.* San Francisco: Jossey-Bass.

Kirkman, B. L., Shapiro, D. L., Novelli, L., & Brett, J. M. (1996). Employee concerns regarding self-managing work teams: A multi-dimensional justice perspective. *Social Justice Research, 9,* 47–67.

Kotter, J. P. (1990, May–June). What leaders really do. *Harvard Business Review,* pp. 103–111.

Kotter, J. P., & Schlesinger, L. A. (1979, March–April). Choosing strategies for change. *Harvard Business Review,* pp. 106–114.

Kozlowski, S. W. J., & Kirsch, M. P. (1987). The systematic distortion hypothesis, halo, and accuracy: An individual-level analysis. *Journal of Applied Psychology, 72,* 252–261.

Kramer, R. M. (1995). Power, paranoia, and distrust in organizations: The distorted view from the top. In R. J. Bies, R. J. Lewicki, & B. H. Sheppard (Eds.), *Research on negotiation in organizations* (Vol. 5, pp. 199–154). Greenwich, CT: JAI Press.

Lind, E. A., Kanfer, R., and Earley, P. C. 1990. Voice, control, and procedural justice: Instrumental and non-instrumental concerns in fairness judgments. *Journal of Personality and Social Psychology, 59,* 952–959.

Lind, E. A., & Tyler, T. R. (1988). *The social psychology of procedural justice.* New York: Plenum.

Louis, M. R. (1980). Surprise and sensemaking: What newcomers experience in entering unfamiliar organizational settings. *Administrative Science Quarterly, 25,* 226–251.

Loy, P. H., & Stewart, L. P. (1984). The extent and effects of sexual harassment of working women. *Sociological Focus, 17,* 31–34.

Manz, C. C., & Sims, H. P., Jr. (1993). *Business without bosses: How self-managing teams are building high performance companies.* New York: Wiley.

Markham, S. E., & McKee, G. H. (1995). Group absence behavior and standards: A multi-level analysis. *Academy of Management Journal, 38*(4), 1174–1190.

Markus, H., & Zajonc, R. B. (1985). Cognitive perspectives in social psychology. In G. Lindzey & E. Aronson (Eds.), *Handbook of social psychology (3rd ed.)* (Vol. 1, pp. 137–230). New York: Random House.

Mathieu, J., & Kohler, S. (1990). A cross-level examination of group absence influences on individual absence. *Journal of Applied Psychology, 75,* 217–220.

Mayer, R. C., Davis, J. H., & Schoorman, F. D. (1995). An integrative model of organizational trust. *Academy of Management Review, 20,* 709–734.

Nathan, B., Mohrman, A. M., & Milliman, J. (1991). Interpersonal relations as a context for the effectiveness of appraisal interviews on performance and satisfaction: A longitudinal study. *Academy of Management Journal, 34,* 352–369.

Nicholson, N., & Johns, G. (1985). The absence culture and the psychological contract: Who's in control of absence? *Academy of Management Review, 10,* 397–407.

Novelli, L., Kirkman, B. L., & Shapiro, D. L. (1995). Effective implementation of organizational change: An organizational justice perspective. In C. L. Cooper & D. M. Rousseau (Eds.), *Trends in organizational behavior* (Vol.2, pp. 15–36). New York: John Wiley & Sons.

Petrini, C., & Hultman, K. E. (1995). Scaling the wall of resistance. *Training & Development, 49,* 15–18.

Robinson, S. L. (1996). Trust and breach of the psychological contract. *Administrative Science Quarterly, 1,* 574–599.

Rogers, C. (1977). *On personal power: Inner strength and its revolutionary impact.* New York: Dalacorte.

Rosnow, R. L. (1980). Psychology of rumor reconsidered. *Psychological Bulletin, 87,* 578–591.

Sanchez, J., & Brock, P. (1996). Outcomes of perceived discrimination among Hispanic employees: Is diversity management a luxury or a necessity? *Academy of Management Journal, 39,* 704–719.

Sandroff, R. (1992, June). Sexual harassment: The inside story. *Working Woman,* pp. 47–51.

Saunders, D. M. (1987, April). *Employee voice.* Paper presented at the annual meeting of the Institute of Management Science/Operations Research Society of America. New Orleans, LA.

Saunders, D. M., Sheppard, B. H., Knight, V., & Roth, J. D. (1992). Employee voice to supervisors. *Employee Rights and Responsibilities Journal, 5,* 241–259.

Schelling, T. (1960). *The strategy of conflict.* Cambridge, MA: Harvard University Press.

Shapiro, D. L. (1991). The effects of explanations on negative reactions to deceit. *Administrative Science Quarterly, 36,* 614–630.

Shapiro, D. L. (1993). Reconciling theoretical differences among procedural justice researchers by re-evaluating what it means to have one's views "considered." Implications for third-party managers. In R. Cropanzano (Ed.), *Justice in the workplace: Approaching fairness in human resource management* (pp. 51–78). Hillsdale, NJ: Lawrence-Erlbaum Associates.

Shapiro, D. L., & Brett, J. M. (1993). Comparing three processes underlying judgments of procedural justice: A field study of mediation and arbitration. *Journal of Personality and Social Psychology, 65,* 1167–1177.

Shapiro, D. L., Buttner, H. B., & Barry, B. (1994). Explanations: What factors enhance their perceived adequacy? *Organizational Behavior and Human Decision Processes, 58,* 346–368.

Shapiro, D. L., & Kirkman, B. L. (1999). Employees' reaction to the change to work teams: The influence of "anticipatory" injustice. *Journal of Organizational Change Management, 12,* 51–66.

Shapiro, D. L., Lewicki, R. J., & Devine, P. (1995). When do employees choose deceptive tactics to stop unwanted organizational change? A relational perspective. In R. J. Bies, R. J. Lewicki, & B. H. Sheppard (Eds.), *Research on negotiation in organizations* (Vol. 5, pp. 155–184). Greenwich, CT: JAI Press Inc.

Shaw, R. B. (1997). *Trust in the balance: Building successful organizations on results, integrity, and concern.* San Francisco: Jossey-Bass.

Shibutani, T. (1966). *Improvised news: A sociological study of rumor.* Indianapolis: Bobbs-Merrill.

Siegall, M. (1992). The effect of rater expectations on the evaluation of a hypothetical subordinate. *The Journal of Psychology, 126,* 453–463.

Sitkin, S. B., Rousseau, D. M., Burt, R. S., & Camerer, C. (Eds). (1998). Special issue on trust. *Academy of Management Review, 23.*

Sitkin, S. B. & Stickel, D. (1996). The road to hell: The dynamics of distrust in an era of quality. In R. M. Kramer & T. R. Tyler (Eds.), *Trust in organizations: Frontiers of theory and research* (pp. 196–215). Thousand Oaks, CA: Sage.

Smolinski, C., & Shapiro, D. L. (2000). *Perceived justice for all? Race and gender differences in perceptions of fairness and job satisfaction.* Working paper: University of North Carolina-Chapel Hill.

Snyder, M., & Swann, W. B., Jr. (1978a). Behavioral confirmation in social interaction: From social perception to social reality. *Journal of Experimental Social Psychology, 14,* 148–162.

Snyder, M., & Swann, W. B., Jr. (1978b). Hypothesis-testing processes in social interaction. *Journal of Personality and Social Psychology, 36,* 1202–1212.

Thomas, J., Clark, S., & Gioia, D. (1993). Strategic sensemaking and organizational performance: Linkages among scanning, interpretation, action, and outcomes. *Academy of Management Journal, 36,* 239–270.

Tyler, T. R., & Bies, R. J. (1990). Beyond formal procedures: The interpersonal context of procedural justice. In J. S. Carroll (Ed.), *Applied social psychology and organizational settings* (pp. 77–98). Hillsdale, NJ: Lawrence Erlbaum Associates.

Tyler, T. R., & Degoey, P. (1996). Trust in organizational authorities: The influence of motive attributions on willingness to accept decisions. In R. M. Kramer & T. R. Tyler (Eds.), *Trust in organizations: Frontiers of theory and research* (pp. 331–356). Thousand Oaks, CA: Sage.

Van Lange, P. A. M., Liebrand, W. B. G., Messick, D. M., & Wilke, H. A. M. (1992). Social dilemmas: The state of the art. In M. Liebrand, D. Messick, & H. Wilke (Eds.), *Social dilemmas: Theoretical issues and research findings* (pp. 3–28). New York: Pergamon Press.

Weick, K. E. (1995). *Sensemaking in organizations.* Thousand Oaks, CA: Sage.

Wellins, R. S., Wilson, R., Katz, A. J., Laughlin, P., Day, C. R., Jr., & Price, D. (1990). *Self-directed work teams: A study of current practice.* Pittsburgh: Development Dimensions International.

Welsh, D. H. B., Luthans, F., & Sommer, S. M. (1993). Managing Russian factory workers: The impact of U.S.-based behavioral and participative techniques. *Academy of Management Journal, 36,* 58–79.

Wong, R., & Weiner, B. (1981). When people ask "why" questions, and the heuristics of attributional search. *Journal of Personality and Social Psychology, 40,* 650–663.

Zaltman, G., & Duncan, R. (1977). *Strategies for planned change.* New York: Wiley.

6

When Do Elements of Procedural Fairness Make a Difference? A Classification of Moderating Influences

Joel Brockner,
Grant Ackerman,
and
Gregory Fairchild

THE STUDY OF FAIRNESS has been of great interest to philosophers (e.g., Rawls, 1971) and psychologists (e.g., Deutsch, 1985) alike. Recently, numerous scholars have examined the role of fairness in a variety of applied settings, such as legal systems and work organizations (e.g., Bies, 1987; Brockner, 1994; Folger, 1993; Greenberg, 1996; Lind & Tyler, 1988). Initially, theory and research focused on the causes and consequences of *outcome* fairness (e.g., Adams, 1965). In 1975 Thibaut and Walker expanded our understanding of justice by calling attention to *procedural* fairness: the legitimacy of the methods used to plan and implement resource allocation decisions. Thibaut and Walker originally conceived of procedural justice in terms of the degree of input people were allowed to have into the decision-making process; the greater the input,

We are greatly indebted to Russell Cropanzano, Jerry Greenberg, and Batia Wiesenfeld for their helpful comments on earlier versions of the chapter.

the more likely it was for people to perceive procedures as fair. Thibaut and Walker also distinguished between two types of input: (a) process control, in which people were allowed to provide evidence to a decision-making authority, and (b) decision control, in which people were allowed to have some say in the actual rendering of the decision.

Whereas the control dimensions identified by Thibaut and Walker (1975) are major determinants of procedural fairness, they are by no means the only ones. Leventhal, Karuza, and Fry (1980) identified many other factors that influence perceptions of fairness, including whether procedures are implemented consistently, on the basis of accurate information and with opportunities for correction, to name a few. An important commonality to the control dimensions recognized by Thibaut and Walker and the factors identified by Leventhal et al. is that they refer to *structural* aspects of the decision-making process.

Recent evidence suggests, however, that peoples' perceptions of procedural fairness also depend upon the *interpersonal conduct* of the parties responsible for planning and implementing decisions. Two features are central to the interpersonal aspect of procedural justice, also known as "interactional justice" (Bies, 1987): (a) whether those responsible for planning or implementing decisions provide social accounts of their actions (e.g., the extent to which they provide adequate explanations of the bases of their decisions to the affected parties), and (b) whether the implementers of decisions treat the affected parties with dignity and respect (Bies & Moag, 1986; Greenberg, 1993; Tyler & Bies, 1990). In sum, people's perceptions of procedural fairness are multiply determined. From this point forward we use the term "procedural elements" to refer to the various aspects of procedures that influence people's perceptions of procedural fairness.

Initially, research on procedural elements showed that they influenced a variety of dependent measures, even when perceptions of outcome fairness or outcome favorability were held constant (e.g., Lind & Tyler, 1988; Thibaut and Walker, 1975). Having shown the pervasive effects of procedural elements, researchers have more recently identified moderating influences on procedural elements; that is, they have analyzed the conditions under which procedural elements are differentially impactful. The primary purpose of the present chapter is to organize previous research that has examined moderating influences on procedural elements. In so doing, we hope not only to make sense of research that has come before but also to stimulate future research in organizational justice and related areas.

Theoretical as well as practical considerations motivate our quest to understand better the moderating influences on various procedural elements. At the theoretical level, by identifying *when* procedural elements have more or less of an impact, we may be better able to explain *why* procedural elements affect peoples' beliefs and behaviors.

At the practical level, the identification of moderating influences may help managers make more informed decisions about how to plan and implement decisions. In the best of worlds, managers should strive to be procedurally fair. This recommendation may be easier said than done, however. For one thing, perceptions of procedural fairness may be affected by multiple factors. As a result, managers may need to devote a considerable amount of time and energy to ensure that their procedures will be perceived as fair. Moreover, most managers operate under severe time constraints. Although they may wish to be procedurally fair, they simply may not have the time to be attentive to all procedural elements. For example, managers may find that giving process control or decision control to their subordinates is more time consuming than autocratic descision-making.

Moreover, it may be necessary for managers to expend a considerable amount of energy to achieve certain aspects of interactional justice, such as frequently explaining why decisions are made, being readily available to answer questions and address concerns, and generally reducing the psychological distance between themselves and those who are affected by difficult resource allocation decisions (Folger & Skarlicki, 1998). The present analysis recognizes managers' constraints and recommends that they need to consider the *relative* degree of importance of various procedural elements. In certain instances, it may be particularly important to provide process control or decision control. In other cases, it may be especially important to invoke the procedural element of correctability. By identifying moderating influences on procedural elements, we may help managers make more accurate judgments about when they need to devote more attention to certain procedural elements rather than others.

Moderating Influences on Procedural Elements: Some Organizing Dimensions

Before describing the specific dimensions that organize the ensuing discussion of moderating influences on procedural elements, we need to locate our analysis on the broader terrain of organizational justice. Greenberg's (1987a) taxonomy of organizational justice theories suggested that approaches to the study of organizational justice may be classified along two dimensions. One dimension refers to whether the theory is concerned with outcome fairness (content focus) or procedural fairness (process focus). The other dimension refers to whether the theory is concerned with individuals' reactions to perceived levels of fairness (reactive focus) or the process by which people create outcome or procedural fairness (proactive focus). Each of the four cells created by Greenberg's 2×2 taxonomy raise important, albeit different, questions about the antecedents, nature, and consequences of organizational justice.

Given our goal to delineate moderating influences on procedural elements, the analysis is located in Greenberg's (1987a) procedural/reactive cell, which focuses on people's reactions to procedural fairness. Studies exploring moderating influences on procedural elements have proliferated to such an extent that it may be useful to impose some conceptual order on them. We attempt to do so by calling attention to two (orthogonal) dimensions, along which moderating influences on procedural elements may be differentiated. One is a temporal dimension, that is, the time at which the moderating influence takes shape or is introduced. The other is a generality/specificity dimension, that is, the extent to which the moderator applies to multiple procedural elements rather than one.

We are not suggesting that these two dimensions are the only ones along which moderating influences on procedural elements may be sorted. However, the two dimensions help distinguish many recent efforts to study moderating influences on procedural elements. Moreover, a number of theories may account for the various moderating influences on procedural elements. An important purpose served by the current framework is to clarify each theory's domain of relevance, that is, the conditions under which the theory is best suited to account for certain moderating influences on procedural elements. The organizing dimensions are described next in greater detail.

Temporal Dimension

In some instances, the moderator variable takes shape *prior to* people's exposure to the procedural element in the focal situation.[1] For example, suppose that one wished to examine the effect of the procedural element of correctability (Leventhal, Karuza, & Fry, 1980) on people's reactions in the focal situation. The impact of correctability may depend upon events that transpired well before people's exposure to correctability in the focal situation, such as the extent to which correctability was present in similar situations in the past. The historical presence of correctability heightens its legitimacy in the present, focal situation. The more that people's previous experience leads them to perceive correctability to be legitimate in the focal situation, the more likely is correctability to influence their beliefs and behaviors in that situation.

In other instances the moderating influence takes shape *during* the focal situation in which people are exposed to the procedural element. For example, one important factor accompanying procedural information is the favorability of the outcomes associated with the decision. Based on the results of many recent studies, we suggest that people will be more influenced by procedural elements in the focal situation when their outcomes are relatively unfavorable (Brockner & Wiesenfeld, 1996).

One noteworthy aspect of the temporal dimension is its implication that people are concerned with procedural fairness at multiple times. Thus, people's reactions to procedural elements depend not only on factors that they encounter in the focal situation (e.g., outcome favorability) but also on variables that affect what they bring to the focal situation (e.g., the extent to which the procedural element has been encountered in previous situations).

Generality Dimension

The second organizing factor refers to the extent to which the moderating influence generalizes across procedural elements. Some factors moderate the influence of many procedural elements. For example, the notion that the legitimacy of correctability moderates the extent to which people will be influenced by the correctability that they experience in the focal situation could be extended to many procedural elements. That is, the impact of process control, consistency in treatment, and other procedural elements may be greater when previous experience with these elements imbues them with greater legitimacy in the present, focal situation.

Other moderators exert influence on a particular procedural element but may have little or no effect on other procedural elements. Certain procedural elements may have relatively unique properties that make them more susceptible than other procedural elements to the moderating influence of a given factor. For example, providing people with a causal account is likely to have a greater effect when people are seeking explanations in the first place (Bies, 1987). When people are motivated to understand why things turned out as they did, they are more likely to be influenced by the presence of a clear and adequate causal account than when they are not asking the why question. If so, then theory and research on attributional instigation, which concerns itself with when people ask why (e.g., Wong & Weiner, 1981) may help us to identify moderators of the effects of causal accounts. Moreover, factors derived from the attributional instigation literature may be less helpful in accounting for moderators of other procedural elements that are less directly related to the question of when people ask why.

Note that different, but equally worthwhile, theoretical purposes may be served by efforts to identify general vs. specific moderators. As Greenberg (1990) has suggested, conceptual progress in the procedural justice literature may be achieved through processes of both integration and differentiation. Theory and research showing that the same factor moderates the influence of many procedural elements exemplifies integration, whereas theory and research showing that a factor moderates the impact of a certain procedural element more than others reflects differentiation.

There may or may not be an empirical overlap between the two dimensions. In either event, they are clearly conceptually distinct and will be treated as such. Treating the two dimensions as orthogonal gives rise to four categories of moderating influences, as exhibited in Table 6.1: (1) factors that take shape prior to people's exposure to the procedural element in the focal situation that apply to procedural elements in general (prior/general quadrant), (2) factors that take shape during the focal situation that apply to procedural elements in general (during/general quadrant), (3) factors that take shape prior to exposure to the procedural element in the focal situation that apply to a specific procedural element (prior/specific quadrant), and (4) factors that take shape during the focal situation that apply to a specific procedural element (during/specific quadrant).

Table 6.1. A Two-Factor Taxonomy of Moderating
Influences on Procedural Elements.

Time in Which the Moderating Influence Takes Shape	GENERALITY OF THE MODERATING INFLUENCE ACROSS PROCEDURAL ELEMENTS	
	General	Specific
Prior to exposure to the procedural element in the focal situation	Prior/General	Prior/Specific
During the focal situation	During/General	During/Specific

The following sections present exemplars of moderating influences within each of the four categories just noted and in Table 6.1. Furthermore, we present theory and research pertinent to each category of moderating influence.

Factors from the Prior/General Quadrant

Prior to their exposure to procedural elements in the focal situation, people develop beliefs about the legitimacy of those elements. The legitimacy of a procedural element refers to the extent to which people accept the element as normatively correct. Legitimacy is at once the perception that "this is how things are done around here" as well as a tacit endorsement of that perception.

Procedural elements are predicted to have more of an influence on people's beliefs and behaviors when they are legitimate. Legitimacy reflects the combination of what people believe will happen (i.e., their expectancies) and what they believe should happen (i.e., their values). Of course, the underlying constructs of expectancies and values have had a long history in psychological theory in general (e.g., Tolman, 1935) and organizational psychology in particular. For example, Vroom (1964) suggested that motivational force is greatest when people both *expect* to succeed and *want* to succeed. In the present context, we refer to the bases of another psychological force: legitimacy. Following Vroom, we suggest that the psychological force or influence of a procedural element will be high when people both expect and value the element, in other words, when the element has legitimacy.

Antecedents of Legitimacy: Distal and Proximal Factors

The notion that procedural elements will be more influential when they have legitimacy is reasonably straightforward. What the notion does not suggest, however, is that numerous factors may influence the legitimacy of procedural elements. Factors affecting the legitimacy of procedural elements should moderate the impact of those elements on people's reactions. One determinant of the legitimacy of procedural elements is the extent to which the element was present in the past. For example, process control should have legitimacy in the focal situation when people have been given process control in similar situations in the past. In other words, the more that a procedural element has been legitimated by culturally or historically based norms, the more likely people are to believe that it will and should be present in the current, focal situation. We refer

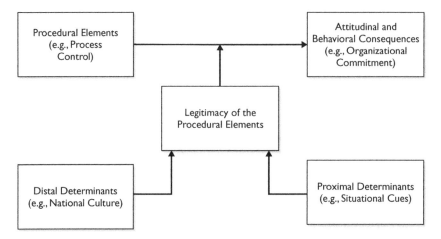

Figure 6.1. Summary of Relationships between Variables in the
Prior/General Quadrant.

to determinants of legitimacy that are deeply embedded in culture and
prior history as *distal* causes.

The legitimacy of a procedural element is not simply the product of distal causes, however. Legitimacy perceptions may also be shaped by cues in
the focal situation to which people are exposed shortly before their
encounter with the procedural element. For example, information provided by one's co-workers may influence the legitimacy that people attach
to certain procedural elements (Salancik & Pfeffer, 1978). We refer to
determinants of legitimacy that people encounter in the focal situation
shortly before their exposure to the procedural element as *proximal*
causes. For a summary of the relevant variables in the Prior/General quadrant (and the hypothesized relationships between them), see Figure 6.1.

Empirical Evidence

Recently we and others have investigated how the impact of procedural
elements is moderated by various distal and proximal antecedents of the
legitimacy of those elements (Brockner, Ackerman, et al., in press; Greenberg, Eskew, & Miles, 1991).

CULTURE AS A DISTAL DETERMINANT   One study investigated whether
cultural differences in power distance beliefs have a moderating influence
on the procedural element of process control. Power distance (Hofstede,
1980) refers to the extent to which people view inequality between persons

occupying different positions of hierarchical status to be an appropriate and desirable aspect of the social order. The lower the power distance, the less apt people are to endorse the legitimacy of hierarchy-based inequality. In low (rather than high) power distance cultures authorities are more likely to share their decision-making responsibilities with people in lower status positions. As a result of having decision-making responsibilities shared with them, people in lower status position in low power distance cultures should be more apt to believe that they will and should have process control, relative to their counterparts in high power distance cultures.

If process control is indeed more legitimate in the eyes of people in low than high power distance cultures, then people with low power distance beliefs should be more influenced by the level of process control that they actually experience in the focal situation. In particular, whereas people may be expected to react negatively to low levels of process control, this tendency should be more pronounced among people who assign greater legitimacy to process control. In one study participants were drawn from two cultures that have been shown to endorse different levels of power distance beliefs: the United States (low power distance) and the People's Republic of China (high power distance). The two samples read a scenario in which they were asked to imagine that they were working in an organization that was experiencing a great deal of change in technology, structure, and work arrangements. The process control variable contained three levels. In the high process control condition, participants were told that their manager "repeatedly consults with you and others about what changes are being considered and whether you think they are good ideas." In the low process control condition, participants were told that their manager "does not consult with you or others about what changes are being considered and whether you think they are good ideas." A third group (no information condition) was not told anything about their manager's decision-making style.

The primary dependent variable was a measure of organizational commitment. As predicted, culture interacted with process control such that the tendency for people to respond with less organizational commitment in the low process control than the high process control condition was more pronounced in the culture believed to be lower than higher in power distance beliefs (the United States vs. the Peoples' Republic of China, respectively).[2] In addition, we evaluated the role of power distance more directly. Specifically, participants completed a measure of power distance beliefs.

Several findings provided additional support for the notion that differences between the two cultures in their responsivity to process control were attributable to power distance beliefs. First, when people were sorted on the basis of their power distance beliefs rather than their country of origin, we found a significant interaction effect between power distance and process control: The tendency for people to respond with lower commitment in the low process control condition than the high process control condition was significantly more pronounced among those with relatively low power distance beliefs. Second, the interaction between culture and process control was reduced to nonsignificance when we controlled for the interaction between power distance and process control. Such findings suggest that it was not culture per se but rather the concomitant dimension of power distance that interacted with process control to influence participants' organizational commitment.

In addition to lending support to the specific notion that power distance moderates the impact of process control, the study illustrates a more general conceptual strategy that may be used to evaluate how culture and procedural elements interactively combine to influence peoples' reactions. The strategy requires articulation of how cultural factors affect the legitimacy that people attach to certain procedural elements. Just as power distance was hypothesized to influence the legitimacy of process control, other culturally produced psychological factors may influence the legitimacy that people assign to other procedural elements. Cultural factors that influence people's perceptions of the legitimacy of a procedural element should moderate the impact of that element on peoples' reactions to it in the focal situation.

For example, Kluckhohn and Strodtbeck (1961) suggested that cultures differ in the way that they view the basic character of human nature. In certain cultures people see human nature as fundamentally positive, whereas in others they view basic human nature more negatively, perhaps even evil. Cultural differences in the perceived character of human nature could influence the extent to which people assign legitimacy to the procedural element of dignified and respectful treatment when decisions are implemented. In cultures that view human nature more positively, people may be more likely to assign legitimacy to dignified treatment, relative to cultures with darker views of human nature. For example, in cultures with a more positive view of human nature, the people who implement decisions may be expected to do so in a more respectful and dignity-preserving way. If so, then the extent to which decisions are implemented in a respectful and dignified fashion in the focal situation may have more of an effect on people from cultures that have a positive rather than a negative view of human nature. Whereas people may generally respond negatively to decisions implemented in a disrespectful way, this may be particularly true for people in cultures with a positive view of human nature.

In summary, the globalization of the workplace has led to a perhaps unprecedented interest in cross-cultural differences in work attitudes and behaviors. The theory and research just presented offer one way to extend the study of cross-cultural differences into the arena of procedural fairness.

PRIOR EXPERIENCE AS A DISTAL DETERMINANT National culture is not the only distal determinant of the legitimacy that people assign to procedural elements. Even within a given national culture, people have different histories that lead them to develop different beliefs about the legitimacy of procedural elements. Those who have experienced high levels of the procedural elements in the past are likely to believe that high levels of those elements will and should be present in the focal situation. As a result, they should be more influenced by their perceptions of the procedural element in the focal situation.

We recently tested this hypothesis in a broader dataset examining survivors' reactions to an organizational layoff, portions of which have been published elsewhere (e.g., Brockner, Konovsky, Cooper-Schneider, Folger, Martin, & Bies, 1994). Previous studies have shown that survivors' reactions such as their work motivation and organizational commitment are influenced by various procedural elements (e.g., Brockner, Wiesenfeld, & Martin, 1995). As in nonlayoff domains, employees were found to respond more favorably when procedural fairness was relatively high. For instance, survivors' organizational commitment was greater when they felt that they had been given: (a) ample advance notification of the impending layoffs, and (b) a clear and adequate explanation of the reasons for the layoffs.

In the present analysis we also evaluated survivors' reactions as a function of these two procedural elements. We expected that the legitimacy that survivors assigned to these two procedural elements would vary, depending upon their perceptions of the organization's previous history in handling other important events. The more survivors believed that they received ample advance notification and clear explanations from organizational authorities in the past, the more they would assign legitimacy to, and as a result be affected by, these two elements in the organization's implementation of the layoff.

To test this hypothesis we assessed survivors' organizational commitment as a function of their perceptions of these two procedural elements in past situations and in the focal situation. An example of an item designed to measure perceptions of a procedural element in the past was,

"Prior to the layoffs, when important changes were going to be made in the daily lives of employees, how much did the company provide clear explanations of why such changes were necessary?" An example of an item measuring the same procedural element in the present was, "How clearly were the reasons for the layoff explained to you by management?" As might be expected, survivors expressed lower organizational commitment when they perceived that they had received relatively low levels of advance notification of the layoffs or relatively inadequate explanations of the reasons for the layoffs. Of greater importance, these relationships were moderated by survivors' prior perceptions of these two procedural elements. The more that the two elements were perceived to have been present in prior situations (which presumably influenced their legitimacy in the current situation), the more likely survivors were to express reduced organizational commitment in response to the perception that the current layoffs were accompanied by little advance notification or inadequate explanations.

PROXIMAL DETERMINANTS   The extent to which people assign legitimacy to procedural elements in the focal situation is not simply the product of their distal past. Cues encountered in the focal situation may also affect the legitimacy of procedural elements and, as a consequence, moderate the impact of the procedural element in the focal situation. This hypothesis was tested in an experiment (Greenberg, Eskew, and Miles, 1991), in which undergraduate students read a scenario describing a hypothetical situation that took place on the first meeting of a class. The procedural element under consideration was process control. Half of the participants were led to believe that students enrolled in the course would and should have input into the grading process (high legitimacy condition). The other half (low legitimacy condition) were led to believe that students would and should not have input. Furthermore, half were told that the professor actually gave students a high degree of input into the grading process (high process control condition), whereas the remaining half were told that the professor did not allow students to have input (low process control condition).

The primary dependent variable was the perceived fairness of the professor's actions. As might be expected, the professor was seen as much less fair in the low process control condition than in the high process control condition. Of greater importance, this tendency was moderated by the legitimacy of process control. The effect of process control on fairness perceptions was much more pronounced among those who were led to believe that process control was more legitimate. For further consideration of how proximal determinants of legitimacy have a moderating influence on procedural elements, see recent empirical findings of van den Bos, Vermunt, and Wilke (1996) and the discussion by Cropanzano and Ambrose (2001) in this volume.

Future Considerations

Taken together, the results of several studies provide converging evidence that people are more affected by procedural elements that have greater legitimacy in the focal situation. Although offering a clear and consistent set of findings, however, the studies leave several important matters unresolved. First, legitimacy was found to have much more of an effect on people's reactions when they encountered low rather than high levels of the procedural elements in the focal situation. In most instances, the findings suggest that, when people encounter high levels of the procedural elements, their reactions did not differ much as a function of the factors believed to influence legitimacy. In contrast, however, consistently sizable effects of legitimacy were found when people encountered low levels of the procedural elements.[3]

It should be noted that analogously asymmetric findings have appeared elsewhere in the justice literature. For example, equity theorists originally proposed that people find the state of equity to be far more pleasing than inequity (e.g., Walster, Walster, & Berscheid, 1978). Inequity, however, can take two forms: negative or positive. Negative inequity refers to a state of affairs in which perceived outcomes are less than those to which the person feels entitled, whereas positive inequity occurs when perceived outcomes are greater than those to which the person feels entitled. Research has consistently shown that people find negative inequity far more objectionable than positive inequity (Greenberg, 1982).

Taken together, the results of studies of outcome fairness and procedural fairness suggest that people's reactions are differentially affected by negative or positive discrepancies between the events they actually experience and those that they define as legitimate. The magnitude of their reactions in the focal situation will be greater in response to negative than positive discrepancies. Or, as Kahnemean and Tversky (1983) pointed out in a somewhat different context, "losses loom larger than gains." Perceiving outcomes or procedures as legitimate (i.e., "taken for granted") and not receiving them elicits more negative reactions than not defining them as legitimate but receiving them elicits positive reactions. Future research needs to shed additional light on why people respond more to negative than positive discrepancies between fairness standards of legitimacy and the level of fairness they experience in the focal situation.

Future research should also be devoted to another matter of great theoretical significance: how expectancies and values contribute to peoples' legitimacy beliefs about procedural elements. All that can be said at this point is that peoples' legitimacy beliefs about a procedural element are based on the extent to which they believe the element will and should be present, that is, how much they expect and want the element to be present. Moreover, the more people define a given procedural element as legitimate, the more likely they are to be affected by the level of the element they experience in the focal situation.

Although reasonably straightforward, the preceding assertions leave a number of important questions unanswered. For example, are expectancies and values equally important components of legitimacy beliefs, or is one more influential than the other? Moreover, in what manner (i.e., additively or multiplicatively) do expectancies and values combine *with each other* to influence the legitimacy (and hence impact) of various procedural elements? To address these questions, future researchers should examine individuals' reactions as a function of three independent variables: (a) peoples' expectancies regarding a particular procedural element, (b) their desire for that same element, and (c) the level of the element to which they are exposed in the focal situation. Such a study may not only contribute to the procedural justice literature; it also may shed light on more basic theoretical issues by examining how expectancies and values shape conceptions of legitimacy (be they about procedural elements or otherwise; Shah & Higgins, 1997).

Factors from the During/General Quadrant

In the present section we posit that factors that accompany (rather than precede) people's exposure to procedural elements in the focal situation may also have a moderating influence on procedural elements. One of the most crucial concerns to people in the focal situation is not simply *how* things were done (process information) but also *what* was done (i.e., outcome information). For example, social exchange theorists (e.g., Blau, 1964; Homans, 1961) have shown that outcomes that are more favorable to people (economically, psychologically, or both) elicit more positive attitudinal and behavioral reactions.

Many recent studies have shown that outcome favorability moderates the impact of procedural elements on individuals' judgments and behaviors (for a review, see Brockner & Wiesenfeld, 1996). Procedural elements were found to be much more influential when the outcomes people encountered in the focal situation were relatively unfavorable. This pattern emerged in a variety of laboratory and field settings. Moreover, it applied to a host of procedural elements including process control (Cropanzano & Konovsky, 1995), advance notice (Brockner et al., 1994), legitimacy of information (Greenberg, 1987b), causal accounts (Folger, Rosenfield, & Robinson, 1983; Schaubroeck, May, & Brown, 1994), and interpersonal sensitivity (Greenberg, 1993, 1994).

Numerous explanations may account for the interactive relationship between procedural elements and outcome favorability (for further discussion, see Brockner & Wiesenfeld, 1996). Despite differences between the various explanations, all suggest that the receipt of unfavorable outcomes arouses peoples' sense-making concerns. For example, people may wonder why they received unfavorable outcomes, and they may question the longer-term implications of having received such outcomes. Concerns about unfavorable outcomes may lead people to focus on the procedures associated with the outcomes they received. In other words, the sense making elicited by unfavorable outcomes may have heightened the salience of procedural elements, thereby increasing the impact of procedural elements on people's beliefs and behaviors. This reasoning further suggests that when people receive relatively favorable outcomes, sense-making concerns are not elicited nearly so much; as a result, procedural elements are less salient and hence have less of an impact.

Because the interactive relationship between procedural elements and outcome favorability has been reviewed elsewhere in great detail, we will not rehash those findings. Instead, we describe three noteworthy developments since the publication of Brockner and Wiesenfeld's (1996) review: (a) further evidence that outcome favorability moderates the effect of procedural elements, (b) the role of trust in accounting for the interactive relationship between procedural fairness and outcome favorability, and (c) the possibility that people may react differently to various combinations of procedural fairness and outcome favorability.

Further Evidence of the Moderating Effect of Outcomes

Although the interaction between outcome favorability and procedural fairness has been replicated repeatedly—Brockner and Wiesenfeld (1996) reported the same basic pattern in 45 independent samples—we are aware of at least eight additional studies conducted subsequent to the earlier review that show similar results (e.g., Brockner, Chen, Mannix, Leung, & Skarlicki, 2000; Garonzik, Brockner & Siegel, 2000; Skarlicki & Folger, 1997). For example, Garonzik et al. examined the extent to which expatriate managers were seriously thinking about departing prematurely from their overseas assignment. Independent variables included the favorability of the outcomes associated with their overseas assignment (i.e., whether the benefits of the job outweighed the costs), as well as the fairness of the organization's decision-making procedures. Procedural fairness bore little relationship with managers' thoughts of premature departure when outcome favorability was high. However, when outcome favorability was low, procedural fairness was significantly (and inversely) related to managers' thoughts of premature departure.

The Role of Trust

Recent research has also shed additional light on why procedural elements interact with outcome favorability. Apparently, procedural elements matter because they provide information on how much people can *trust* the other party involved in the exchange relationship. That is, people whose sense-making concerns are aroused by unfavorable outcomes may ultimately be trying to evaluate the trustworthiness of the other party. As people look toward the future, their perceptions of procedural elements in the focal situation may inform them about the trustworthiness of the other party. The fairer the other party's decision-making procedures are, the more likely that party will be seen as trustworthy. Moreover, to the extent that the other party is seen as trustworthy, people are likely to support that party's decisions or the institution that the party represents (Lind & Tyler, 1988). In short, we are suggesting that it is not the level of procedural fairness per se that interacts with outcome favorability. Rather, it is the degree of trust elicited by procedural elements that interacts with outcome favorability to influence people's reactions.

This reasoning gave rise to two recently tested hypotheses (Brockner, Siegel, Daly, Tyler, & Martin, 1997). First, trust and outcome favorability should interact. When outcomes are unfavorable, the extent to which people trust the other party will be more strongly related to their reactions to the other party (or the institution represented by the other party), relative to what would be observed when outcomes are more favorable. Second, the interaction between procedural elements and outcome favorability is attributable to the interaction between trust and outcome favorability. See Figure 6.2 for a summary of the hypothesized relationships between variables.

These hypotheses were examined in three different field settings. In all cases, independent variables included employees' trust in organizational authorities, procedural elements used by organizational authorities, and the perceived favorability of the outcomes associated with the authorities' decisions. Dependent variables included a variety of measures of support

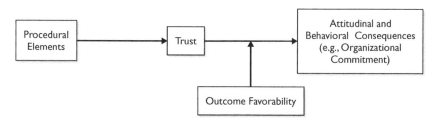

Figure 6.2. Hypothesized Relationships between Procedural Fairness, Trust, and Outcome Favorability.

for the authorities as well as the institution that the authorities represented. For example, in one study (Brockner et al., 1997, Study 3), layoff survivors indicated their level of organizational commitment as a function of the independent variables mentioned earlier. Replicating previous findings (Brockner & Wiesenfeld, 1996), the results showed that procedural fairness and organizational commitment were more strongly related to one another when outcomes were unfavorable than when they were favorable.

Extending the earlier findings, we found that trust and outcome favorability also combined interactively: Trust and organizational commitment were more strongly related to one another when outcomes were perceived to be unfavorable than when they were favorable. A final analysis showed that when the interactions between: (a) procedural fairness and outcome favorability, and (b) trust and outcome favorability were entered into the same regression equation, only the latter remained significant. Such findings suggest that it was not procedural fairness per se but rather the degree of trust associated with procedural fairness that interacted with outcome favorability to influence survivors' organizational commitment.

These findings may help to explain why outcome favorability has a moderating influence on many procedural elements. Theory (e.g., Lind & Tyler, 1988) and research (e.g., Konovsky & Pugh, 1994) have suggested that procedural elements and trust are strongly associated with one another. These findings suggest that procedural elements may have more of an impact on people's reactions when outcomes are less favorable *because* of the impact of procedural elements on trust.

Differences in Reactions as a Function of Procedure and Outcome

Cross-cutting procedural fairness and outcome favorability creates four sets of conditions: high procedural fairness/high outcome favorability, high procedural fairness/low outcome favorability, low procedural fairess/high outcome favorability, and low procedural fairness/low outcome favorability. As shown in Figure 6.3, one way to describe the interaction between procedural elements and outcome favorability is that people react particularly negatively under conditions of low procedural fairness and low outcome favorability. Moreover, their reactions in the remaining three conditions appear to be *similar* to one another. The presentation of the interaction in Figure 6.3 may be overly simplistic, however. That is, there may be differences in people's experiences of the conditions in which either procedural fairness or outcome favorability is high, or when both are high.

One way to illustrate possible differences in the various cells created by the factorial crossing of procedural fairness and outcome favorability is to consider the emotional experience of people within each condition. As suggested by Folger's (1986) referent cognitions theory, when unfair procedures are combined with unfavorable outcomes (i.e., when insult is added to injury), people are likely to feel angry and resentful. Moreover, the joint presence of favorable outcomes and fair procedures is likely to produce a relatively positive emotional state (e.g., contentment or even happiness).

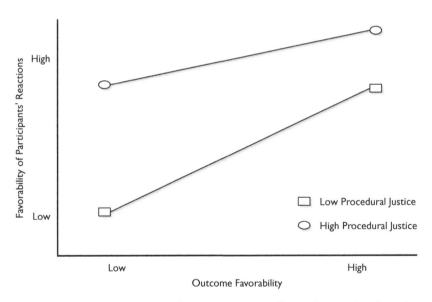

Figure 6.3. Representation of the Interactive Effect of Procedural Justice and Outcome Favorability.

It seems unlikely that people will feel similarly positive, however, when procedures are fair while outcomes are unfavorable, or when outcomes are favorable while procedures are unfair. Consider the latter condition. People who receive favorable outcomes in the face of unfair procedures may feel somewhat guilty or anxious. Although they may appreciate their favorable outcomes, the presence of unfair procedures may cause them to feel undeserving of (and hence guilty about) the outcomes (e.g., Brockner, Davy, & Carter, 1985) or worried that they will not be so lucky in the future (anxiety).

In contrast, when outcomes are unfavorable while procedures are fair, people may experience sadness or depression. This assertion stems from: (a) research showing that the effect of outcome favorability on self-evaluations is more pronounced when people perceive their outcomes to be more internally caused (Weiner, 1974), and (b) the notion that people will perceive their outcomes as more internally caused when the procedures giving rise to them are relatively fair (Van den Bos, Bruins, Wilke, & Dronkert, 1999). After all, when outcomes result from unfair procedures, it is relatively easy for people to make external outcome attributions. They may reason that the outcomes had little to do with them; rather, the outcomes were the result of whimsical procedures. Alternatively, when procedures are fair, people may feel that they were more deserving of (or causally responsible for) whatever outcomes they received.

This reasoning suggests that people should feel better about themselves when favorable outcomes result from fair rather than unfair procedures, and worse about themselves when unfavorable outcomes result from fair rather than unfair procedures. In fact, this pattern has been found on at least three different occasions (Gilliland, 1994; Schroth & Shah, 2000, Studies 1 and 2). In short, fair procedures that give rise to unfavorable outcomes may lead people to blame themselves for their outcomes. One of the psychological tendencies of depressed individuals is to blame themselves for their plight. That is, unfavorable outcomes by themselves do not necessarily induce depression. It is the tendency to attribute unfavorable outcomes to internal causes that predisposes people toward sadness and depression (Abramson, Seligman, & Teasdale, 1978). Thus, we tentatively suggest that people may experience sadness/depression in the unfavorable outcome/low procedural fairness condition.

Clearly, there is a need for further research on the interactive relationship between procedural fairness and outcome favorability. Conditions that may appear at first to be eliciting equivalent reactions may actually be giving rise to different emotional reactions. Future research needs to examine the extent to which people do in fact have different emotional experiences as a function of the various combinations of procedural fairness and outcome favorability. If so, it will also be worth examining the attitudinal and behavioral consequences of their differing emotional states (Brockner & Higgins, in press; Weiss & Cropanzano, 1996). The work attitudes and behaviors of employees who are angry and resentful may differ from those shown by anxious employees, which in turn may differ from those exhibited by employees who are feeling sad or depressed (Higgins, Roney, Crowe, & Hymes, 1994). For example, angry employees may be more apt to engage in sabotage relative to their counterparts who are feeling anxious or depressed. Anxious workers may be overly rigid in their information-processing tendencies (Staw, Sandelands, & Dutton, 1981). Finally, the overall energy levels of depressed employees should be less than that shown by angry or anxious workers. These are merely some of the speculations that await further research.

Factors from the Prior/Specific Quadrant

The previous two sections identified factors that have been found to have a moderating influence on numerous procedural elements. The guiding question considered in the previous sections was, "What factors moderate the impact of procedural elements *in general?*" In contrast, the next two sections treat procedural elements in a more differentiated manner. The starting point for conceptual analysis is on a specific procedural element, and the guiding question is, "What factors moderate the impact of *this particular* procedural element?" Moderators of a particular procedural element may or may not moderate the influence of other procedural elements.

The specific procedural element to be considered in the current section is process control. First, we suggest how process control differs from other procedural elements. Based on the analysis of how process control differs from other procedural elements, we identify a factor (taking shape prior to people's exposure to process control in the focal situation) that may have a moderating influence on process control.

Process control differs from other procedural elements in that it incorporates individuals' behavioral input. Other procedural elements simply refer to external conditions, such as whether decisions are implemented consistently, or whether decision makers provide explanations for their actions. High degrees of process control require behavioral responses from people. In contrast, high levels of other procedural elements do not, or at least not as much. More than high levels of other procedural elements, high levels of process control may force people to consider their level of efficacy. That is, high levels of process control may cause people to contemplate the extent to which they believe their input could make a meaningful difference.

Expectancy theory (e.g., Vroom, 1964) suggests that people will be more motivated to have process control to the extent that they believe that their input could make a meaningful difference. Moreover, the more motivated people are to have input, the more influenced they should be by the amount of input (process control) they experience in the focal situation. This reasoning suggests that the beliefs people maintain about their ability to provide meaningful input prior to their exposure to process control in the focal situation should moderate the impact of process control that they experience in the focal situation. People who are more confident that their input can make a meaningful difference should be more influenced by the level of process control they experience in the focal situation. Put differently, the well-documented tendency for people to respond more favorably to high levels of process control than to low levels (Lind & Tyler, 1988; Thibaut & Walker, 1975) should be stronger among those who believe more that their input can make a meaningful difference.

Empirical Evidence

The hypothesis that individuals with stronger beliefs about the efficacy of their input will be more influenced by process control has been tested in a variety of field and laboratory settings. In some cases the independent variable pertaining to the perceived efficacy of one's input has been experimentally manipulated (Bazerman, 1982). For example, Brockner, Heuer, Siegel, Wiesenfeld, Martin, Grover, Reed, and Bjorgvinsson (1998) measured participants' satisfaction with a third party's decision about whether to include them in a desirable activity as a function of whether they: (a) were allowed to have input into the third party's decision about including them in the activity, and (b) believed that they were highly qualified to contribute to the activity. An interaction effect emerged, showing that process control or input into the third party's decision enhanced participants' satisfaction when they believed that they were highly qualified to contribute to the activity, but that process control had no effect when people did not feel highly qualified to contribute.

Brockner et al. (1998) also examined reactions to process control as a function of a personality variable likely to be related to the perceived efficacy of one's input: self-esteem. The sample in one study consisted of a group of layoff survivors who were asked to indicate their degree of trust in and support for the organizaton. The independent variable of process control was measured rather than manipulated. Self-esteem interacted with process control to influence survivors' trust in and support for the organization. Whereas survivors' perceptions of process control were significantly related to their trust in and support for the organization among high self-esteem persons, no such relationship emerged among low self-esteem individuals.

In another study, Brockner et al. (1998) examined the moderating effect of organization-based self-esteem on the relationship between process control and organizational attitudes of employees whose organization had recently introduced several changes. Organization-based self-esteem (OBSE) refers to "the self-perceived value that individuals have of themselves as organizational members acting within an organizational context" (Pierce, Gardner, Cummings, & Dunham, 1989, p. 625). As such, it is more situationally specific than global self-esteem. OBSE and process control interactively combined to influence the favorability of employees' organizational attitudes. Process control was positively related to organizational attitudes among those high in OBSE; among those low in OBSE, process control and organizational attitudes were unrelated.

The literature on psychological reactance (e.g., Brehm & Brehm, 1981) also provides evidence that the effect of the procedural element of process control depends upon one's perceived ability to provide meaningful input. Studies of reactance examine peoples' reactions to the explicit *removal* of being able to provide input. A frequently used method for studying reactance consists of exposing participants to a persuasive communication designed to influence their attitudes. After hearing the persuasive communication, individuals receive a coercive message informing them that they have "no choice" but to agree with the persuasive communication. Such coercion is obviously antithetical to their sense of having process control or input.

The typical "reactance effect" is that people are *less* likely to agree with the persuasive communication when they have been exposed to the coercive message about having no choice, relative to when they are not given the coercive message. Of greater relevance to the present analysis, Brockner and Elkind (1985) found that the expression of reactance was stronger among people with high self-esteem than low self-esteem. One interpretation is that high self-esteem persons, feeling more confident about their ability to provide meaningful input, were more motivated to have input than their low self-esteem counterparts. When confronted with the coercive message designed to eliminate their input, high self-esteem persons experienced greater reactance than their low self-esteem counterparts.

In summary, the independent variables of process control and beliefs about one's ability to provide meaningful input when given process control have been operationalized in a variety of laboratory and field settings. In spite of the many methodological differences between studies, the results have been highly consistent; process control has a greater impact on people who are more likely to believe that their input can make a meaningful difference.

This is not to suggest, however, that beliefs about one's ability to provide meaningful input will necessarily moderate the impact of other procedural elements. Rather, the nature of process control may make salient to people beliefs about their ability to provide meaningful input. As a result, such beliefs would have a moderating influence on process control in particular. In fact, several of the studies that showed interactive relationships between process control and self-esteem included measures of other procedural elements (e.g., advance notice, explanations, and accuracy). In no instance, however, did self-esteem moderate the influence of these other procedural elements. Thus, the moderating influence of beliefs about one's ability to provide meaningful input is greater on process control than on other procedural elements.[4]

Factors from the During/Specific Quadrant

Bies (1987) suggested that procedural elements include the interpersonal behavior of the parties responsible for planning and implementing decisions. Such behavior includes the extent to which the responsible parties provide causal accounts of their decisions. Perceived fairness will be heightened to the extent that the causal account is judged to be clear and/or adequate. Causal accounts differ from other procedural elements in that they refer to a particular type of sense-making activity in which individuals engage during the focal situation: efforts to understand *why* events turned out as they did.

The search for moderators of causal accounts may be facilitated by the following question: When are people motivated to understand the causes of events? The very conditions that prompt people to seek causal understanding should be those in which people will be more affected by the presence of a clear and adequate causal account. In contrast, when people are less eager to know why certain outcomes occurred, they should be less affected by the presence of a clear and adequate causal account.

Attribution theory (e.g., Kelley, 1972) and research following from it has identified various types of causal attributions that people make for their own and others' behavior. Relevant dimensions include whether the attributions are internal vs. external, stable vs. unstable, and global vs. specific (Abramson, Seligman, & Teasdale, 1978). Researchers have also studied the psychological and behavioral consequences of individuals' causal attributions (e.g., Seligman & Schulman, 1986). A more basic question that has also been examined (albeit to a lesser extent) pertains to the onset of attributional processing as a dependent variable. That is, under what conditions do people ask why?

Several studies have shown that the unexpectedness of the event is one antecedent of attributional instigation. The more unexpected the event is, the more likely it is that people will be motivated to understand why it occurred (Pyszczynski & Greenberg, 1981; Wong & Weiner, 1981). In contrast, events that are consistent with individuals' prior expectations are much less likely to elicit a sense-making process in which people seek causal understanding of events.

This reasoning suggests that the unexpectedness of an event that unfolds during the focal situation should have a moderating influence on causal accounts. Specifically, the presence of a clear and adequate causal account should have a greater impact when the event to which the person is exposed during the focal situation is more unexpected. This hypothesis was tested on a group of layoff survivors whose organization had initiated layoffs for the first time in recent corporate history (Brockner, DeWitt, Grover, & Reed, 1990). One independent variable was survivors' ratings of the unexpectedness of the layoffs. The other independent variable was their evaluation of the quality of the causal accounts offered by management for the layoff.

The two independent variables interactively combined to influence survivors' work effort and desire to remain with the organization. Replicating the work of Bies (1987), Brockner et al. (1990) found that the perceived quality of the causal accounts was positively related to the favorability of participants' reactions. Of greater importance, these positive relationships were much more pronounced among those who perceived the layoff to be more of an unexpected event.

It also is worth noting that although the perceived unexpectedness of the layoffs moderated the impact of causal accounts on survivors' reactions, the perceived unexpectedness of the layoffs did not moderate the influence of other procedural elements. For example, survivors were asked to indicate the extent to which they believed that various criteria were used to determine whether employees would be targeted to be laid off or chosen to remain with the organization (e.g., seniority, merit, job function, and politics). After having made these judgments, participants evaluated the fairness of the criteria that they believed had been used. This judgment corresponds to Leventhal, Karuza, and Fry's (1980) procedural element of accuracy, in which decisions will be seen as more fair to the extent that they are based on valid information. In fact, survivors' reactions were positively related to the perceived fairness of the decision criteria. However, the magnitude of this relationship did not depend on the perceived unexpectedness of the layoffs. These findings suggest that the moderating influence of unexpectedness on procedural elements does not generalize across all procedural elements. Whereas unexpectedness moderated the impact of causal accounts, it did not have a similar moderating effect on other procedural elements.

More generally, procedural elements may be influential when they satisfy individuals' sense-making needs. When events are unexpected, clear and adequate causal accounts may be useful—and thereby contribute to perceived fairness—because they help people determine why the events occurred. As the same events become more typical or less unexpected, clear and adequate causal accounts should be less in demand, less likely to be provided, and less influential if they are in fact provided. The last point is underscored by the finding that survivors who perceived the layoffs to be less unusual in light of their organization's culture were not affected by the perceived quality of management's explanation of the reasons for the layoff (Brockner et al., 1990).

A recent study across many downsizing organizations provides evidence that causal accounts are less likely to be offered as layoffs become more typical (Lamertz & Baum, 1998). The authors tracked over a seven-year period (January 1988 through December 1994) the frequency with which causal accounts were offered in Canadian newspapers in articles describing middle-management layoffs in Canadian companies. At the outset of the seven-year time frame, layoffs targeted at middle managers were relatively unusual. Over time, however, they became an increasingly prevalent form of downsizing. Thus, middle-management layoffs in the later stages of the seven-year time period were much less unusual than they were during the earlier stages. Accompanying the repeated occurrence of layoffs among the ranks of middle managers was a sharp decline in the use of causal accounts in newspaper articles.

These findings suggest that readers' needs to understand the reasons for middle-management layoffs were less intense as the event had become a more typical form of business practice. This is not to say, however, that, once people understand the reasons for previously unexpected layoffs, they no longer need to make sense of them. Rather, the nature of their sense-making activities may change. For example, when expectancy-violating layoffs occur, one of survivors' initial reactions may be to seek to understand the reasons for them. Having made sense of the reasons for the layoffs, they may then become more concerned with appraising the longer-term implications of the layoffs, leading to questions such as, "What does this organization stand for?" and "What will life be like in this organization down the road?" Later stages of sense making may heighten survivors' need for information that reassures them that the basic values of the organization are still intact.

The underlying motivation of account givers is to make them appear less responsible for inappropriate behaviors. Causal accounts imply that the behavior is inappropriate but deny that the actor is responsible for bringing about its negative consequences. Bies (1987) has identified other forms of accounts (e.g., ideological, referential) that concede that the actor is responsible but counter the claim that the behavior is not legitimate (Lamertz & Baum, 1997). An ideological account labels "the action or the outcome in more positive value-laden terms" (Bies, 1987, pp. 300–301). For example, an ideological account of downsizing is that the organization will be able to reduce its costs and thereby improve its competitiveness. A referential account also puts a positive spin on things "by providing a temporal, social, or aspirational referent standard in comparison to which the act in question appears . . . less unacceptable" (Lamertz & Baum, 1997, p. 96). An example of a referential account of downsizing is that the scope of the downsizing is less than that observed in other comparable organizations.

In summary, accounts are a component of interactional justice that have the potential to satisfy individuals' sense-making needs. To determine moderating influences on various types of accounts, it is necessary to specify the particular sense-making concern that is salient to people at a given time. In the face of unexpected events, people may first need to know why they occurred. If so, then the presence of clear and adequate causal accounts should be particularly influential. As the unexpectedness of the event becomes less salient, other sense-making concerns may become more pronounced, thereby increasing the potential impact of other types of accounts. Interestingly, Lamertz and Baum (1998) discovered not only that causal accounts became less prevalent over time in newspaper reports of middle-management layoffs but also that ideological and referential accounts became more prevalent. Perhaps the increasing prevalence of ideological and referential accounts was to help readers deal with different sense-making concerns that may have accompanied the continuation, rather than the onset, of middle-management layoffs.

Future Directions

For both theoretical and practical purposes, it is important to understand when various procedural elements will have more or less impact on peoples' perceptions, attitudes, and behaviors. We have provided four different types of moderating influences on procedural elements, organized by the taxonomic dimensions of the point in time in which the moderating influence takes shape and the generality of the moderating influence across procedural elements. Although some progress has been made, it is likely that we have merely scratched the surface in the search for moderating influences on procedural elements. Looking toward the future, we envision at least two forms of further investigation: (a) work *within* the boundaries of each of the four quadrants set forth in Table 6.1, and (b) research that spans the boundaries *between* the quadrants in Table 6.1. Examples of each form follow.

Working within the Quadrants

Of the following two examples of suggestions for future research, one is suggested by the generality dimension of moderating influences whereas the other is related to the temporal dimension of moderating influences. First, the impact of certain procedural elements has been studied much more than the impact of others. For example, we know much more about the effects of, and moderating influences on, process control and decision control (e.g., Lind & Tyler, 1988; Thibaut & Walker, 1975) and interactional justice (e.g., Bies, 1987; Brockner et al., 1994; Greenberg, 1993, 1994) than we do about the Leventhal et al. (1980) procedural elements of consistency, correctability, and accuracy. Future efforts need to redress this imbalance. As work on the moderating influences on specific procedural elements mounts, we will be better able to perform the conceptual tasks of integration and differentiation called for by Greenberg (1990). That is, some moderating influences may be shown to generalize across procedural elements, whereas others may be more element-specific in scope.

Second, in discussing factors that take shape *during* the focal situation we merely provided one example: the favorability of the outcomes associated with the decision procedures. People are exposed to other information in the focal situation, however, that could moderate the effect of procedural elements. For instance, people's reactions to procedural elements may be influenced not only by the information they acquire about the elements from their own direct observations but also by social cues from relevant others (Cropanzano & Ambrose, Chapter 4). What their co-workers say about the procedural elements may interact with their own judgments of the procedural elements to influence their reactions to those elements. When social cues are ambiguous (e.g., such as when some co-workers report that procedures are fair while others do not), peoples' reactions are likely to depend on their own (independent) judgments of the procedural elements. In contrast, when social cues provide a clear and consistent message concerning procedural fairness that differs from their own judgments, they may be less influenced by their own judgments of the procedural elements.

Spanning the Boundaries between the Quadrants

The temporal dimension of the taxonomy suggests that moderating influences materialize both prior to and during the focal situation in which people are exposed to procedural elements. Thus far we have tried to illustrate the utility of bifurcating the moderating influences along the temporal dimension. Moderating influences that take shape prior to people's exposure to a procedural element in the focal situation may reflect the legitimacy of the procedural element; moderating influences that take shape during the focal situation may result from a retrospective sense-making process elicited by the receipt of unfavorable outcomes.

A question worth examining in future research is how moderators that take shape prior to exposure to procedural elements in the focal situation combine with those that materialize during the focal situation to influence people's reactions to procedural elements. Based on results to date, we predict that the effect of a given procedural element in the focal situation should be most pronounced when the element has legitimacy *and* when the outcomes associated with the procedural element are unfavorable. To state the prediction differently, the procedural element should have the least impact when it lacks legitimacy *and* when the associated outcomes are favorable. Left unspecified by these predictions is whether the moderating influences that take shape prior to people's exposure to procedural elements in the focal situation (that is, antecedents of legitimacy) will combine additively or interactively with the moderating influences that materialize during the focal situation (that is, outcome favorability). To address this matter three independent variables need to be incorporated into a single design: (a) a procedural element in the focal situation, (b) a factor influences the legitimacy of the procedural element in the focal situation, and (c) the favorability of the outcomes associated with the procedural element. More generally, empirical research that spans the boundaries between the quadrants set forth in Table 6.1 may lead to the development of a more integrative explanation of when procedural elements will be more or less influential.

Conclusions

This chapter was designed to organize recent attempts to delineate moderating influences on procedural elements. Our goals were twofold: to make sense of past efforts and to suggest needed areas for future research. The two-factor framework illustrates a variety of approaches that have been taken in the (recent) past, as well as the ways in which those approaches differ from one another. Moreover, the framework provides guidance to researchers who wish to further explore moderating influences on procedural elements.

Regardless of whether our organizing framework proves to be a useful heuristic for future research, researchers who further examine moderating influences on procedural elements should capitalize on potential opportunities to contribute to literatures outside the realm of organizational justice. We have hinted at several possibilities along the way, such as cross-cultural effects on work attitudes and behaviors, the question of how expectancies and values influence judgments of legitimacy, and the affective consequences of different combinations of procedural fairness and outcome favorability. The theoretical yield from the future research we have advocated could be considerable. Finally, in support of Lewin's famous dictum that there is nothing quite so practical as a good theory, the present and future research on moderating influences on procedural elements may help managers make more informed decisions about when to be procedurally fair, as well as the ways in which to be so.

NOTES

1. The "focal situation" is the setting in which people's reactions to procedural elements are assessed.
2. Gelfand (1998) also discovered a tendency for people to respond less favorably to low process control than high process control in a low power distance country than a high power distance country. Importantly for purposes of convergent validity, the participants in the Gelfand study came from two countries other than the United States and the People's Republic of China: Costa Rica (low power distance) and Turkey (high power distance).
3. Van den Bos, Wilke, and Vermunt (1996) did find a significant effect of legitimacy when people were exposed to high process control in the focal situation. That is, people who received process control felt that they had been treated more fairly when having process control was legitimized than when not having process control had been legitimized. Consistent with the previously reported findings, however, Van den Bos et al. found an even larger effect of legitimacy when people were exposed to low process control in the

focal situation. That is, people who did not receive process control exhibited a very pronounced tendency to feel that they had been treated less fairly when having process control was legitimized than when not having process control was legitimized.

4. Moreover, recent research provides suggestive evidence that self-esteem may have a *different* moderating influence on other procedural elements. Vermunt et al. (1998) found that the relationship between people's perceptions of dignified interpersonal treatment and outcome fairness was more pronounced among low self-esteem than high self-esteem individuals.

REFERENCES

Abramson, L. Y., Seligman, M. E. P., & Teasdale, J. (1978). Learned helplessness in humans: Critique and reformulation. *Journal of Abnormal Psychology, 87*, 49–74.

Adams, J. S. (1965). Inequity in social exchange. In L. Berkowitz (Ed.), *Advances in experimental social psychology* (Vol. 2, pp. 267–299). New York: Academic Press.

Bazerman, M. (1982). Impact of personal control on performance: Is added control always beneficial? *Journal of Applied Psychology, 67*, 472–479.

Bies, R. J. (1987). The predicament of injustice: The management of moral outrage. In L. L. Cummings & B. M. Staw (Eds.), *Research in organizational behavior* (Vol. 9, pp. 289–319). Greenwich, CT: JAI Press.

Bies, R. J., & Moag, J. S. (1986). Interactional justice: Communication criteria of fairness. In R. J. Lewicki, B. H. Sheppard, & M. Bazerman (Eds.), *Research on negotiation in organizations* (Vol. 1, pp. 43–55). Greenwich, CT: JAI Press.

Blau, P. (1964). *Exchange and power in social life.* New York: Wiley.

Brehm, J. W., & Brehm, S. (1981). *Psychological reactance: A theory of freedom and control.* New York: Academic Press.

Brockner, J. (1994). Perceived fairness and layoff survivors' reactions, or how downsizing organizations can do well by doing good. *Social Justice Research, 7*, 345–364.

Brockner, J., Ackerman, G., Greenberg, J., Gelfand, M., Francesco, A. M., Chen, Z. X., Leung, K., Bierbrauer, G., Gomez, C., Kirkman, B. L., & Shapiro, D. (in press). Culture and procedural justice: The influence of power distance on reactions to voice. *Journal of Experimental Social Psychology.*

Brockner, J., Chen, Y., Mannix, E., Leung, K., & Skarlicki, D. (2000). Culture and procedural fairness: When the effects of what you do depend upon how you do it. *Administrative Science Quarterly, 45*, 138–159.

Brockner, J., Davy, J., & Carter, C. (1985). Layoffs, self-esteem, and survivor guilt: Motivational, affective, and attitudinal consequences. *Organizational Behavior and Human Decision Processes, 36*, 229–244.

Brockner, J., DeWitt, R. L., Grover, S., & Reed, T. (1990). When it is especially important to explain why: Factors affecting the relationship between managers' explanations of a layoff and survivors' reactions to the layoff. *Journal of Experimental Social Psychology, 26,* 389–407.

Brockner, J., & Elkind, M. (1985). Self-esteem and reactance: Further evidence of attitudinal and motivational consequences. *Journal of Experimental Social Psychology, 21,* 346–361.

Brockner, J., Heuer, L. B., Siegel, P. A., Wiesenfeld, B. M., Martin, C., Grover, S., Reed, T., & Bjorgvinsson, S. (1998). The moderating effect of self-esteem in reaction to voice: Converging evidence from five studies. *Journal of Personality and Social Psychology, 75,* 394–407.

Brockner, J., & Higgins, E. T. (in press). Regulatory focus theory: Implications for the study of emotions at work. *Organizational Behavior and Human Decision Processes.*

Brockner, J., Konovsky, M., Cooper-Schneider, R., Folger, R., Martin, C., & Bies, R. J. (1994). The interactive effects of procedural justice and outcome negativity on the victims and survivors of job loss. *Academy of Management Journal, 37,* 397–409.

Brockner, J., Siegel, P. A., Daly, J., Tyler, T. R., & Martin, C. (1997). When trust matters: The moderating effect of outcome favorability. *Administrative Science Quarterly, 42,* 558–583.

Brockner, J., & Wiesenfeld, B. M. (1996). An integrative framework for explaining reactions to decisions: The interactive effects of outcomes and procedures. *Psychological Bulletin, 120,* 189–208.

Brockner, J., Wiesenfeld, B. M., & Martin, C. (1995). Decision frame, procedural justice, and survivors' reactions to job layoffs. *Organizational Behavior and Human Decision Processes, 63,* 59–68.

Cropanzano, R., & Folger, R. (1991). Procedural justice and worker motivation. In R. M. Steers & L. W. Porter (Eds.), *Motivation and work behavior* (2nd ed., pp. 131–143). New York: McGraw-Hill.

Cropanzano, R., & Konovsky, M. A. (1995). Resolving the justice dilemma by improving the outcomes: The case of employee drug screening. *Journal of Business and Psychology, 10,* 221–243.

Deutsch, M. (1985). *Distributive justice: A social-psychological perspective.* New Haven, CT: Yale University Press.

Folger, R. (1986). Rethinking equity theory: A referent cognitions model. In H. W. Bierhoff, R. L. Cohen, & J. Greenberg (Eds.), *Justice in social relations* (pp. 145–162). New York: Plenum.

Folger, R. (1993). Reactions to mistreatment at work. In J. K. Murnighan (Ed.), *Social psychology in organizations: Advances in theory and research* (pp. 161–183). Englewood Cliffs, NJ: Prentice-Hall.

Folger, R., Rosenfield, D., & Robinson, T. (1983). Relative deprivation and procedural justification. *Journal of Personality and Social Psychology, 45,* 268–273.

Folger, R., & Skarlicki, D. (1998). When tough times make tough bosses: Managerial distancing as a function of layoff blame. *Academy of Management Journal, 41,* 79–87.

Garonzik, R., Brockner, J., & Siegel, P. (2000). Identifying international assignees at risk for premature departure: The interactive effect of outcome favorability and procedural fairness. *Journal of Applied Psychology, 85,* 13–20.

Gelfand, M. (1998). Unpublished data, University of Maryland.

Gilliland, S. W. (1994). Effects of procedural and distributive justice on reactions to a selection system. *Journal of Applied Psychology, 79,* 691–701.

Greenberg, J. (1982). Approaching equity and avoiding inequity in groups and organizations. In J. Greenberg & R. L. Cohen (Eds.), *Equity and justice in social behavior* (pp. 389–435). New York: Academic Press.

Greenberg, J. (1987a). A taxonomy of organizational justice theories. *Academy of Management Review, 12,* 9–22.

Greenberg, J. (1987b). Reactions to procedural injustice in payment allocations: Do the means justify the ends? *Journal of Applied Psychology, 72,* 55–61.

Greenberg, J. (1990). Organizational justice: Yesterday, today, and tomorrow. *Journal of Management, 16,* 399–432.

Greenberg, J. (1993). Stealing in the name of justice: Informational and interpersonal moderators of theft reactions to underpayment inequity. *Organizational Behavior and Human Decision Processes, 54,* 81–103.

Greenberg, J. (1994). Using socially fair treatment to promote acceptance of a work site smoking ban. *Journal of Applied Psychology, 79,* 288–297.

Greenberg, J. (1996). *The quest for justice on the job: Essays and experiments.* Thousand Oaks, CA: Sage.

Greenberg, J., Eskew, D. E., & Miles, J. (1991, August). *Adherence to participatory norms as a moderator of the fair process effect: When voice does not enhance procedural justice.* Paper presented at the meeting of the Academy of Management, Miami Beach, Florida.

Higgins, E. T., Roney, C. J. R., Crowe, E., & Hynes, C. (1994). Ideal versus ought predilections for approach and avoidance: Distinct self-regulatory systems. *Journal of Personality and Social Psychology, 66,* 276–286.

Hofstede, G. (1980). *Culture's consequences.* London: Sage.

Homans, G. C. (1961). *Social behaviour: Its elementary forms.* London: Routledge and Kegan Paul.

Kahneman, D., & Tversky, A. (1983). Choices, values, and frames. *American Psychologist, 39,* 341–350.

Kelley, H. H. (1972). Attribution in social interaction. In E. E. Jones, D. E. Kanouse, H. H. Kelley, R. E. Nisbett, S. Valins, & B. Weiner (Eds.), *Attribution: Perceiving the causes of behavior* (pp. 1–26). Morristown, NJ: General Learning Press.

Kluckhohn, F. R. & Strodtbeck, F. L. (1961). *Variations in value orientations.* Evanston, IL: Row, Peterson.

Konovsky, M. A., & Pugh, S. D. (1994). Citizenship behavior and social exchange. *Academy of Management Journal, 37,* 656–669.

Lamertz, K., & Baum, J. (1998). The legitimacy of organizational downsizing in Canada: An analysis of explanatory media accounts. *Canadian Journal of Administrative Sciences, 15,* 93–107.

Leventhal, G. S., Karuza, J., & Fry, W. R. (1980). Beyond fairness: A theory of allocation preferences. In G. Mikula (Ed.), *Justice and social interaction* (pp. 167–218). New York: Springer-Verlag.

Lind, E. A., & Tyler, T. R. (1988). *The social psychology of procedural justice.* New York: Plenum.

McFarlin, D. B., & Sweeney, P. D. (1992). Distributive and procedural justice as predictors of satisfaction with personal and orangizational outcomes. *Academy of Management Journal, 35,* 626–637.

Pierce, J. L., Gardner, D. G., Cummings, L. L., & Dunham, R. B. (1989). Organization-based self-esteem: Construct definition, measurement, and validation. *Academy of Management Journal, 32,* 622–648.

Pyszcznski, T. A., & Greenberg, J. (1981). Role of disconfirmed expectancies in the instigation of attributional processing. *Journal of Personality and Social Psychology, 40,* 31–38.

Rawls, J. A. (1971). *A theory of justice.* Cambridge, MA: Harvard University Press.

Salancik, G. R., & Pfeffer, J. (1978). A social information processing approach to job attitudes and task design. *Administrative Science Quarterly, 23,* 224–253.

Schaubroeck, J., May, D. R., & Brown, F. W. (1994). Procedural justice explanations and employee reactions to economic hardship: A field experiment. *Journal of Applied Psychology, 79,* 455–460.

Schroth, H., & Shah, P. P. (2000). Procedures, do we really want to know them? *Journal of Applied Psychology, 82,* 434–443.

Seligman, M. E. P., & Schulman, P. (1986). Explanatory style as a predictor of productivity and quitting among life insurance sales agents. *Journal of Personality and Social Psychology, 50,* 832–838.

Shah, J., & Higgins, E. T. (1997). Expectancy × value effects: Regulatory focus as determinant of magnitude *and* direction. *Journal of Personality and Social Psychology, 73,* 447–458.

Skarlicki, D. P., & Folger, R. (1997). Retaliation in the workplace: The roles of distributive, procedural, and interactional justice. *Journal of Applied Psychology, 82,* 434–443.

Staw, B. M., Sandelands, L. E., & Dutton, J. E. (1981). Threat-rigidity effects in organizational behavior. *Administrative Science Quarterly, 26,* 501–524.

Thibaut, J. W., & Walker, L. (1975). *Procedural justice: A psychological analysis.* Hillsdale, NJ: Lawrence Erlbaum Associates.

Tolman, E. C. (1935). *Purposive behavior in animals and men.* New York: Century.

Tyler, T. R., & Bies, R. J. (1990). Interpersonal aspects of procedural justice. In J. S. Carroll (Ed.), *Applied social psychology and organizational settings* (pp. 77–98). Hillsdale, NJ: Erlbaum.

Tyler, T. R., & Lind, E. A. (1992). A relational model of authority in groups. In M. Zanna (Ed.), *Advances in experimental social psychology* (Vol. 25, pp. 115–192). San Diego: Academic Press.

Van den Bos, K., Bruins, J., Wilke, H. A. M., & Dronkert, E. (1999). Sometimes unfair procedures have nice aspects: On the psychology of the fair process effect. *Journal of Personality and Social Psychology, 77,* 324–336.

Van den Bos, K., Vermunt, R., & Wilke, H. A. M. (1996). The consistency rule and the voice effect: The influence of expectations on procedural fairness judgments and performance. *European Journal of Social Psychology, 26,* 411–428.

Vermunt, R., Blauuw, E., van Knippenberg, B., & van Knippenberg, D. (1998). *The influence of self-esteem on the use of outcome information and procedural information to evaluate the fairness of outcomes.* Manuscript under editorial review.

Vroom, V. H. (1964). *Work and motivation.* New York: Wiley.

Walster, E., Walster, G. W., & Berscheid, E. (1978). *Equity: Theory and research.* Boston: Allyn & Bacon.

Weiner, B. (1974). *Achievement motivation and attribution theory.* Morristown, NJ: General Learning Press.

Weiss, H. M., & Cropanzano, R. (1996). Affective events theory: A theoretical discussion of the structure, causes and consequences of affective experiences at work. In B.M. Staw & L.L. Cummings (Eds.), *Research in organizational behavior* (Vol. 18, pp. 1–74). Greenwich, CT: JAI Press.

Wong, P. T. P., & Weiner, B. (1981). When people ask "why" questions, and the heuristics of attributional search. *Journal of Personality and Social Psychology, 40,* 650–663.

7

Ethnic Diversity and the Viability of Organizations: The Role of Procedural Justice in Bridging Differences

Yuen J. Huo
and
Tom R. Tyler

THE WORKFORCE OF 21ST CENTURY AMERICA will be characterized by racial, ethnic, and cultural diversity. This new face of the workforce was shaped by demographic trends that began in the 1980s. During that period, the large majority of additions to the workforce were women and racial and ethnic minorities. Whereas white males of European descent had historically constituted the greater portion of the workforce, they will soon come to represent less than 50% of the working population (Johnston & Packer, 1987). Given these dramatic changes, it is not surprising that organizational researchers and practitioners have taken it

The data described in this chapter were collected as part of a larger project on diversity and authority relations conducted in collaboration with Allan Lind of Duke University. The project was supported by National Science Foundation Grants SES-9113863 and SES-9113752 and by the American Bar Foundation.

We thank Jerry Greenberg and Russell Cropanzano for their very helpful comments and suggestions on an earlier version of this chapter.

upon themselves to explore the impact of diversity on the workplace. A central concern is how diversity may affect the viability of organizations. Can diversity hinder the ability of managers and other organizational leaders to coordinate action and to carry out institutional goals? This is the question we address in this chapter. We do so by describing a theoretical framework for understanding the exercise of authority in organizations, presenting data collected from a survey of employees to test aspects of this theory, and discussing the implications of the findings for the management of diversity in the workplace.

We turn our attention to the effect of diversity on the exercise of authority because authorities play an important role in maintaining the viability of organizations. Among other things, authorities manage internal conflicts and coordinate the efforts of individuals and teams (Messick, Wilke, Brewer, Kramer, Zemke, and Lui, 1983; Rutte, Wilke, & Messick, 1987; Samuelson, 1991; Sato, 1987; Wit, 1989; Yamagishi, 1986). With the introduction of large numbers of ethnic minorities into the workforce, authorities in organizations are faced with meeting the additional challenge of managing conflicts and disagreements among employees with diverse interests and values. We propose that one mechanism through which differences in interests and values can be bridged is the use of fair decision-making procedures. Studies of organizational, political, and legal authorities have demonstrated that perceptions of fair treatment are linked to endorsement of authorities, the decisions they make about how to resolve a problem or conflict, and the policies they enact (see Tyler & Lind, 1992; Tyler, Smith, & Huo, 1996, for reviews of relevant studies). Such voluntary deference is important to social coordination because it empowers authorities to effectively resolve difficult problems and to enact basic changes that are necessary to the successful attainment of organizational goals.

Our goal is to argue that concerns about fair treatment ("procedural justice concerns") can help authorities to bridge differences among employees with vastly different interests and values. We then explore the manner in which diversity might diminish the effectiveness of a procedural justice approach to the exercise of authority. Empirical evidence was generated through analysis of data collected from a mail survey of Asians, Blacks, Latinos, and Whites employed at a public sector organization. We focus on two factors that may disrupt the exercise of authority in diverse work settings: 1) ethnic group differences in the importance placed on procedural justice and in the way procedural justice is defined; and 2) potential intergroup conflicts created by the introduction of ethnicity as an organizing framework for social relations within an organization. Our findings indicate that a procedural justice strategy is somewhat less effective in a diverse context. We discuss the implications of this finding for the viability of organizations and offer some strategies organizations can adopt to ensure the successful coordination of action in the face of competing interests, values, and loyalties introduced by a diverse workforce.

The Theoretical Framework: Procedural Justice and the Exercise of Authority

In their effort to coordinate action, group authorities are sometimes able to generate decisions or policies that subordinates agree with and accept. However, in many instances, it is not possible to generate solutions that accord with the interests and values of all those involved. If people's willingness to voluntarily comply with the directives of an authority depend wholly on whether they agree with or benefit from those directives, then the authority's effectiveness is seriously diminished. The authority's inability to manage internal disagreements about how problems should be resolved would lead to heightened levels of conflicts within the organization.

However, a number of studies have demonstrated that in addition to instrumental concerns about the benefits of authorities' actions, concerns about fair treatment also play an important role in shaping attitudes toward authorities in work organizations. Perceptions that authorities have acted in a fair or an unfair manner are linked to a variety of important attitudes including willingness to accept the authority's decisions (Tyler & Degoey, 1996), organizational commitment (Folger & Konovsky, 1989; Konovsky & Brockner, 1993), and endorsement of workplace policies (Greenberg, 1994). These findings suggest that authorities who are perceived by their subordinates to have acted in a fair way are better able to garner support for their decisions and policies even among those who disagree with the substance of the decision or policy.

Such support empowers authorities to make difficult decisions that benefit the organization as whole but which may not accord with the desires of some of the employees. For example, when managers are charged with evaluating employees for salary increases, they typically have a limited amount of money to distribute among all the employees they supervise. In the interest of advancing organizational goals, managers need to have the discretion to distribute salary increases in the way they feel is most appropriate. If the procedure through which such decisions are made is perceived by the subordinates to be fair, then the manager can act in the interest of the collective without losing the support of the individuals who did not get the salary increases they were expecting or hoping for.

Similar dynamics should be at work in situations in which conflicts arise out of more fundamental disagreements about how business should be conducted. Consider three such issues. Should employees be able to communicate to each other in their native language, or should they have to speak English when at work? To what extent is the workplace obligated to accommodate employees' request to be granted time off to observe ethnic holidays or religious practices? And should the organization make special efforts to recruit and retain members of traditionally underrepresented groups? There are no easy answers to such difficult questions. Inevitably, a position will have to be taken by management—probably one with which not all employees will agree. Regardless of whether each individual or subgroup within the organization agrees with the decision, the crucial issue is the extent to which they are willing to accept the outcome and go along with the decision.

Research on procedural justice developed out of Thibaut and Walker's early work on legal disputes (Thibaut & Walker, 1975). The Thibaut and Walker control model of procedural justice is based on the premise that concerns about the fairness of decision-making procedures stem from instrumental, self-interested motives. For example, when individuals approach a third-party authority (e.g., arbitrator, judge) for help in resolving a dispute, the decision about how to resolve the problem rests in the hands of the authority. Although the disputants have lost decision control in this situation, they retain process control over the presentation of evidence. In a series of experiments, Thibaut and Walker found that procedures that afford "voice" or the opportunity to explain one's case are considered to be more fair than procedures that do not offer such an opportunity because voice is the primary mechanism through which people can influence outcomes when they do not have decision control. According to the Thibaut and Walker model, in the absence of direct control, people seek indirect control over outcomes. This instrumental perspective suggests that concerns about procedural justice arise out of the desire to influence outcomes for personal gain.

Since the early work of Thibaut and Walker, subsequent research has implicated noninstrumental motives as underlying the procedural justice effect (Lind, Kanfer, & Earley, 1990; Tyler, 1987). Lind and Tyler (1988) developed the group-value model of procedural justice to account for such noninstrumental motives. The group-value model was extended to the context of authority relations in the relational model of authority (Tyler & Lind, 1992). It is the relational model and its assumptions that form the basis of our working theoretical framework.

The relational model proposes that three types of concerns are linked to procedural justice judgments: neutrality (the belief that the authority is unbiased and is acting on the basis of facts rather than prejudices), trust in benevolence (the belief that the authority is considering one's needs and concerns), and status recognition (the feeling that one is treated with dignity and respect by the authority). When these relational concerns are satisfied, authorities are viewed as fair, and their decisions and policies are more readily accepted. This is true even when they make decisions that individuals disagree with or do not benefit from. If such justice concerns are not satisfied, authorities are viewed as unfair, and their decisions and policies are often not accepted unless they accord with people's preferences.

According to the relational model, people care about being treated fairly by group authorities because such treatment communicates information about one's status as an important and valued member of the organization. In contrast, unfair treatment communicates the message that one is unimportant or marginal. The relational model draws from social identity theory's premise that people look to groups and the actions of group authorities for information about their self-worth (Tajfel & Turner, 1986). Research provides empirical evidence that fair/unfair treatment affects both people's perceptions of their standing within important reference groups as well as their self-esteem (Koper, Van Knippenberg, Bouhuijs, Vermunt & Wilke, 1993; Smith, Tyler, Huo, Ortiz, & Lind, 1998; Tyler, Daubenmier, Huo, & Smith, 2000; Tyler, Degoey, and Smith, 1996).

The relational model and the control model share the assumption that the acceptance of the decisions and policies of third-party authorities is linked to perceptions of procedural justice. However, the relational model departs from the control model in its explanation of *why* people are motivated to care about procedural fairness. Whereas the control model suggests an instrumental motive, the relational model suggests a social motive. It argues that people want fair treatment because such treatment reflects favorably on their social standing within important reference groups.

The two models also differ in their implications for the management of internal disagreements within organizations and other groups. Because the control model suggests that self-interest is a key motive in social relations, authorities are limited in their ability to bridge differences in values and interests. The allocation of resources and the resolution of conflicts are often a zero-sum game. People do not always end up with the kind of outcomes they want or feel they deserve. In contrast, if people are motivated by relational concerns, then there is a more optimistic outlook for the viability of diverse organizations. Relational affirmations provide a basis for the acceptance of and deference to authorities independent of competing interests.

Empirical tests of the relational model of authority have generated support for the hypothesis that judgments of neutrality, trust in benevolence, and status recognition are linked to judgments of procedural justice (Tyler, 1994). Such relational judgments are also linked to general evaluations of authorities and to the willingness to voluntarily accept the decisions the authorities make or the policies they adopt (see Chapter 8 in Tyler, Boeckmann, Smith, & Huo, 1997, for a review of relevant studies). However, much of that research has overlooked the possible moderating effects introduced by ethnic, racial, and cultural diversity. The validity of our claim that procedural justice can bridge differences in interests and values among members of a diverse work organization depends on the extent to which the factors associated with diversity disrupt the psychological processes proposed in the relational model.

We examine the influence of diversity on the relational underpinnings of procedural justice from two perspectives. The first focuses on the existence of subgroups within an organization. To what extent do people from different backgrounds agree that procedural justice is an important aspect of authority relations, and do they agree about which elements distinguish fair treatment from unfair treatment?

The second perspective focuses on changes in the social dynamics within diverse organizations. As more ethnic minorities join the workplace, ethnic group membership may take on greater importance as a form of self-categorization. When ethnic boundaries become an important basis for defining social relations, then the potential for intergroup conflicts rises. For our purposes, we examine the extent to which the group context affects the relational processes we describe. To do so, we contrast intragroup contexts (i.e., situations in which the authority and subordinate share the same ethnicity) with intergroup contexts (i.e., situations in which the authority and subordinate are from different ethnic backgrounds).

Beliefs and Values about Procedural Justice

Researchers have suggested that cultural differences in values and beliefs between citizens of different nations or among members of different ethnic groups within a nation may play an important role in shaping justice-related attitudes and behaviors (Feather, 1994; James, 1993; Leung, 1988;

Lind, Tyler & Huo, 1997). This line of thought suggests that ethnicity should influence perceptions of procedures and attitudes about procedural justice. Indeed, studies that focus on individual differences in value orientations find that justice-related values shape judgments of the fairness of social policies and political figures (Peterson, 1994; Rasinski, 1987; Tetlock & Mitchell, 1993). Moreover, cross-cultural studies of attitudes about conflict-resolution procedures find that culture influences perceptions of the various attributes of different procedures (Leung, 1987; Leung & Lind, 1986).

Although the studies we just described suggest that ethnicity and culture should exert an important influence on the hypothesized procedural mechanisms, findings from several of our own recent studies indicate that such influence may be limited. In a study of Asian, Black, Latino, and White college students, we explored attitudes about interpersonal disputes (Lind, Huo, & Tyler, 1994). When asked to evaluate how they would resolve a hypothetical dispute, respondents across all ethnic groups expressed general agreement about the kind of procedures through which they want their disputes to be resolved. Moreover, in examining the antecedents of affective reactions to real disputes, we found that the most important factor across all ethnic groups was procedural justice.

Tyler (1988) reported the findings of a study in which a sample of Black and White residents of Chicago were interviewed about their experiences with the local police and courts. The study examined the effect of race on procedural concerns. No race effects were found in respondents' judgments about what makes a procedure fair. Moreover, the study found that other respondent characteristics such as gender and political ideology also had little to do with the manner in which individuals judged how they were treated by authorities.

A similar conclusion can be drawn from studies reported in Tyler (1994). A series of three studies explored the extent to which procedural justice can bridge disagreements about national-level social policy decisions (i.e., cutting federal funding for hospitals that perform abortions, federal aid for a program that provides job training to African Americans). In all of the studies, the United States Congress was the decision maker and the authority under evaluation. The findings suggest that: (1) process concerns shaped general support for Congress and (2) they influenced the willingness to accept the policies Congress adopted. Race, gender, income, and education had no direct influence on assessments of the legitimacy of Congress. Nor did such demographic variables interact with either procedural elements or outcome favorability to determine acceptance of Congress as a national decision-making body.

It appears that people from different ethnic groups within the United States concur that fair treatment is an important component of their experiences with group authorities. Moreover, people agree about what makes a procedure fair or unfair. These findings provide an optimistic outlook for relying on a procedural justice strategy to bridge the kinds of differences in interests and values that are likely to arise in diverse organizations.

In this chapter we present the results from a study we designed to directly test the effectiveness of a procedural justice strategy for bridging differences in a diverse work environment. In the organization from which we drew our respondents, diversity is a salient feature of the environment in several respects. First, the employees in the organization represent a wide range of ethnic groups including Asians, Blacks, Latinos, and Whites. Second, they belong to informal employee associations that are ethnically based. Because of the unique environment in which these individuals work, we speculate that they are likely to identify with their ethnic group and to hold values and beliefs that are consistent with their ethnic background. Hence, the characteristics of this sample should provide a strong test for the procedural justice approach.

In the study, we focus on two possible ways in which values and beliefs arising out of different cultural experiences may affect the relationship between perceptions of procedural justice and attitudes toward organizational authorities. One issue is whether individuals from all ethnic groups evaluate their experiences by judging the fairness of the procedures they have experienced. The viability of organizations will be enhanced to the extent that procedural justice is the primary antecedent of the acceptance of authorities and their directives for members of all ethnic groups. If, on the other hand, the psychology of authority relations differs across different groups, then procedural justice cannot be viewed as a general strategy for managing conflict within organizations. In this scenario, it will be necessary to qualify the general procedural justice argument to take into account context issues such as the background of the people involved when formulating strategies for the management of internal conflicts within diverse organizations.

A second issue involves the extent to which people of varying ethnic backgrounds define the meaning of procedural justice in a similar way. It might be that people agree that procedures ought to be fair but differ in their definitions of fairness. Again, such differences would pose problems for authorities. All parties to a dispute may be willing to defer to the judgments of an authority who acts fairly but disagree about the information they use to form these judgments.

Ethnicity as Social Category

In addition to possible differences in values and beliefs, there is a second way in which diversity may affect the viability of organizations. The introduction of ethnicity as a basis of social categorization may change the way in which members of the same organization respond to each other. Research on group processes suggests that the perception of differences brought about by a salient social attribute such as ethnicity shapes the resulting group dynamics in fundamental ways (Kramer, 1991). The changes are linked to the way people categorize others in their social world. Social categorization processes can lead to increased escalation of conflicts among group members (Brewer & Kramer, 1986; Kramer & Brewer, 1984).

The processes outlined are linked to the manner in which people define themselves via important reference groups. In an organization, everyone may think of themselves as members of an overarching social category. For example, employees may think of themselves as members of the "Microsoft family." Or group members may think of themselves as members of smaller units within the organization (e.g., the marketing department). These subgroup categorizations change the dynamics of interactions by creating an intergroup context within the organizational structure (i.e., marketing vs. human resources).

Ethnic diversity provides another type of subgroup framework that may serve as the basis for categorization. An example is provided by the structure of the organization that is the focus of our study. Instead of organizing themselves by traditional subgroups (i.e., employees and managers), the public sector employees we studied were organized into ethnic employee associations. Each association is composed of both employees and managers who share a common ethnic group membership. Our concern is with the influence of such subgroup framing on the dynamics of authority relations.

In the study, we compare respondents who report an interaction with an authority who shares their ethnicity with respondents who report an interaction with an authority from a different ethnic background. Our attention to social categorization processes stems from the relational model of authority (Tyler & Lind, 1992), which suggests that the social context of an interaction should influence the basis of reactions to authorities. The central premise of the relational model is that people look to their interactions with authorities for relational information about their standing within important reference groups. Fair treatment characterized by neutrality, benevolence, and treatment with dignity and respect signals legitimacy and inclusion within a group, whereas unfair treatment characterized by favoritism, mistrust, and treatment with a lack of respect signals marginalization and exclusion. Because outgroup authorities are by definition outside of the individual's reference group, their actions would carry less of the social identity information that people seek in interactions with ingroup authorities. Hence, whether the individual views the authority as an ingroup representative or as an outsider has important implications for how they respond to that authority and the decisions he or she makes.

The question we address is the extent to which social categorization moderates the hypothesized relational processes such that the link between procedural justice judgments and support for authorities and their actions should be stronger when the authority shares one's ethnicity and weaker when the authority is from a different ethnic background. One can make the argument that in addition to fair treatment, authorities can signal inclusion by handing out positive outcomes and tangible resources. However, research suggests that feelings of inclusion are largely distinct from outcome effects (Smith, Tyler, Huo, Ortiz, & Lind, 1998).

There are studies that suggest that the influence of procedural fairness on reactions to others and to organizations varies as a function of the nature of the outcome (Brockner & Wiesenfeld, 1996; Lind & Tyler, 1988; van den Bos, Lind, Vermunt, & Wilke, 1997). This line of thought suggests that procedural justice has the greatest influence when outcomes are unfair or bad and when social comparison information about other people's outcomes is available. Such suggestions are interesting and make significant contributions to the understanding of organizational justice. However, we limit our focus to the interaction of social categorization with process judgments and with outcome judgments. We do so because the relational model predicts that perceptions of group boundaries would change the relative weight assigned to procedural considerations, but it does not predict the interaction between process and outcome judgments.

The Data: Survey of Employees at an Ethnically Diverse Organization

The ideas we have outlined are tested using a survey dataset based on responses to a written survey administered to staff employees at a large public university. We contacted ethnicity-based employee associations on campus for their assistance in recruiting potential respondents. The executive committee of each association agreed to provide us with a mailing list of their membership. Questionnaires were mailed to all members included on the mailing list. The questionnaire was written in English. An optional Spanish version of the questionnaire was also provided. We enlisted the help of three ethnicity-based associations including an Asian American employee association, a Black employee association, and a Chicano and Latino employee association. We also recruited respondents from a nonethnicity-based association in an effort to recruit White respondents.

Each respondent was asked to describe a recent encounter with his or her work supervisor. They were asked to think about the last time they went to their supervisor for help in resolving a work-related problem, conflict, or disagreement about an issue that mattered to them. Respondents indicated that they spoke to their supervisor about a number of issues, including "making decisions or settling disagreements about how work should be done" (mentioned by 40% of the respondents), "discussing issues of pay, promotion, work hours, or similar issues" (27%), "getting help in resolving a dispute with a customer, a co-worker, or with the supervisor" (39%), and "other issues and problems" (34%).

Respondents were asked to report their own ethnicity based on 14 categories used in the United States Census. They were also asked to indicate their supervisor's racial or ethnic background. A total of 305 employees returned completed questionnaires including 117 Asians, 45 Blacks, 58 Latinos, 56 Whites, 25 multiple-ethnic-heritage individuals, and four respondents who did not indicate their ethnic background. Women represented the large majority of respondents (74%).

The response rate for the study is 29%. Although the response rate is reasonable for a mailed questionnaire, it is low in absolute terms. Nevertheless, we believe that the dataset we developed has some desirable qualities. First, it is likely that individuals who join an ethnicity-based employee association are more likely to identify with their ethnic group and to hold interests and values that are more consistent with others in their ethnic group. Compared to White respondents ($M = 2.28$, $SD = .90$), the minority respondents reported greater identification with their ethnic group ($M = 1.53$, $SD = .51$) on a scale ranging from 1 ("agree strongly") to 4 ("disagree strongly"), $t(261) = 9.23$, $p < .01$. Second, it is likely that the types of interactions reported by our respondents are negative experiences because such experiences are more likely to be recalled. The data confirm that a large proportion of respondents indicated that the interaction with their supervisor had left them frustrated (72%), irritated (64%), and angry (60%). If concerns about the fairness of the decision-making process shape reactions to these negative experiences, then we can be more confident that this mechanism can be effective in managing serious conflicts.

The diversity of the sample provided us with the opportunity to study interactions among individuals with different values and interests. It also provides us with the opportunity to compare two types of interactions: one between individuals from different ethnic backgrounds and one between individuals from the same ethnic background. With the introduction of ethnicity as a basis on which subgroup boundaries are drawn, we can compare intragroup interactions with intergroup interactions and test the validity of the hypothesis that the former can be characterized as more relational than the latter.

Does Ethnicity Matter?

The first issue we explore in our analysis of the dataset is the extent to which people from different ethnic groups share a similar psychology when reacting to their experiences with organizational authorities. Two questions are addressed: 1) whether members of different ethnic groups place equal importance on procedural justice and 2) whether they use similar criteria to form procedural justice judgments.

We begin by examining across ethnic groups the reactions of respondents to the decision their supervisor made about how to handle the problem or how to resolve the conflict that they reported in the questionnaire. The analysis focuses on three general antecedents of reactions to authorities and the decisions they made: outcome favorability, distributive fairness, and procedural fairness. Outcome favorability refers to the instrumental judgment that the decision serves one's self-interest. Distributive fairness refers to the fairness of the outcome of the decision. Procedural fairness refers to the fairness of the decision-making process. Ratings of respondents' willingness to accept the decisions made by their supervisor were regressed on judgments of outcome favorability, distributive fairness, and procedural fairness. A similar analysis was conducted on ratings of support for the authority. The exact wordings for the items used to measure these constructs can be found in the appendix to this chapter.

Table 7.1 presents the results of the analysis. Two patterns should be noted. First, voluntary decision acceptance and support for authority have different antecedents. The instrumental motive to maximize personal gain is an important antecedent of decision acceptance but is not related to support for the supervisor. In contrast, perception of distributive fairness is related to support for authority but not to decision acceptance. Interestingly, perception of fair treatment is related to both decision acceptance and support for authority. Procedural justice appears to be a factor people seriously considered when evaluating their supervisors.

Table 7.1. Influence of Ethnicity on the Importance
of Procedural Justice.

	Voluntary Decision Acceptance		Support for Authority	
Outcome Favorability (A)	.29**	.27	.05	.21
Distributive Fairness (B)	.13	.11	−.20*a	−.41
Procedural Fairness (C)	.49**	.45**	.86**	.89**
Asian		−.03		.09
Asian * A		.03		−.10
Asian * B		.09		.20
Asian * C		−.03		−.03
Black		.04		.04
Black * A		.00		−.16
Black * B		.00		.18
Black * C		.06		−.11
Latino		−.05		.07
Latino * A		.02		−.01
Latino * B		−.05		−.01
Latino * C		.05		.07
R-squared	72%	73%	55%	57%

Note: Entries are beta weights for an equation in which all terms are entered simultaneously. Dummy codes for ethnicity compare each minority group with Whites.

aThe zero-order correlation between distributive fairness and support for authority is positive (i.e., perception of distributive fairness is associated with greater support). [This applies *only* to the "−.20*" coefficient. It does *not* apply to any other negative coefficients.]

*$p < .05$.

**$p < .01$.

Second, it is important to note that the weight associated with outcome favorability, distributive fairness, and procedural fairness in the two regression equations does not differ significantly across ethnic groups. Interaction terms testing whether ethnicity influenced the importance of outcome favorability, distributive fairness, and procedural fairness in shaping judgment of decision acceptance and support for authority were created and entered into regression equations along with the main effects of ethnicity. The results indicate that no interaction terms were statistically significant. Moreover, there were no direct effects of ethnicity. These findings suggest that the Asians, Blacks, Latinos, and Whites in our sample share a similar psychology of authority relations. What matters to our respondents, regardless of their ethnic background, is how fairly their supervisors treat them in the process of discussing and resolving problems that arise at work.

The second issue relevant to the influence of ethnicity is the extent to which people from different ethnic groups agree on how they define what is procedurally fair. Even if people agree that procedural justice is an important concern in forming judgments about authorities, its utility as a mechanism for bridging differences would be limited if people disagree about what is or is not fair. A further qualification is needed. A procedural strategy will help manage internal conflicts to the extent that concerns about fair treatment are driven by the relational motive to seek understanding about one's social status within the organization. If, on the other hand, concern about procedural fairness is simply a mask for the more instrumental motive of serving one's self-interest, then a procedural strategy would fail as a mechanism for preserving the viability of organizations.

An analysis was conducted to examine the influence of ethnicity on how people define procedural justice. Again we considered respondents who identified themselves as members of the following ethnic groups: Asian, Black, Latino, and White. We asked all respondents to evaluate their experience with their work supervisor on five dimensions: outcome favorability, voice, neutrality, trust in the benevolence of the authority, and status recognition. Outcome favorability represents an instrumental judgment of gain and loss. In contrast, the other four dimensions—voice, neutrality, trust, and status recognition—are procedural elements that represent a relational motive. Respondents' evaluations of how fairly they were treated by their supervisors were regressed on their ratings on these five dimensions along with ethnicity main effects and ethnicity interaction terms.

Table 7.2 shows that both instrumental and relational motives underlie judgments of procedural fairness. In particular, trustworthiness and status recognition are the primary factors that define procedural fairness, with outcome favorability also showing an important influence. Again, what is striking is the absence of any significant interaction effects. It appears that across the different ethnic groups, people generally share a similar conception of the elements of fair treatment.

Table 7.2 also shows the results of analysis in which the relative contributions of instrumental and relational factors in explaining variance in decision acceptance and support for authority were examined. Again, instrumental concerns seem to be an important factor in explaining decision acceptance but not support for authority. In contrast, relational concerns

Table 7.2. Influence of Ethnicity on the Antecedents of Procedural Justice and Reactions to Authority.

	Procedural Justice		Voluntary Decision Acceptance		Support for Authority	
Outcome Favorability (A)	.27**	.21*	.42**	.12	−.04	.05
Voice (B)	.05	−.05	.11*	.46**	.01	.01
Neutrality (C)	.12**	.13	.04	−.24	.23**	.19
Trustworthiness (D)	.33**	.40**	.27**	.43**	.36**	.17
Status Recognition (E)	.29**	.37**	.14**	.24	.33**	.46**
Asian		−.01		−.14**		.07
Asian * A		.05		.17		.02
Asian * B		.14		−.07		−.09
Asian * C		−.07		.23		.03
Asian * D		−.08		−.24*		.11
Asian * E		−.07		−.10		.00
Black		.01		−.02		.02
Black * A		.03		.17*		−.12
Black * B		.04		−.22**		−.02
Black * C		.05		.11		.00
Black * D		−.10		−.04		.13
Black * E		−.01		−.06		−.10
Latino		.06		−.07		.10
Latino * A		.00		.15		−.07
Latino * B		.06		−.21*		.03
Latino * C		.04		.09		−.02
Latino * D		.00		.04		.18
Latino * E		−.08		−.09		−.06
R-squared	84%	86%	72%	75%	66%	69%

Note: Entries are beta weights for an equation in which all terms are entered simultaneously. Dummy codes for ethnicity compare each minority group with Whites.
*$p < .05$.
**$p < .01$.

are related to both types of judgments. What is more interesting is that there appears to be considerable consensus among the different ethnic groups in terms of the weight assigned to the various antecedents of decision acceptance and support for authority. Only 4 of 30 interaction terms involving ethnicity (13%) were significant. All of the significant interaction terms involved decision acceptance. These results indicate that the antecedents of decision acceptance differ somewhat for each of the three minority groups compared to Whites.

Additional analyses examined how the various ethnic groups differed in the weight they placed on the antecedents of decision acceptance. Compared to Whites, Asians were less concerned about the trustworthiness of the supervisor; Blacks were more concerned about getting a favorable outcome but less concerned about having an opportunity to voice their concerns; and similar to Blacks, Latinos were less concerned about voice. There was also one direct effect of ethnicity. Compared to Whites, Asians were more willing to accept the decision their supervisor made.

In summary, the results of the analysis of this multiethnic sample of employees suggests that there is a striking consensus both that procedural justice is important and that it is defined in a relational manner. Hence, the first concern we raised about the effects of diversity—that there would be variations across ethnic groups in terms of the value placed on fair treatment and in the criteria used to define what is or is not fair is largely unsupported in our sample. Although some differences are found, the most robust finding is that the members of different ethnic groups are more alike than different in their reactions to authorities who make decisions that affect how they do their work. All in all, the preceding analyses suggest an optimistic outlook for the use of a procedural justice strategy in maintaining the viability of diverse work organizations.

Does the Ethnicity Match between Employee and Supervisor Matter?

Our analysis in the previous section treats diversity as a property of the employee. However, diversity also involves ethnicity match or mismatch between the employee and the supervisor. It is to this latter issue that we now turn our attention. Work force diversity brings not only a diversity of perspectives and beliefs but also introduces new situations in which employees and supervisors of different backgrounds and loyalties come into contact with each other. In this section, we focus on comparing two types of situations: one in which the employee and the supervisor are from the same ethnic group and one in which they are from different ethnic groups. The relational model predicts that procedural concerns would be more relevant in interactions with a same-ethnicity authority (ingroup context) and would be less important in interactions with a different-ethnicity authority (intergroup context).

Our first step in testing this social-categorization-based hypothesis was to conduct regression analyses to predict decision acceptance and support of authority. Interaction terms were created to examine whether the ethnicity match (e.g., Latino employee interacting with Latino supervisor) or mismatch (e.g., Latino employee interacting with White supervisor) of the respondents and their supervisors moderated the relative weight associated with each of three judgments: outcome favorability, distributive fairness, and procedural fairness. The results of the regression analyses presented in Table 7.3 indicate that none of the six possible interactions was significant. Feelings that one has been treated fairly by an authority are closely linked to willingness to support that authority and his or her decision regardless of whether the two parties share a common ethnic group membership.

These findings suggest that social categorization does not influence the importance people attach to procedural justice. However, it is possible that social categorization influences the factors that underlie judgments of procedural justice such that people base their judgments more heavily on instrumental concerns when dealing with an outgroup authority and are more relational when dealing with an ingroup authority. To explore this

Table 7.3. Effect of Ethnicity Match vs. Mismatch on the Importance of Procedural Justice.

	Voluntary Decision Acceptance	Support for Authority
Outcome Favorability (A)	.00	−.36
Distributive Fairness (B)	.23	−.38
Procedural Fairness (C)	.49*	.83**
Ethnicity Match/Mismatch	.02	.11*
Match/Mismatch * A	.32	.41
Match/Mismatch * B	−.12	.23
Match/Mismatch * C	−.01	−.01
Asian	−.05	.02
Black	.03	−.02
Latino	−.06	−.01
R-squared	73%	55%

Note: Entries are beta weights for an equation in which all terms are entered simultaneously. Dummy codes for ethnicity compare each minority group with Whites.

$*p < .05.$

$**p < .01.$

possibility, we conducted regression analysis to test whether the relative contributions of an instrumental motive (i.e., outcome favorability) and a relational motive (i.e., voice, neutrality, trustworthiness, and status recognition; for ease of analysis, items were combined to form one scale, alpha = .94) in shaping procedural fairness judgments differ depending on the ethnicity match or mismatch of the employee and his or her supervisor.

The results are presented in Table 7.4. The findings indicate that procedural justice is defined both relationally and instrumentally. Moreover, the analysis generated a significant interaction between the social categorization variable (i.e., ethnicity match or mismatch) and relational judgments. Further analysis shows that as predicted, individuals were more relational when involved in an interaction with a supervisor from the same ethnic group than when they dealt with a supervisor from a different ethnic group.

These findings suggest that the way in which procedural fairness is defined is different depending on whether the individual is dealing with an ingroup or with an outgroup supervisor. Additional analysis examined whether social categorization exerts a similar influence on decision acceptance and support for authority. Table 7.4 shows that both relational and

Table 7.4. Effect of Ethnicity Match vs. Mismatch on the Antecedents of Procedural Justice and Reactions to Authority.

	Procedural Justice		Voluntary Decision Acceptance		Support for Authority	
Instrumental Judgments (A)	.25**	.08	.43**	.03	−.07	−.39*a
Relational Judgments (B)	.72**	.99**	.48**	.86**	.86**	.52**
Ethnicity Match/Mismatch		−.03		−.01		.09*
Match/Mismatch * A		.18		.43*		.32
Match/Mismatch * B		−.28*		−.40*		.34
Asian		.00		−.07		−.01
Black		.01		.03		−.05
Latino		.06		−.03		.02
R-squared	84%	85%	71%	73%	66%	68%

Note: Entries are beta weights for an equation in which all terms are entered simultaneously. Dummy codes for ethnicity compare each minority group with Whites.
aThe zero-order correlation between instrumental judgments and support for authority is positive (i.e., favorable outcome is associated with greater support).
*p < .05.
**p < .01.

instrumental judgments shaped voluntary decision acceptance. Moreover, both the interaction between the social categorization variable and instrumental judgments and the interaction between the social categorization variable and relational judgments were significant. Further analysis suggests that employees were less concerned with instrumental matters in same ethnicity interactions than in cross-ethnic interactions. In contrast, they were more concerned with relational matters in same-ethnicity interactions than in cross-ethnic interactions. What these findings suggest is not that relational factors are unimportant in the intergroup context but that the influence of relational judgments in shaping decision acceptance diminishes somewhat when the employee and his or her supervisor are from different ethnic groups.

Table 7.4 also presents the results of analysis involving support for the supervisor. Although the pattern of findings is similar to that found for decision acceptance, there are some notable differences. Again, relational judgments were important in shaping support for authority. However, neither of the interaction terms were significant. Support for authorities appears to be shaped primarily by relational concerns regardless of whether the authority involved was from the same ethnic group as the respondent or from a different ethnic group. In addition, there was a significant main effect for group context such that support for the authority was greater in the ethnicity match situation than in the ethnicity mismatch situation.

The empirical evidence supports the idea that relational concerns are attenuated when the authority represents a salient outgroup (i.e., an ethnic group different from one's own). Although relational considerations are important in shaping procedural fairness judgments, voluntary decision acceptance, and attitudes consistent with support for authority, the relative weight placed on such concerns changes depending on whether the interaction occurred within the context of shared group membership (employee and supervisor are from same ethnic background) or not (employee and supervisor are from different ethnic backgrounds). The results indicate that a procedural strategy for bridging differences is most effective in same-ethnicity interactions and becomes less so in cross-ethnic interactions. This finding suggests an important limitation of using a procedural justice strategy to bridge differences that occur within an ethnically diverse organization. As the work force becomes more diverse, the likelihood of cross-ethnic interactions within an organization will increase substantially. Accordingly, managers' ability to resolve conflicts may be somewhat diminished when they deal with subordinates who do not share their ethnicity.

Implications for the Management of Diversity in Organizations

Our analysis presents a mixed outlook for the viability of diverse organizations. On the one hand, the values, beliefs, and perspectives that individuals from different ethnic groups are assumed to hold do not seem to influence the basis of reactions to interactions with their work supervisors. Regardless of their self-reported ethnic group affiliation, the respondents in our study place importance on procedural fairness in addition to their concerns about distributive fairness and outcome favorability. Moreover, they define procedural fairness in primarily relational terms. It appears that our respondents are driven not so much by self-interest as they are by the desire to be connected to important groups and to be acknowledged as a valued member of those groups.

Further analyses show that diversity can hinder the use of a procedural justice strategy by introducing ethnicity as a basis for social categorization. In a diverse organization such as the one we studied, ethnicity is one basis upon which subgroup boundaries are drawn. The fact that our respondents were recruited from informal work associations that are organized by ethnic group membership is a case in point. In such a situation, interactions between two people of the same ethnicity are likely to be viewed as an intragroup exchange. In contrast, interactions between two people of different ethnic backgrounds are likely to be viewed as an intergroup exchange. What we have found is that the way in which people define procedural fairness is moderated by the ethnicity of the supervisor they interact with. The pattern of findings indicates that procedural fairness is defined more relationally when the individual and his or her supervisor are from the same ethnic group than when they are from different ethnic groups. When contrasting the relative importance of relational and instrumental concerns in predicting voluntary decision acceptance, a similar moderating effect of social categorization was also found.

The general finding that social categorization moderates the importance of relational concerns in shaping reactions to work supervisors suggests a potential problem for the viability of diverse work organizations. When employees report to supervisors who share their ethnic background, the processes hypothesized by the relational model of authority are at work. In this situation, employees defer to the judgments of their supervisors when they perceive that they have been treated fairly. In contrast, when employees report to supervisors who are from different ethnic backgrounds, relational concerns diminish in importance. In this situation, supervisors' ability to elicit cooperation and support from their employees is threatened when they are unable to generate decisions that are favorable or instrumentally beneficial to the employee.

A closer examination of the incidents reported provides some interesting insights about the dynamics of ethnic relations in diverse work organizations. Table 7.5 shows that while the majority of White respondents reported an interaction with a White supervisor, the large majority of Asians, Blacks, and Latinos reported interactions with a supervisor who did not share their ethnic background. Furthermore, most of the mismatched minorities reported interactions with White supervisors and not with supervisors from another ethnic minority group (122 out of 172 cases). Even though our sample is drawn from an ethnically diverse organization, it appears that most of our minority respondents report to White supervisors.

This pattern of minority employees reporting to White managers is consistent with larger societal trends. Although there is a rapid movement of minorities into the workforce, it appears, at least in the organization we studied, that few have made it up the ranks into supervisory or managerial positions. Our findings suggest that the scarcity of minorities in supervisory positions may have negative consequences for the management of internal conflicts within diverse organizations. In organizations such as the one we studied, ethnicity is an important source of social identification for employees. As such, ethnicity also serves as a dividing line that defines subgroups of employees within one organization. And, although ethnicity is a socially constructed concept (Betancourt & Lopez, 1993), it is also typically directly observable and a means through which people define who they are. To the extent that minorities view White supervisors as

Table 7.5. Frequencies of Matched vs. Mismatched
Ethnicity Interactions.

	CORRESPONDENCE OF SUPERVISOR-EMPLOYEE ETHNICITY	
	Matched	*Mismatched*
Asians	18	87
Blacks	10	38
Latinos	10	47
Whites	46	9

Note: Entries indicate the number of matched or mismatched interactions within each ethnic group.

being part of an outgroup, the ability of these authorities to bridge differences and conflicts would be diminished.

What Can Organizations Do to Cope with Social Categorization Effects?

What can organizations do to address the problem that we have identified? Here we present some general suggestions for actions that organizations can consider taking in their efforts to deal with the effects of ethnicity-based subgroup categorization.

ADVANCEMENT OF MINORITIES INTO MANAGERIAL POSITIONS Our analysis suggests that, should ethnicity retain its importance as an organizing framework in businesses as it has historically in American society, then the issue of underrepresentation of minorities in positions of power is a problem that deserves serious scrutiny. The findings from our study suggest that in some situations, a minority manager may have a distinct advantage over a White manager. Consider the situation in California, where Latinos are predicted to become the largest ethnic group in the state (California Department of Finance, 1993). If individuals of White European descent continue to dominate the upper echelon of power in organizations while minorities, Latinos in particular, form the core of the labor force, then the exercise of authority would be diminished and the viability of organizations would be threatened.

There are multiple arguments in favor of the introduction of diversity into organizations. Diversity of perspectives may lead to innovations, and it also places businesses in an advantageous position to compete in an increasingly global economy. Our findings suggest that we need to think carefully about the roles that members of minority and majority groups play within organizations. If an organization is diverse but minorities are relegated to subordinate positions, then managers in that organization will find it difficult to resolve problems that arise in the workplace and to achieve organizational goals that require coordination and cooperation. Efforts to advance a greater number of minorities into supervisory and managerial positions could provide organizations with the flexibility they need to effectively manage a workforce of individuals from varying backgrounds in an environment where ethnicity has become an important organizing principle for social relations.

DEVELOPMENT OF SUPERORDINATE IDENTITY Another viable route for reducing the negative impact of social categorization is suggested in our earlier research on levels of social identification. In Huo, Smith, Tyler, and Lind (1996), we used a subset of the dataset presented in this chapter to look at how different patterns of social identifications influence the way people respond to outgroup (i.e., different ethnicity) supervisors. We found that individuals who are highly identified with the organization are more inclined to view interactions with an outgroup authority relationally than are individuals who are less identified with the organization. Hence, to the extent that individuals can be primed or motivated to adopt strong identification with the organization, the problems we described in this chapter as occurring in cross-ethnic interactions would be minimized.

Our argument flows from the idea that ingroup and outgroup distinctions are subjective in nature and as such can be reframed. According to social categorization theory (Turner, Hogg, Oakes, Reicher, & Wetherell, 1987), people simultaneously belong to many groups, and at any one point in time, some group membership may be more salient than others. This logic is consistent with other research that points to the importance of a sense of common group membership in promoting more positive intergroup attitudes (Gaertner, Mann, Murrell, & Dovidio, 1989; Gaertner, Rust, Dovidio, Bachman, & Anastasio, 1994) and in encouraging cooperative behavior in social dilemma situations (Brewer & Kramer, 1986).

Because of the importance of superordinate identification in facilitating a reliance on the relational aspects of the process, an interesting question for future research is how people become more or less identified with and attached to an organization, group, or society. We suggest at least two avenues through which superordinate identification is developed. The first is fair treatment by authorities. As we have suggested earlier, such treatment sends a signal of inclusion. In contrast, consistent and repeated unfair treatment sends a message of marginalization (Huo, 1999; Lind, Kray, & Thompson, 1998). Over time, individuals who experience injustice or perceive that others like them are victims of systematic discrimination may withdraw from the group. Relational evaluations of group authorities will carry less weight for individuals who feel excluded. As a consequence, they may focus more on short-term, instrumental gains.

The second is socialization. To the extent that new members to an organization or new immigrants to a nation are given the opportunity to understand and learn the prevailing values and norms, they would be assimilated into the new culture and develop a healthy sense of superordinate identification. The education system, for example, has served as the primary institution through which generations of Americans have become acculturated.

We have suggested two approaches to deal with the problem resulting from cross-ethnic authority-subordinate relations: 1) moving more minorities into supervisory positions; 2) building superordinate identification through either fair treatment or socialization. Although these approaches provide hope for maintaining the viability of diverse organizations, there are limitations associated with each. The hiring or promotion of minorities into supervisory positions will take time and may not be a realistic quick fix. Building identification with and loyalty to the organization through sincere efforts to develop relationships based on trust and respect may be difficult given the perception among traditionally disadvantaged groups that discrimination and bias are prevalent in organizations and in society (Crocker, Luhtanen, Broadnax, & Blaine, 1999; Davidson & Friedman, 1998).

Most problematic, however, are the problems that are associated with building superordinate identification through socialization. Efforts to build organizational loyalty and commitment through activities such as retreats, workshops, and holiday parties are aimed at creating a sense of unity and positive feelings about the workplace. Such efforts when coupled with the equitable distribution of collectively shared benefits and burdens enhance the state of social relations within an organization. However, the problem of "false consciousness" (Cohen, 1985; Lind & Tyler, 1988; Jost, 1995) or "hollow justice" (Greenberg, 1990) arises when authorities take advantage of the benefits of strong identification with the organization without ensuring the fair distribution of outcomes among their subordinates.

The potential misuse of procedural justice is particularly serious when members of traditionally disadvantaged groups are involved. Research on women and their perceptions of gender inequality at the workplace has shown that although most women recognize the disadvantage that women as a group experience, they deny their own cases of personal discrimination (Crosby, 1984). Similarly, research on the phenomenon of tokenism shows that members of disadvantaged groups are unwilling to engage in collective protest even when there is no real possibility that they would be accepted into an advantaged group (Wright, Taylor, & Moghaddam, 1990). The concern in both situations is that members of disadvantaged groups do not take action to correct distributive injustices. A procedural emphasis in evaluations of group authorities contributes to this problem to the extent that it supports the functioning of a system in which some groups are worse off materially than others by virtue of their subgroup membership. Although procedural justice can enhance the effective exercise of authority and the viability of organizations, the opportunity for misuse of such power is ever present. Hence, our enthusiasm for procedural justice and its beneficial consequences for organizational dynamics must be tempered with the knowledge that it can also produce some unintended, adverse effects.

Why Do Social Categorization Effects Occur?

Given the significance of the social categorization effects for the viability of diverse organizations, an important avenue for future research is to explore in detail the source of such effects. At this point, we offer our thoughts on three possible explanations for the observed categorization effect: 1) social identity investment; 2) ambiguity in interpretation; and 3) differing expectations. We offer these three tentative explanations for the observed categorization effects in the hope that they will stimulate future research that tests their validity.

One possible explanation for the observed categorization effect is that in interactions that cross group boundaries, the individual is less invested in the social identity information that can be gleaned from observing the actions of authorities. Support for this explanation can be found in a series of recent studies (Koper et al., 1993, Smith et al., 1998; Tyler et al., 1997). These studies provide evidence that our perceptions of how an ingroup authority treats us (fairly/unfairly) shape our self-esteem and feelings of whether we are respected. In contrast, how an outgroup authority treats us does not have similar effects on our self-concept.

A second explanation suggests that procedural justice concerns diminish in cross-ethnic interactions because of the ambiguity introduced in that particular situation. When dealing with an outgroup authority, we may not know which norms are in place and do not know how to interpret the behavior of outgroup authorities. When we are unsure about how to infer the motives of authorities, we may fall back on more concrete information, such as the extent to which we receive favorable outcomes. Imagine the situation when a foreigner is sent to the United States to help develop a joint venture project. The visitor arrives at work the first day and finds that his supervisor is particularly friendly—more so than would be appropriate in his home country. How should he interpret the actions of the friendly manager? Does the manager want to make him feel at ease? Or is the manager stepping beyond the bounds of propriety due to some sinister motive? This ambiguity or cultural misunderstanding explanation for the social categorization effect observed in the dataset suggests that future research should examine whether people interpret the same actions differently depending on the social context of the situation.

A third explanation is based on the assumption that we have different expectations for ingroup and outgroup authorities. In particular, although we may expect fair treatment from an ingroup authority, we do not have similar expectations for outgroup authorities. This explanation is consistent with recent research indicating that members of traditionally disadvantaged groups (e.g., African Americans) tend to mistrust governmental authorities (Crocker, Luhtanen, Broadnax, & Blaine, 1999) and that they are less responsive to actions taken to explain negative events in work organizations (Davidson & Friedman, 1998). If individuals do not expect to be treated fairly, then they may rely more heavily on instrumental considerations for information about the quality of their relationship with group authorities.

Summary and Conclusion

We began the chapter by suggesting that procedural justice can bridge differences in interests and values and thereby allow authorities to effectively manage internal conflicts in work organizations that are ethnically and culturally diverse. We found that procedural justice is a viable strategy for managing a diverse workforce. People from different ethnic groups appear to share the belief that procedural fairness is an important aspect of interactions with authorities. Moreover, they generally agree about the elements that distinguish fair from unfair treatment. Diversity of the workforce, in and of itself, does not appear to diminish the viability of organizations.

However, we also found that the social dynamics created by diversity do affect how people respond to authorities. When the authority and his or her subordinate are from different ethnic groups, the procedural mechanisms we described are weakened. In this situation, the authority's ability to bridge differences and manage conflicts is correspondingly reduced. We suggested some possible ways for dealing with the problems that arise in organizations where ethnicity has become an important basis for social division. To the extent that these suggestions prove to be useful, authorities in diverse work organizations stand a good chance of retaining their ability to encourage cooperation among subordinates, manage conflicts, and maintain the stability of the organization in the midst of unprecedented social changes.

Appendix

Questionnaire Items

Voluntary Decision Acceptance (alpha = .70)

- If this problem or issue were to occur again in the future, how willing are you to see it be resolved in a similar way?

- How willing were you to voluntarily accept the decision(s) your supervisor made?

Support for Authority (alpha = .70)

- When you think about your supervisor, to what extent do you . . .

  Trust your supervisor?

  Respect your supervisor?

  Like your supervisor?

  Feel loyal toward your supervisor?

- I can count on my supervisor to help me out when I need it.

- My supervisor is willing to help me solve problems.

Outcome Favorability (alpha = .86)

- Overall, how satisfied were you with the outcome?
- How favorable was the outcome to you?
- In terms of your outcome, how much did you gain or lose?

Distributive Fairness (alpha = .90)

- Given the rules in your organization, did you get more or less than you deserved?
- How fair was the outcome you received?
- To what extent did you deserve the outcome you received?

Procedural Fairness (alpha = .91)

- Overall, how fair were the procedures used to handle the problem?

- Overall, how fairly were you treated by your supervisor?

- Given the rules of your organization, how appropriate were the procedures used by your supervisor to handle your problem?

Voice

- How much of an opportunity were you given to describe your problem before any decisions were made about how to handle it?

Neutrality (alpha = .78)

- How honest was your supervisor in what he or she said to you?

- To what extent did your supervisor get all the information needed to make good decisions about how to handle the issues involved?

Trust in Benevolence (alpha = .92)

- How hard did your supervisory try to take account of your needs in the situation?

- How hard did your supervisor try to bring the issues into the open so that they could be resolved?

- How hard did your supervisor try to do the right thing by you?

Status Recognition (alpha = .89)

- How politely were you treated by your supervisor?

- How dignified was your supervisor's treatment of you?

REFERENCES

Betancourt, H., & Lopez, S. R. (1993). The study of culture, ethnicity, and race in American psychology. *American Psychologist, 48,* 629–637.

Brewer, M. B., & Kramer, R. M. (1986). Choice behavior in social dilemmas: Effects of social identity, group size, and decision framing. *Journal of Personality and Social Psychology, 50,* 543–549.

Brockner, J., & Wiesenfeld, B. M. (1996). An integrative framework for explaining reactions to decisions: Interactive effects of outcomes and procedures. *Psychological Bulletin, 120,* 189–208.

California Department of Finance. (1993). *Projected Total Population of California Counties* (Report 93 P-3). Sacramento, CA: Author.

Cohen, R. L. (1985). Procedural justice and participation. *Human Relations, 38,* 643–663.

Crocker, J., Luhtanen, R., Broadnax, S., & Blaine, B. E. (1999). Belief in U.S. government conspiracies against blacks among black and white college students: Powerless or system blame? *Personality and Social Psychology Bulletin, 25,* 941–953.

Crosby, F. (1984). The denial of personal discrimination. *American Behavioral Scientist, 27,* 371–386.

Davidson, M. N., & Friedman, R. (1998). When excuses don't work: The persistent injustice effect among black managers. *Administrative Science Quarterly, 43,* 154–183.

Feather, N. T. (1994). Human values and their relations to justice. *Journal of Social Issues, 50,* 129–151.

Folger, R., & Konovsky, M. A. (1989). Effects of procedural and distributive justice on reactions to pay raise decisions. *Academy of Management Journal, 32,* 115–130.

Gaertner, S. L., Mann, J., Murrell, A., & Dovidio, J. F. (1989). Reducing intergroup bias: The benefits of recatgorization. *Journal of Personality and Social Psychology, 57,* 239–249.

Gaertner, S. L., Rust, M. C., Dovidio, J. F., Bachman, B. A., & Anastasio, P. A. (1994). The contact hypothesis: The role of a common ingroup identity on reducing intergroup bias. *Small Group Research, 22,* 267–277.

Greenberg, J. (1990). Looking fair vs. being fair: Managing impressions of organizational justice. In B. Staw & L. Cummings (Eds.), *Research in organizational behavior* (Vol. 12, pp. 111–157). Greenwich, CT: JAI Press.

Greenberg, J. (1994). Using socially fair treatment to promote acceptance of a work site smoking ban. *Journal of Applied Psychology, 79,* 288–297.

Huo, Y. J. (1999). *Defining moral communities: Normative and functional bases of the allocation of social goods.* Unpublished manuscript, University of California, Los Angeles.

Huo, Y. J., Smith, H. J., Tyler, T. R., & Lind, E. A. (1996). Superordinate identification, subgroup identification, and justice concerns: Is separatism the problem; Is assimilation the answer? *Psychological Science, 7,* 40–45.

James, K. (1993). The social context of organizational justice: Cultural, intergroup, and structural effects on justice behaviors and perceptions. In R. Cropanzano (Ed.), *Justice in the workplace: Approaching fairness in human resource management* (pp. 21–50). Hillsdale, NJ: Lawrence Erlbaum Associates.

Johnston, W. B., & Packer, A. E. (1987). *Workforce 2000: Work and workers for the 21st century.* Indianapolis: Hudson Institute.

Jost, J. T. (1995). Negative illusions: Conceptual clarification and psychological evidence concerning false consciousness. *Political Psychology, 16,* 397–424.

Konovsky, M. A., & Brockner, J. (1993). Managing victim and survivor layoff reactions: A procedural justice perspective. In R. Cropanzano (Ed.), *Justice in the workplace: Approaching fairness in human resource management* (pp. 171–192). Hillsdale, NJ: Lawrence Erlbaum Associates.

Koper, G., Van Knippenberg, D., Bouhuijs, F., Vermunt, R., & Wilke, H. (1993). Procedural fairness and self-esteem. *European Journal of Social Psychology, 23,* 313–325.

Kramer, R. M. (1991). Intergroup relations and organizational dilemmas: The role of categorization processes. *Research in Organizational Behavior, 13,* 191–228.

Kramer, R. M., & Brewer, M. B. (1984). Effects of group identity on resource use in a simulated commons dilemma. *Journal of Personality and Social Psychology, 46,* 1044–1057.

Leung, K. (1987). Some determinants of reactions to procedural models for conflict resolution: A cross-national study. *Journal of Personality and Social Psychology, 53,* 898–908.

Leung, K. (1988). Theoretical advances in justice behavior: Some cross-cultural inputs. In M. H. Bond (Ed.), *The cross-cultural challenge to social psychology* (pp. 218–229). Newbury Park, CA: Sage Publications.

Leung, K., & Lind, E. A. (1986). Procedural justice and culture: Effects of culture, gender, and investigator status on procedural preferences. *Journal of Personality and Social Psychology, 50,* 1134–1140.

Lind, E. A., Huo, Y. J., & Tyler, T. R. (1994). And justice for all: Ethnicity, gender, and preferences for dispute resolution procedures. *Law and Human Behavior, 18,* 269–290.

Lind, E. A., Kanfer, R., & Earley, C. (1990). Voice, control, and procedural justice: Instrumental and noninstrumental concerns in fairness judgments. *Journal of Personality and Social Psychology, 1990,* 952–959.

Lind, E. A., Kray, L., & Thompson, L. (1998). The social construction of injustice: Fairness judgments in response to own and others' unfair treatment by authorities. *Organizational Behavior and Human Decision Processes, 75,* 1–22.

Lind, E. A., & Tyler, T. R. (1988). *The social psychology of procedural justice.* New York: Plenum Press.

Lind, E. A., Tyler, T. R., & Huo, Y. J. (1997). Procedural context and culture: Variation in the antecedents of procedural justice judgments. *Journal of Personality and Social Psychology, 73,* 767–780.

Messick, D. M., Wilke, H., Brewer, M. B., Kramer, R. M., Zemke, P. E., & Lui, L. (1983). Individual adaptations and structural change as solutions to social dilemmas. *Journal of Personality and Social Psychology, 44,* 294–309.

Peterson, R. S. (1994). The role of values in predicting fairness judgments and support of affirmative action. *Journal of Social Issues, 50,* 95–115.

Rasinski, K. A. (1987). What's fair is fair—or is it? Value differences underlying public views about social justice. *Journal of Personality and Social Psychology, 53,* 201–211.

Rutte, C. G., Wilke, H., & Messick, D. M. (1987). Scarcity or abundance caused by people or the environment as determinants of behavior in the resource dilemma. *Journal of Experimental Social Psychology, 23,* 208–214.

Samuelson, C. D. (1991). Perceived task difficulty, causal attributions, and preferences for structural change in resource dilemmas. *Personality and Social Psychology Bulletin, 17,* 181–187.

Sato, K. (1987). Distribution of the cost of maintaining common resources. *Journal of Experimental Social Psychology, 23,* 19–31.

Smith, H. J., Tyler, T. R., Huo, Y. J., Ortiz, D., & Lind, E. A. (1998). The self-relevant implications of the group-value model: Group membership, self-worth, and procedural justice. *Journal of Experimental Social Psychology, 34,* 470–493.

Tajfel, H., & Turner, J. C. (1986). The social identity theory of intergroup behavior. In S. Worchel & W. G. Austin (Eds.), *Psychology of intergroup relations.* Chicago: Nelson-Hall.

Tetlock, P. E., & Mitchell, G. (1993). Liberal and conservative approaches to justice: Conflicting psychological portraits. In B. A. Mellers & J. Baron (Eds.), *Psychological perspectives on justice: Theory and application* (pp. 234–255). New York: Cambridge University Press.

Thibaut, J., & Walker, L. (1975). Procedural justice: A psychological analysis. Hillsdale, NJ: Erlbaum.

Turner, J. C., Hogg, M. A., Oakes, P. J., Reicher, S., & Wetherell, M. S. (1987). *Rediscovering the social group: A self-categorization theory.* Oxford: Basil Blackwell.

Tyler, T. R. (1987). Conditions leading to value expressive effects in judgments of procedural justice: A test of four models. *Journal of Personality and Social Psychology, 52,* 333–344.

Tyler, T. R. (1988). What is procedural justice? Criteria used by citizens to assess the fairness of legal procedures. *Law & Society Review, 22,* 103–135.

Tyler, T. R. (1994). Governing amid diversity: The effect of fair decisionmaking procedures on the legitimacy of government. *Law & Society Review, 28,* 809–831.

Tyler, T. R., Boeckmann, R. J., Smith, H. J., & Huo, Y. J. (1997). *Social justice in a diverse society.* Boulder, Co: Westview Press.

Tyler, T. R., Daubenmier, J. J., Huo, Y. J., & Smith, H. J. (2000). *Comparative and noncomparative status judgments in intragroup settings: When is it important to be better than others?* Unpublished manuscript, New York University.

Tyler, T. R., & Degoey, P. (1996). Trust in organizational authorities: The influence of motive attribution on willingness to accept decisions. In R. M.

Kramer & T. R. Tyler (Eds.), *Trust in organizations: Frontiers of theory and research* (pp. 331–356). Thousand Oaks, CA: Sage Publications, Inc.

Tyler, T. R., Degoey, P., & Smith, H. (1996). Understanding why the justice of group procedures matters: A test of the psychological dynamics of the group-value model. *Journal of Personality and Social Psychology, 70,* 913–930.

Tyler, T. R., & Lind, E. A. (1992). A relational model of authority in groups. In M. Zanna (Ed.), *Advances in experimental social psychology* (Vol. 25, pp. 115–191). San Diego: Academic Press.

Van den Bos, K., Lind, E. A., Vermunt, R., & Wilke, H. A. M. (1997). How do I judge my outcome when I do not know the outcome of others? The psychology of the fair process effect. *Journal of Personality and Social Psychology, 72,* 1034–1046.

Wit, A. P. (1989). *Group efficiency and fairness in social dilemmas: An experimental gaming approach.* Unpublished doctoral dissertation, University of Groningen, the Netherlands.

Wright, S. C., Taylor, D. M., & Moghaddam, F. M. (1990). Responding to membership in a disadvantaged group: From acceptance to collective protest. *Journal of Personality and Social Psychology, 58,* 994–1003.

Yamagishi, T. (1986). Seriousness of social dilemmas and the provision of sanctioning system. *Social Psychology Quarterly, 51,* 32–42.

8

The Seven Loose Can(n)ons
of Organizational Justice

Jerald Greenberg

ACCORDING TO THE *Random House Unabridged Dictionary* (1993), a *canon* is a "body of rules, principles, or standards, accepted as axiomatic and universally binding in a field of study" (p. 306). I believe that, although generally unacknowledged, the field of organizational justice is predicated on several canons. However, because these tend not to be as well established as a canon strictly should be, I prefer to think of them as "loose canons." Curiously, this is just one *n* away from the term *loose cannon,* which the same dictionary defines as "a person whose reckless behavior endangers the efforts or welfare of others" (p. 1135).

Depersonalizing this definition, I argue that several canons of organizational justice may be considered loose cannons insofar as they may potentially mislead scientists intending to promote our understanding of organizational justice—that is, unless their limitations are recognized. In other words, the qualifications that make the canons considered loose must be readily acknowledged to avoid drawing premature and misleading conclusions about organizational justice. With this in mind, I identify seven such canons, describing their status as loose canons and as loose cannons.

Loose Canon 1: Justice Matters in All Organizational Settings

The importance of justice and fairness in organizations has been recognized by professionals from many disciplines. The philosopher Rawls (1971), for example, has referred to justice as "the first virtue of social institutions" (p. 3). Sociologists (e.g., Rytina, 1986) have used the concept of justice to explain collective reactions to institutions. Economists, who traditionally embraced self-interest-based models of behavior, also have acknowledged that employees are strongly motivated by a sense of moral duty (e.g., Etzioni, 1988). Even evolutionary psychologists (e.g., Wright, 1994) have taken a stand, claiming that people's justice motivations are "hardwired" insofar as justice breeds cooperation, which promotes survival of the species. More familiar to readers of this book are likely to be various theories and empirical findings from social psychologists suggesting that matters of justice are involved in all social settings (e.g., Lerner, 1980; Walster, Walster & Berscheid, 1978).

Given this background, it is not surprising to find that organizational behavior experts accept the idea that justice matters in all organizational settings (Folger & Cropanzano, 1998). However, the suggestion that justice is an omnipresent concern of people in organizations is misleading insofar as it ignores the possibility that naturally occurring characteristics of organizations differentially prompt the salience of justice concerns. After all, differences in such dimensions as status, role obligations, and pay inevitably will trigger questions of fairness—but not always, and not equally. Justice might always be a potential concern, but that potential will materialize only sometimes. This leads us to ask: When are concerns about justice most likely to come to people's attention in organizations?

Research has revealed that concerns about organizational justice has several key triggers. First, concerns about justice are triggered when people receive negative outcomes. Indeed, people are unlikely to consider the fairness of procedures when they benefit from the implementation of those procedures (Greenberg, 1987). After all, when people get what they want, they are likely to be so satisfied with their outcomes as to not raise questions about them. Moreover, to the extent that the receipt of positive outcomes is not likely to be the result of a norm violation, there is no triggering event making issues of justice salient. However, when people do *not* get what they want, they then tend to raise questions about the procedures that lead to those outcomes, such as in the case of negative performance appraisals (Greenberg, 1986b). The same also could be said with respect to interactional justice. Specifically, when people are treated with dignity and respect, they are unlikely to have any concerns about how fairly they have been treated (Greenberg, 1994). Thus, it might be said that organizations make employees' concerns about justice salient by virtue of violating their expectations of fairness.

This leads to my second point regarding the triggering of justice concerns: Justice evaluations are made salient by change. This is consistent with Lind's (1995) fairness heuristic theory, according to which the processing of judgments about fairness is most likely to occur when relationships (such as those between employer and employee) are in a state of flux. So, for example, employees evaluating what life might be like in their organization after it merges with another might be especially sensitive to issues of justice that arise. However, when things are stable, concerns about justice are likely to be limited. The same also may be said about changes in organizations that stem from demographic shifts in the workplace. Indeed, the growing prominence of minority group employees in the workforce has been promoting concerns about the fairness of their treatment (Azzi, 1992). Change makes justice concerns salient, so not surprisingly, employees are likely to accept organizational changes as fair to the extent that these have been made following fair procedures (Cobb, Wooten, & Folger, 1995; Novelli, Kirkman, & Shapiro, 1995).

A third condition under which concerns about justice are salient is when resources are scarce. Indeed, concerns about the allocation of resources become trivial when there are more than enough resources to go around (Greenberg, 1981). Simply put, when everyone gets what he or she wants, questions about justice do not emerge (Hogan & Emler, 1981). However, when resources are scarce, people not only become concerned about justice in general, but in particular, are concerned about the manner in which justice is defined (Tyler, Boeckmann, Smith, & Huo, 1997). For the most part, when resources are scarce, self-serving perceptions of justice tend to prevail (Greenberg, 1981). It is with this in mind that strikes and slowdowns (responses to injustice) result when resources are scarce (e.g., the money to grant desired pay raises), leading both labor and management to perceive its own interests as fairest. However, when economic conditions make it possible for labor and management both to get what they want, not only are displays of perceived injustice not in evidence, but concerns about justice are unlikely to arise in the first place.

A fourth trigger of concerns about justice in organizations is likely to emerge simply because of the power differences created by role differentiation between people in organizations. Justice concerns are more likely to arise among interactants having different levels of power than among those for whom the balance of power is equal (Cohen, 1986). For example, managers, by virtue of their obligations to allocate rewards fairly, must be proactive, taking into account macrojustice concerns, such as the good of their entire units. However, their subordinates are more likely to take a reactive stance in evaluating justice, considering what they got and how they got it. By contrast, employees interacting at the same levels are less likely to take into account such concerns. With the power differential removed, concerns about fairness between people often are likely to be limited. Although people may be concerned about how fairly they have been treated during the course of an informal personal relationship, the removal of a power differential between people often makes moot the issue of the allocation of rewards between them.

   In view of the evidence we have reviewed here, it would be misleading to claim that concerns about justice are salient in all organizational settings. Indeed, justice is a far greater concern to people under some circumstances than others. This qualification of the canon is important from a practical perspective insofar as it suggests that to be maximally effective, efforts to promote fairness in organizations should be reserved for those settings in which concerns about justice are greatest.

Loose Canon 2: Organizational Justice Research Promotes Justice in Organizations

Of all the endeavors in which organizational scholars participate, few may be considered more noble than promoting justice in the workplace. After all, not only is justice a universally accepted value, but it is also one whose role in promoting the well-being of individuals and institutions has been broadly acknowledged (Greenberg, 1996; Tyler et al., 1997). Not surprisingly, widespread effort has been directed toward using justice concepts to explain organizational phenomena (for a review, see Cropanzano & Greenberg, 1997). However, it is mostly at this stage of explaining phenomena through an organizational justice lens that our contributions lie. Very few studies directly have applied organizational justice principles to the task of intentionally promoting justice in organizations (Greenberg & Lind, 2000). Because interventions based on organizational justice research have been limited, the field of organizational justice may be characterized as having a gap between research and practice—one that is not unlike that found in other areas of organizational behavior (Rynes, McNatt, & Bretz, 1999).

   This gap would not be problematic if people routinely did things to promote justice in organizations. I am not presumptuous enough to believe that managers never behaved fairly until we came along to tell them what to do. Clearly, they did. However, the accumulated literature on organizational justice suggests that there are specific ways in which impressions of fairness may be promoted that are being ignored or underutilized. Illustrating this, Folger and Skarlicki (1998) asked students in a laboratory study to perform an exercise that required them to explain their decisions to lay off employees. They did so either under a condition in which they themselves were blamed for having made the bad decisions that led to the layoff or a condition in which the layoffs were said to result from unforeseen economic conditions. Although participants who were blamed for the layoffs stood to benefit most by explaining and apologizing for their actions, these individuals spent significantly less time explaining their layoff decisions than those who were able to attribute the layoffs to external conditions. Folger and Skarlicki suggest that these "truncated dismissals" represent participants' efforts at distancing themselves from individuals they have harmed, allowing them to escape an uncomfortable situation. Importantly, although the participants most needed to promote their image as being interpersonally fair when they were associated with the dismissal, they ignored an opportunity to do so. These findings and others (e.g., Korsgaard, Roberson, & Rymph, 1998) suggest that people do *not* always behave in ways that promote maximal impressions of fairness.

Fortunately, executives of several organizations have had enough foresight to allow organizational justice researchers to train their managers in ways to promote fairness. The effectiveness of these efforts has been documented in the literature. For example, Cole and Latham (1997) trained supervisors on six key aspects of procedural justice: (1) explanation of the performance problem, (2) the demeanor of the supervisor, (3) subordinates' control over the process, (4) arbitrariness, (5) employee counseling, and (6) privacy. The training consisted of role-playing exercises conducted in small groups held over 5 half-days. Two groups of expert judges evaluated the behavior of the participants who role-played supervisors administering discipline in various test scenarios. Not only did the judges agree that managers who were trained behaved more fairly than those in an untrained, control group, but they also predicted that those in the trained group would perform better as supervisors. Although Cole and Latham's (1997) findings do not assess the effectiveness of training on the job, they suggest that managers can be trained to emulate specific behaviors that enhance procedural justice.

Two additional studies have shown that managers trained in various aspects of procedural justice do, in fact, behave in ways that yield beneficial organizational results. For example, Skarlicki and Latham (1996) trained managers in various aspects of procedural justice, including ways of providing voice and techniques for facilitating the fairness of the social interaction between labor and management. Trainees heard lectures and completed various exercises over a total of 12 hours. The objective of the training was to enhance the level of organizational citizenship behavior (OCB) among a group of union laborers. Results indicated that the training was effective: Three months after training, incidents of OCB were higher among employees of the trained managers than among employees of the untrained managers. Before the study was conducted, we knew only that fairness perceptions were related to OCB (Organ & Moorman, 1993). However, this study showed that OCB can be enhanced directly by training managers to behave fairly toward their employees.

In another study, I trained managers of retail stores in ways of enhancing procedural justice (Greenberg, 1999). The study was conducted in an effort to curb an alarming level of employee theft that stemmed from widespread job dissatisfaction. Indeed, pretesting revealed that employees believed their managers were disrespectful, uncaring, insensitive, and generally unconcerned with their welfare and that supervisory personnel routinely failed to involve them in decisions, keeping them in the dark about the reasons underlying various company policies. In short, procedural justice was low. I designed an intervention to turn this around by systematically training managers in techniques of delegation, supportive communication, and other aspects of procedural justice. The training occurred in one store (randomly selected from several in the chain) for 2 hours per week over an 8-week period. It consisted of involving the participants in a variety of role-playing exercises, having them read and analyze several cases, and discussing managerial problems at their stores. Compared to a second store location whose managers received training on an unrelated topic and a third whose managers received no training at all, I found that the training was effective not only at improving employees' job satisfaction, commitment, and turnover intentions, but also at cutting the rate of employee theft in half.

These few studies suggest that organizational justice research can be used to promote justice in organizations and that organizations derive benefits from such efforts. However, insofar as these efforts are recent, we cannot determine how long-lasting the benefits may be. Also, because there have been so few investigations in this area, we do not know precisely what forms of training are most effective at improving specific dependent variables. Despite these uncertainties, it appears as if the benefits of systematically attempting to promote procedural justice in organizations are very promising. As a field, it appears that we are approaching the point at which the cumulative knowledge we have gained from studies showing how organizational justice concepts can be used to explain organizational phenomena can be used to change those phenomena for the better. Until then, statements about the organizational benefits associated with promoting organizational justice may be considered loose canons.

Loose Canon 3: Favorable Outcomes Are Fair Outcomes

As Miller (1999) has recently chronicled, the norm of self-interest is a powerful motive in all walks of life. Not surprisingly, the idea that people act and perceive so as to pursue their own best interests has been a dominant theme in the justice literature (Törnblom, 1977). After all, given that it is almost never completely clear what constitutes fairness, people have a ready-made opportunity to perceive justice in a manner that benefits themselves (Greenberg, 1983).

We have seen this in several studies. For example, assessing drivers' perceptions of the fairest practices for allocating gasoline (a scarce resource at the time of the study), I found that people believed that whatever allocation schemes most benefited themselves were the fairest (e.g., equal allocations were favored by those driving economy cars because this practice would likely meet their needs amply). In a similar vein, Grover (1991) found that employees' perceptions of the fairness of parental-leave policies was related to their experiences with these benefits themselves: Those who either took parental leaves or who planned to do so believed the practice was fairer than those who did not. From a more macro level, Azzi (1992) found that members of social majority groups and minority groups differed in their preferences for governmental representation in ways that advantaged themselves: Equal representation was favored by minorities, and proportional representation was favored by majorities. Not only do people perceive as fair outcomes that benefit themselves, but they also perceive themselves as being more fair as individuals than others (Messick, Bloom, Boldizar, & Samuelson, 1985).

Despite such evidence and the general tendency for people to behave in a self-interested fashion (Miller, 1999), it would be misleading to conclude that self-serving interests completely dictate perceptions of justice and reactions to injustice. There are several reasons for this. First, classic research on equity theory (for a review, see Greenberg, 1982) has shown that people respond so as to reduce overpayment inequities, suggesting that fairness sometimes demands lowering one's outcomes. Although such behavior is ostensibly not self-serving, at least in the short term, it may be considered to be beneficial to their overall best interests insofar as promoting justice in the workplace stands to benefit everyone over the long run (Walster et al., 1978).

Second, the idea that people perceive as fair whatever outcomes that benefit themselves overlooks the important contribution of procedural justice. Indeed, the matter of how those outcomes came about is important in this regard. Considerable research has shown that people may, in fact, be convinced of the fairness of even undesirable outcomes if these have followed from enactment of a fair procedure (Brockner & Weisenfeld, 1994). Even litigants who lose court cases, for example, perceive the verdicts against them as being fair when they recognize that the legal process used was fair (Thibaut & Walker, 1975). Again, this may be the result of an underlying belief that institutions (such as courts and organizations) that enact procedures fairly are, in fact, acting in their own long-term best interest, even if the immediate outcomes are less than desirable (Tyler et al., 1997).

A third qualification of the self-interest view of justice comes from another classic literature—the work on relative deprivation (e.g., Merton & Kitt, 1950). Here, the relevant question is: Against what standards do people compare themselves in making judgments about the fairness of their outcomes? If people were always interested in feeling better about themselves, they would choose to compare themselves to others who fare worse—but they do not (Levine & Moreland, 1998). In fact, it is not at all unusual for people to be motivated to compare themselves to those who are doing better, satisfying their interest in self-evaluation and self-improvement (Wood, 1989). Clearly, these motives must also be considered along with self-interest in understanding people's perceptions of justice.

A fourth line of research qualifying the self-interested view of justice comes from evidence showing that sometimes even those who are unfairly advantaged relative to others recognize this and willingly reduce their outcomes (Montada & Schneider, 1989). This tendency toward sympathetic recognition of the disadvantaged by the advantaged has been used to explain the redistribution of resources between people even if it comes at the expense of those who are currently benefiting (Smith & Tyler, 1996). The idea that people may care about justice so much that they are willing to pay with their own resources also comes from evidence showing that people do not always fully exploit their power advantages over others despite opportunities they have to do so (Ochs & Roth, 1989).

To conclude, it would be an overstatement to claim without reservation that self-interest by itself dictates reactions to injustice in organizations. As such, I agree with Tyler et al. (1997), who said the following.

> Many studies that we have noted indicate at least some influence of self-interest on judgments of fairness. However, other studies indicate equally clearly that people are able to distinguish principles of justice from principles of self-interest and often base their evaluations and behaviors on justice principles that are clearly distinct from their own and their groups' interests. *Thus, the relationship of self-interest and justice judgments is a question that needs further study.* (p. 98, emphasis mine)

Loose Canon 4: Reactions to Injustice Are Predictable

When organizational justice researchers perform studies assessing peoples' reactions to injustices, they almost always have some preconceived ideas as to what specific forms those reactions will take. Relying on some of my own research for examples, I have measured various behavioral responses to unfair conditions, such as lowered job performance (Greenberg, 1988) and taking company property (Greenberg, 1990a), as well as behavioral intentions, such as willingness to go along with a smoking ban (Greenberg, 1994) and taking a phone number for purposes of reporting a wrongdoing (Greenberg, 1987). In some of these cases (e.g., Greenberg, 1987, 1994), the dependent variables were made salient by opportunities created by the researcher, serving as paths for expressing one's feelings of injustice. We know what expressions of injustice to look for because these have been built into the research. In the others (e.g., Greenberg, 1988, 1990), however, the behaviors tapped were naturalistic and would have occurred even if no research were being conducted. In such cases, the decisions regarding the expressions of injustice measured are most likely the result of practical factors, such as the opportunity to measure certain variables provided by the host organization.

In both types of research, the possibility exists that the expressions of injustice tapped are neither the most sensitive ones nor the most indicative of how people will choose to respond, although they are available to us as scientists. Indeed, in even the best studies, there are many people who do not respond as intended—individuals we either simply label as aberrant or whom we dismiss as adding to error variance. Of course, as scientists, we have no other choice. However, outliers lead us to think about the possibility that in the real world, reactions to injustice may be nowhere as predictable as we believe. Indeed, there are several good reasons for this.

First, it is apparent that many different types of responses to injustice are possible, both behavioral and psychological. This has been acknowledged by justice theorists ranging from Adams (1965) to contemporary scholars (e.g., Tyler et al., 1997). However, it still remains unclear which particular behavioral expressions of injustice will manifest themselves and when they will do so. For example, although Tyler et al. (1997) described some of the conditions under which people will respond individually (e.g., by showing personal vengeance) or collectively (e.g., by engaging in riots), we are still hard-pressed to tell exactly what form a response might take. Thus, individuals who appear to be unresponsive to an injustice may simply be responding in a manner other than that which we have chosen to measure. In sum, having multiple behavioral options is one reason that responses to injustice are not predictable.

A second reason is that people consciously may decide to disguise their reactions to injustice. For example, it may be considered socially undesirable to express one's dissatisfaction in some traditional ways, such as by lowering performance or engaging in theft or joining others in work slowdowns, strikes, or even riots. To do so would be far too costly. The idea that responses to injustice may be understood from a cost-benefit perspective has been demonstrated by Rusbult (1987). Her research has shown that the more people invest in a relationship, the more interested they are in expressing their feelings of injustice verbally, whereas people making lower investments tend to express themselves by leaving their relationships altogether. In other words, people who care about their relationships invest the energy associated with entering into a discussion about fairness, whereas these costs are too great for those who do not care. The result of leaving a relationship (or quitting a job) is that in the absence of a heart-to-heart discussion (or an exit interview), one never knows that leaving is an expression of injustice. Such disguised responses are yet another reason that reactions to injustice are not perfectly predictable.

This suggests a third factor that makes responses to injustice difficult to predict: Many such responses are covert. Indeed, neglect is a viable response to injustice: One may be seething inside but do nothing about it. Although depression and symptoms of stress may result from living with injustice (Hafer & Olsen, 1993), it is not unusual for people to keep their responses to themselves. As I just noted, this may be because the costs of responding are believed to be too great. However, inaction also may occur because the individual has worked out the injustice psychologically—such as by distorting the facts cognitively or by forgiving the source of the injustice for inflicting harm. Such reactions may be expected from individuals who are only indirectly affected by an organizational injustice—workers whose colleagues are laid off (i.e., survivors) as opposed to those who are victims of layoffs themselves (Brockner & Greenberg, 1990). In some cases, people also may do nothing in response to an apparent injustice because they simply are motivated not to recognize it or because they become resigned to this condition (which seems unfair to others) as the way things are supposed to be (Major, 1994).

In sum, the perceptual and social nature of injustice makes it difficult to predict exactly how and when people will respond to apparent injustices. Assuming that people even recognize injustices, their willingness to take action may be diminished by other concerns. Then, assuming that someone is interested in expressing injustice, the wide variety of options available to individuals makes it difficult to predict how they will respond.

Loose Canon 5: Fair Procedures Enhance Acceptance of Organizational Outcomes

I recently identified a major principle of organizational justice (Greenberg, 2000)—the well-established relationship between fairness of procedures and acceptance of organizational outcomes (for a review, see Lind & Tyler, 1988). We see this principle reflected both with respect to the structural and social determinants of organizational justice.

Structurally, it has been established that people better accept organizational decisions to the extent that these have been made using rules of procedural fairness, such as those suggested by Leventhal, Karuza, and Fry (1980) and by Thibaut and Walker (1975). For example, employees' perceptions of their companies' performance appraisal systems have been positively associated with the opportunities they have to express their own viewpoints regarding their performance (e.g., Dipboye & de Pontbraind, 1981). Similarly, employees' perceptions of their companies' drug-testing procedures (Konovsky & Cropanzano, 1993), personnel selection procedures (Gilliland, 1993), and strategic plans (Kim & Mauborgne, 1993) also have been found to be positively related to the use of a variety of mechanisms associated with procedural fairness (Leventhal et al., 1980).

An analogous relationship also has been demonstrated with respect to the various social determinants of fairness. Specifically, prompting procedural justice socially, such as by giving people sufficient information about the decisions affecting them and by treating them with dignity and respect promotes their acceptance of work outcomes. And, when these practices are violated, employees respond negatively. This has been shown to take many forms, including theft by employees who got their pay cut (Greenberg, 1990b), rejection of a smoking ban by smokers (Greenberg, 1994), and even the filing of lawsuits by former employees who were fired or laid off (Lind, Greenberg, Scott, & Welchans, 2000). In all cases, the socially unfair treatment led to people's rejection of their organizations and their willingness to strike back at them.

Although these findings are well accepted, there are at least three ways in which the link between fair procedures and the acceptance of organizational outcomes is qualified (Greenberg, 2000). First, it is known that the effects of procedural justice on the acceptance of organizational outcomes is moderated by the perceived valence of the outcomes (Brockner & Wiesenfeld, 1994): Fair procedures matter more to people when outcomes are negative than when they are positive. Thus, people's willingness to use fair procedures to promote acceptance of outcomes is likely to be greater when the outcomes involved are negative. As I described earlier in this chapter, employees receiving positive outcomes are so pleased that they are unconcerned about the procedures by which they got them. By contrast, when outcomes are negative, concerns about procedure become highly salient, heightening attention to the promotion of procedural justice.

A second qualification of the relationship between fair procedures and the acceptance of work outcomes has to do with the question of magnitude: If granting voice enhances acceptance of outcomes, then does more voice promote greater acceptance? Recent research suggests not. Demonstrating this, Hunton, Wall, and Price (1998) conducted a study in which they manipulated the number of supervisory decisions over which participants were given voice. Although participants were more satisfied with decisions over which they had any degree of voice than no voice at all, increasingly higher levels of voice had no effects whatsoever. In a similar vein, Peterson (1999) found that inappropriately high levels of voice actually *reduced* satisfaction with outcomes. Specifically, measuring laboratory subjects' satisfaction with leaders who were in conflict with others regarding group decisions, Peterson (1999) found that participants were more satisfied with their leaders when they provided an opportunity to explain their suggestions for solving a group problem than when they were not given such an opportunity. However, when these same leaders behaved inappropriately by giving participants much more voice than expected, participants were less satisfied than when their leaders gave them lower, but more appropriate, levels of voice. Clearly, the effects of voice on outcome satisfaction are not linear, as suggested by Loose Canon 5. Together, the findings of Hunton et al. (1998) and Peterson (1999), although not yet replicated, suggest the need to be aware of the potential limits of the effects of voice.

A third qualification of the effects of voice concerns its perceived sincerity. This is a small, but important, point: For the benefits of voice to accrue, that voice must be sincere. At minimum, it must be listened to. Merely giving employees voice but not taking their ideas into account runs the risk of backfiring, leading to less acceptance—a phenomenon known as the "frustration effect" (Greenberg & Folger, 1983). Sincerity is also important with respect to the nature of the explanations managers give for undesirable organizational outcomes. For perceptions of procedural justice to be enhanced, it is not merely sufficient to explain outcomes but to do so in a manner that is perceived as genuine and sincere (Shapiro, Buttner, & Barry, 1994). In fact, if employees become suspicious that the explanations they were given about outcomes are manipulative, any benefits that might otherwise result by providing explanations may well disappear. In fact, to the extent that the organizational agent's manipulative intent generalizes, suggesting malevolence on the part of the organization, the organization's image of fairness will suffer (Greenberg, 1990c). In sum, for explanations to enhance perceptions of procedural justice, it is necessary for employees to believe that their superiors are "being straight" with them.

To conclude, the well-established finding that fair procedures promote the acceptance of organizational outcomes must be approached with caution. I say this because the effect is qualified in three important ways: (1) the effects of fair procedures on acceptance of outcomes is most prominent when the outcomes in question are negative, (2) the effects of voice on acceptance of outcomes is not linear in nature, and (3) for organizational outcomes to be accepted, the motives underlying the implementation of the procedures leading to them must be perceived to be sincere.

Loose Canon 6: Measuring Organizational Justice Is Straightforward

For the most part, organizational scientists have treated the measurement of justice perceptions rather casually, a state of affairs on which I commented over a decade ago (Greenberg, 1990d). Still, ad hoc measures based primarily on a researcher's casual assessment of fit with the concept at hand have dominated the organizational justice literature (for a summary, see the appendix in Lind & Tyler, 1988). Unfortunately, these assessments are sometimes questionable, even when tapping well-established constructs such as distributive justice and procedural justice.

For example, in their assessment of distributive justice, Fryxell and Gordon (1989) included a question dealing with the ability to assess ideas during a grievance procedure, which is clearly a matter of procedural justice. Similarly, Joy and Witt's (1992) assessment of distributive justice included an item referring to the nature of the treatment respondents had received, which is clearly a matter of interactional justice. More recently, Sweeney and McFarlin (1997) included items referring to the extent to which employees "lose out in the end," an obvious reference to distributive justice, in their assessment of procedural justice. In reviewing various organizational justice measures, Colquitt (in press) has noted that problems of what he calls "cross pollination of items" are even more prevalent when it comes to creating ad hoc measures of interactional justice, a less clearly articulated construct.

A few researchers developed measures of organizational justice by basing them on empirical demonstrations of justice determinants. For example, the measures of organizational justice used by Folger and Konovsky (1989) were derived from Greenberg's (1986d) evidence regarding the determinants of fair performance appraisals. This practice of empirically deriving measurements from conceptually driven empirical findings, although leading to concept-valid assessments, has been rare. When this has been done, efforts have focused on assessing highly specific aspects of fairness, such as pay (Jones & Scarpello, 1992).

In response to my earlier admonitions about measuring organizational justice perceptions (Greenberg, 1990d, 1993), scientists recently have turned attention to developing standardized measures of justice. Some, such as Beugré (1996), have developed scales assessing four distinct sources of justice, including distributive justice, procedural justice, interactional justice, and systemic justice. Similarly, Colquitt (in press) developed a scale measuring essentially the same four facets of organizational justice: distributive justice, procedural justice, interpersonal justice, and informational justice. In contrast, other standardized measures, such as Donovan, Drasgow, and Munson's (1998) Perceptions of Fair Interpersonal Treatment (PFIT) scale, tap a single dimension of organizational justice—in this case, the perceived fairness of interpersonal treatment on the job. Insofar as different facets of organizational justice predict different aspects of organizational behavior (Colquitt, in press; Greenberg, 1990d), the dimensional purity that results from these carefully developed, standardized measures of organizational justice is highly desirable.

The movement from ad hoc measures to standardized measures sends the message that organizational justice as a concept has matured and become legitimized. After all, if a concept is important enough to warrant standardizing, it appears to "have arrived," taking its place among other organizational concepts whose prominence in the organizational sciences is not only showcased but furthered by the existence of established ways to measure it (Greenberg, 1993). With standardization, however, comes a highly casual approach to measurement, freeing scientists to pick previously published measures "off the shelf" and to use them in their studies without much consideration of their appropriateness.

Of course, without standardization, the approach to measurement is casual as well—selecting measures that appear to be relevant to the setting under study as the researcher perceives it. Although I surely recognize the virtues of sound psychometric properties found in standardized measures, I cannot help but note how the use of ad hoc measures forces researchers to pay careful attention to how their measures of justice bridge the gap between a certain conceptualization of justice and the way in which it is materialized in the setting under study. In other words, such measures tend to be "contextualized," enhancing the opportunities for them to be relevant to the attitudes expressed by the participants whose opinions are being surveyed. Taken together, these observations suggest that to achieve the best of both worlds, what is needed is a construct valid measure of organizational justice that is both standardized and immediately relevant to the situation in which fairness is being assessed.

This recommendation is in keeping with Blader and Tyler's (in press) claim that there are likely to be fine, but important, differences in context with respect to how people perceive justice in organizations. Blader and Tyler (in press) wisely recommend that the range of experiences relevant to measuring perceptions of organizational justice be expanded from the formal (e.g., treatment during performance appraisal interviews) to the informal (e.g., treatment at a social function). Indeed, research has shown that employees' perceptions of the fairness of their supervisors is based both on the formal policies and procedures supervisors use as well as the casual, informal ways supervisors treat those employees (Cobb, Vest, & Hills, 1997). With this in mind, I agree that effective measures of the interpersonal aspects of justice should go beyond assessing the extent to which fair treatment is an element of organizational climate (as is done by Donovan et al., 1998) to the more dynamic experiences people have with other individuals in the workplace.

Although this presents a challenge for measuring organizational justice, an approach developed by Colquitt (in press) is promising. To begin,

Colquitt (in press) systematically developed a construct-valid multidimensional measure of organizational justice by carefully selecting items that followed from seminal writings in the field of organizational justice. He then made small adjustments to these items to ensure that they were relevant to the domains of interest to participants completing the scale. Specifically, in one study involving students, Colquitt's items focused on fairness by the teacher in the classroom, and in a second study involving employees of an automotive parts manufacturing company, the items focused on fairness of the treatment and decisions made by the supervisor. In other words, his items were "contextualized" so that they were relevant to the participants. This is in keeping with my earlier plea for "convertability" so as to make justice measures useful in a variety of contexts (Greenberg, 1993). To the extent that this is done, a primary danger of using an off-the-shelf measure of organizational justice is reduced.

For this approach to be most effective, researchers also should incorporate separate sets of questions tapping the perceived fairness of treatment by each of several focal individuals who may be contributing to the employees' overall perceptions of organizational fairness. Although this may mean customizing and lengthening questionnaires, doing so promises to tap the multiple sources that are so relevant to individuals' justice perceptions (Blader and Tyler, in press). For example, it is possible that an employee's perceptions of his or her workplace at a given time is influenced by the actions of a particular supervisor, co-worker, or policy. By asking questions about the fairness of these and other, relevant sources, more meaningful measures of organizational justice are likely to emerge. In all likelihood, this will require extensive pretesting to identify salient foci of justice perceptions and then customizing questionnaire items accordingly. I believe that the effort involved in implementing such a procedure, although considerable, will pay off by creating measures of justice perceptions that are both construct-valid and situationally appropriate.

Loose Canon 7: Concerns about Organizational Justice Are Universal

Citing the influence of common developmental (Piaget, 1948), biological (Wright, 1994), and social (Lerner, 1980) processes, many social scientists have claimed that justice is a universal standard. Even organizational justice scholars have acknowledged that concerns about fairness on the job are universal in nature (James, 1993; Tyler et al., 1997). However, we must be careful how we articulate this canon. It may be argued that whereas *concerns* about distributive justice are universal, *operationalization* of these concerns is highly particularistic. After all, insofar as matters of justice are central to the functioning of societies and organizations are vital institutions in societies, it follows that societal views of justice will manifest themselves in the functioning of organizations (Granovetter, 1985). Specifically, culture's influence on distributive justice appears to manifest itself in at least four ways.

First, Tyler et al. (1997) note that culture may affect the importance of justice in a society. Kidder and Miller (1991), for example, illustrate this point in their analysis of fairness in Japan. Specifically, they note that there is no word for "fair" in the Japanese language. Compared to Americans, who learn early in life to be sensitive to the fairness of the relative size of the rewards they receive, the Japanese have deemphasized this in favor of an elaborate social system that emphasizes respect, politeness, and social harmony. As such, the importance of distributive fairness—at least, as known to most Western cultures—is not as great in Japan.

Second, although people from different cultures may agree that justice is important, they define it differently (James, 1993; Tyler et al., 1997). We see this in studies showing that people from various cultures favor different forms of distributive justice, such as equity, equality, and need (for reviews, see Beugré, 1998; James, 1993; Miles & Greenberg, 1993). For example, studies have shown that whereas Americans favor the norm of equity in making distributive decisions, people from India favor the norm of need (Murphy-Berman, Singh, Pachauri, & Kumar, 1984), and people from the Netherlands favor equality (Natua, 1983). Not surprisingly, the level of anger that people display in response to justice norm violations has been found to be related to the strength by which their preference for that particular norm has been violated (Gundykunst & Ting-Toomey, 1988).

Third, prevailing norms in various cultures may influence what is perceived to be fair in those cultures. For example, in highly individualistic cultures, such as the United States, it follows that equity will prevail insofar as this particular norm of justice recognizes relative individual contributions (Deutsch, 1985). Likewise, justice is also likely to be defined in terms of the equity rule in cultures characterized as being low in power distance (Hofstede, 1980). The idea is that people in such countries, such as Great Britain, recognize differences in power between parties (such as differentiations between people based on their rankings in an organizational hierarchy) as being legitimate, thereby making them willing to use this as a basis for reward differentiation (Miles & Greenberg, 1993). These examples illustrate the point that norms other than justice that prevail within cultures may shape the various standards of justice that prevail in those cultures.

Finally, a fourth way in which the effect of culture may affect distributive justice is by determining the dominance of some groups over others (Bierbrauer, 1990). As Tyler et al. (1997) note, in culturally diverse societies, differences between groups may lead to the marginalization of groups whose members are poorer and politically unconnected, leading to their moral exclusion (Opotow, 1990). This, in turn, sets the stage for justifying the systematic denial of such individuals from the public good. A clear example of this in American society is the tendency for women and members of minority groups to receive systematically lower pay than men and members of majority groups (Cook, 1990). In this manner, culture may play a role in determining how even apparent injustices are tolerated, if not condoned.

Thus far, our discussion has centered around the effects of culture on distributive justice. In the case of procedural justice, although less cross-cultural research has been conducted, it appears that beliefs about fairness are more universal. In other words, some procedures, such as the granting of voice over outcomes, is recognized as fair in different cultures. In one of the earliest studies to demonstrate this, Lind, Erickson, Friedland, and Dickensberger (1978) compared perceptions of the fairness of legal procedures by citizens of the United States and continental Europe. Specifically, they considered the adversary procedure, used in the United States and Great Britain, in which defendants have a say over the choice of attorneys and the evidence used in their defense, and the inquisitorial procedure, used in continental Europe, in which judges exercise control over these procedures. Lind and his associates found that the adversary procedure was perceived as being fairer by citizens from all countries—even those whose cultures did not use this procedure. Such evidence suggests that all people recognize the fairness of voice, even in settings in which the granting of voice runs counter to prevailing cultural norms.

More recent evidence has shown that although members of different ethnic groups may express preferences for different outcome distributions, they are in clear agreement about the fairness of the procedures used to determine those outcomes. For example, Lind, Huo, and Tyler (1994) have found no differences in preferences for various procedures for resolving conflict among various ethnic sub-cultures in the United States. Procedures that provided voice (persuasion and negotiation) were the most strongly preferred by all groups. Similarly, Tyler (1994) found no differences between subcultures with respect to evaluations of the fairness of congressional decision-making procedures. The universal appeal of fair procedures also has been demonstrated in organizations. For example,

Tyler, Huo, and Smith (1995) found strong preferences for voice-granting procedures in employees' evaluations of their supervisors' decisions. Such findings suggest that voice is a key determinant of fairness across both cultures and situations.

Additional research suggests that the universal appeal of fair procedures goes beyond the granting of voice. For example, in a study comparing American and French students' attitudes toward various selection techniques, Steiner and Gilliland (1996) found that people from both cultures perceived the same selection techniques as being fairest—namely, those that provided the most objective information, such as the work sample test. Other structural procedural elements, such as clarity and openness, have also been recognized as contributing to fairness by employees from both the United States and Japan (Sugawara and Huo, 1994).

Although there seems to be cross-cultural agreement with respect to the fairness of the structural determinants of procedural justice, there is good reason to believe that there will not be such agreement with respect to the interpersonal determinants of procedural justice. After all, the interpersonal determinants of justice—based as they are on social norms and customs—are likely to be highly reflective of the cultural nuances that cause justice to be operationalized differently across cultures. Illustrating this point, Itoi, Obhuchi, and Fukuno (1996) compared the kind of mitigating accounts that people from the U.S. and Japan used to cultivate impressions of fairness (Greenberg, 1990c). Specifically, they found that people from Japan were more strongly inclined to use the highly interpersonally sensitive forms of mitigating accounts, such as apologies and excuses, whereas Americans were more likely to use the assertive forms, such as justifications. Commenting on these results, Beugré (1998) said, "These findings suggest that Japanese participants' mitigating styles reflect a stronger concern for relationship and social harmony, whereas American participants' assertive style reveals a stronger concern for personal satisfaction" (p. 108). Although these findings have not been replicated in other cultures, I suspect that they reflect a general tendency for the interpersonal facets of justice to be highly sensitive to differences in culture.

To conclude, caution must be exercised regarding the universality of concerns about justice. Although interest in justice seems to be universal, expressions of that interest are strongly related to cultural differences. This is especially so with respect to people's distributive preferences and the manner in which they are likely to frame arguments regarding explanations for their apparent unfairness. At the same time, there appears to be universal acceptance of various structural determinants of fairness. In other words, although culture may have little effect on the perceived fairness of the processes used to determine outcomes, it has a profound effect on the manner in which those procedures are implemented. In view of this, statements regarding the universality of justice must be interpreted with caution.

Conclusion: Loose Can(n)ons at the Crossroads

The field of organizational justice is at a crossroads. If it turns one direction, it can become a truly mature field—one that promises to provide important insight into organizational theory and practice. But, if it turns the other way, it runs the risk of choking in its own confusion and disappearing into oblivion, leaving in its wake a set of interesting ideas whose value was never completely realized. The challenge is that these roads are not clearly marked, and once we go down the wrong one, there's no turning back. For many years, this was not a problem because the field was (i.e., its roads were) just developing (Greenberg, 1990d, 1993). Today, however, the considerable research and theory (i.e., the huge volume of traffic) that defines the field has placed it squarely at this crossroads.

Although no one effort can save the field, I hope that this chapter may be considered a modest step toward doing so. The reason is that many of our most fundamental canons—seven of which I outlined here—are loose at best, threatening to function as a loose cannon by directing us down the road to scientific oblivion. Given the many important contributions to research, theory, and organizational practice outlined in this book, taking this particular road would be a shame. In pointing to the limitations and ambiguities that make our canons so loose, my intent was not to harm the field of organizational justice but precisely the opposite: to encourage the scientific community to come to its rescue by collectively tightening our understanding of its basic tenets. My rationale is that rescuing the field requires defusing its loose canons, and this begins with acknowledging their existence. And that is precisely why I have laid them bare on these pages.

REFERENCES

Adams., J. S. (1965). Inequity in social exchange. In L. Berkowitz (Ed.), *Advances in experimental social psychology* (Vol. 2, pp. 267–299). New York: Academic Press.

Azzi, A. (1992). Procedural justice and the allocation of power in intergroup relations: Studies in the United States and South Africa. *Personality and Social Psychology Bulletin, 18,* 736–747.

Beugré, C. D. (1996). *Analyzing the effects of perceived fairness on organizational commitment and workplace aggression.* Unpublished doctoral dissertation, Rensselaer Polytechnic Institute, Troy, NY.

Beugré, C. D. (1998). *Managing fairness in organizations.* Westport, CT: Quorum.

Bierbrauer, G. (1990). Toward an understanding of legal culture: Variations in individualism and collectivism between Kurds, Lebanese, and Germans. *Law and Society Review, 28,* 243–264.

Blader, S., & Tyler, T. (in press). Advancing the assessment of procedural justice: What constitutes fairness in work settings? *Human Resources Management Review.*

Brockner, J., & Greenberg, J. (1990). The impact of layoffs on survivors: An organizational justice perspective. In J. Carroll (Ed.), *Advances in applied social psychology: Business settings* (pp. 45–75). Hillsdale, NJ: Lawrence Erlbaum Associates.

Brockner, J., & Weisenfeld, B. M. (1994). The interactive impact of procedural and outcome fairness on reactions to a decision: The effects of what you do depend on how you do it. *Psychological Bulletin, 120,* 189–208.

Cobb, A. T., Vest, M., & Hills, F. (1997). Who delivers justice? Source perceptions of procedural fairness. *Journal of Applied Social Psychology, 27,* 1021–1040.

Cobb, A. T., Wooten, K. C., & Folger, R. (1995). Justice in the making: Toward understanding the theory and practice of justice in organizational change and development. In W. A. Pasmore & R. W. Woodman (Eds.), *Research in organizational change and development* (Vol. 8, pp. 243–295). Greenwich, CT: JAI Press.

Cohen, R. L. (1986). Power and justice in intergroup relations. In H. W. Bierhoff, R. L. Cohen, & J. Greenberg (Eds.), Justice in social relations (pp. 65–84). New York: Plenum.

Cole, N. D., & Latham, G. P. (1997). Effects of training in procedural justice on perceptions of disciplinary fairness by unionized employees and disciplinary subject matter experts. *Journal of Applied Psychology, 82,* 699–705.

Colquitt, J. A. (in press). On the dimensionality of organizational justice: A construct validation of a measure. *Journal of Applied Psychology.*

Cook, S. W. (1990). Toward a psychology of improving justice: Research on extending the equality principle to victims of injustice. *Journal of Social Issues, 46,* 147–162.

Cropanzano, R., & Greenberg, J. (1997). Progress in organizational justice: Tunneling through the maze. In C. L. Cooper & I. T. Robertson (Eds.), *International review of industrial and organizational psychology* (Vol. 12, pp. 317–372). London: Wiley.

Deutsch, M. (1985). *Distributive justice.* New Haven, CT: Yale University Press.

Dipboye, R. L., & de Pontbraind, R. (1981). Correlates of employee reactions to performance appraisals and appraisal systems. *Journal of Applied Psychology, 66,* 248–251.

Donovan, M. A., Drasgow, F., & Munson, L. J. (1998). The perceptions of fair interpersonal treatment scale: Development and validation of a measure of interpersonal treatment in the workplace. *Journal of Applied Psychology, 83,* 683–692.

Etzioni, A. (1988). *The moral dimension: Toward a new economics.* New York: Free Press.

Folger, R., & Cropanzano, R. (1998). *Organizational justice and human resource management.* Thousand Oaks, CA: Sage.

Folger, R., & Konovsky, M. A. (1989). Effects of procedural and distributive justice on reactions to pay raise decisions. *Academy of Management Journal, 32,* 115–130.

Folger, R., & Skarlicki, D. P. (1998). When tough times make tough bosses: Managerial distancing as a function of layoff blame. *Academy of Management Journal, 41,* 79–87.

Fryxell, G. E., & Gordon, M. E. (1989). Workplace justice and job satisfaction as predictors of satisfaction with union and management. *Academy of Management Journal, 32,* 851–866.

Gilliland, S. W. (1993). The perceived fairness of selection systems: An organizational justice perspective. *Academy of Management Review, 18,* 694–734.

Granovetter, M. (1985). Economic action and social structure: The problem of embeddedness. *American Journal of Sociology, 91,* 481–510.

Greenberg, J. (1981). The justice of distributing scarce and abundant resources. In M. J. Lerner, & S. C. Lerner (Eds.), *The justice motive in social behavior* (pp. 289–316). New York: Plenum.

Greenberg, J. (1982). Approaching equity and avoiding inequity in groups and organizations. In J. Greenberg & R. L. Cohen (Eds.), *Equity and justice in social behavior* (pp. 389–435). New York: Academic Press.

Greenberg, J. (1983). Overcoming egocentric bias in perceived fairness through self-awareness. *Social Psychology Quarterly, 46,* 152–156.

Greenberg, J. (1986a). Determinants of perceived fairness of performance evaluations. *Journal of Applied Psychology, 71,* 340–342.

Greenberg, J. (1986b). Organizational performance appraisal procedures: What makes them fair? In R. J. Lewicki, B. H. Sheppard, & M. H. Bazerman (Eds.), *Research on negotiation in organizations* (Vol. 1, pp. 25–41). Greenwich, CT: JAI Press.

Greenberg, J. (1987). Reactions to procedural injustice in payment allocations: Do the ends justify the means? *Journal of Applied Psychology, 72,* 55–61.

Greenberg, J. (1988). Equity and workplace status: A field experiment. *Journal of Applied Psychology, 73,* 606–613.

Greenberg, J. (1990a). Employee theft as a reaction to underpayment inequity: The hidden cost of pay cuts. *Journal of Applied Psychology, 75,* 561–568.

Greenberg, J. (1990b). Employee theft as a reaction to underpayment inequity: The hidden costs of pay cuts. *Journal of Applied Psychology, 72,* 55–61.

Greenberg, J. (1990c). Looking fair vs. being fair: Managing impressions of organizational justice. In L. L. Cummings & B. M. Staw (Eds.), *Research in organizational behavior* (Vol. 12, pp. 111–157). Greenwich, CT: JAI Press.

Greenberg, J. (1990d). Organizational justice: Yesterday, today, and tomorrow. *Journal of Management, 16,* 399–432.

Greenberg, J. (1993). The intellectual adolescence of organizational justice: You've come a long way, maybe. *Social Justice Research, 6,* 135–148.

Greenberg, J. (1994). Using socially fair procedures to promote acceptance of a work site smoking ban. *Journal of Applied Psychology, 79,* 288–297.

Greenberg, J. (1999). *Interpersonal justice training (IJT) for reducing employee theft: Some preliminary results.* Unpublished data. Ohio State University, Columbus, OH.

Greenberg, J. (2000). Promote procedural justice to enhance acceptance of work outcomes. In E. A. Locke (Ed.), *A handbook of principles of organizational behavior.* Oxford, England: Blackwell.

Greenberg, J., & Folger, R. (1983). Procedural justice, participation, and the fair process effect in groups and organizations. In P. B. Paulus (Ed.), *Basic group processes* (pp. 235–256). New York: Springer-Verlag.

Greenberg, J., & Lind, E. A. (2000). The pursuit of organizational justice: From conceptualization to implication to application. In C. L. Cooper & E. A. Locke (Eds.), *Industrial/organizational psychology: What we know about theory and practice* (p. 72–105). Oxford, England: Blackwell.

Grover, S. L. (1991). Predicting the perceived fairness of parental leave policies. *Journal of Applied Psychology, 76,* 247–255.

Gundykunst, W. B., & Ting-Toomey, S. (1988). Culture and affective communication. *American Behavioral Scientist, 31,* 348–400.

Hafer, C. L., & Olson, J. M. (1993). Belief in a just world, discontent, and assertive actions by working women. *Personality and Social Psychology Bulletin, 19,* 30–38.

Hofstede, G. (1980). *Culture's consequences: International differences in work related values.* Beverly Hills, CA: Sage.

Hogan, R., & Emler, N. P. (1981). Retributive justice. In M. J. Lerner & S. C. Lerner (Eds.), *The justice motive in social behavior* (pp. 125–144). New York: Plenum.

Hunton, J. E., Wall, T. W., & Price, K. H. (1998). The value of voice in participative decision making. *Journal of Applied Psychology, 83,* 788–797.

Itoi, R., Obhuci, K. I., & Fukuno, M. (1996). A cross-cultural study of preference of accounts: Relationship closeness, harm severity, and motives of account making. *Journal of Applied Social Psychology, 26,* 913–934.

James, K. (1993). The social context of organizational justice: Cultural, intergroup, and structural effects on justice behaviors and perceptions. In R. Cropanzano (Ed.), Justice in the workplace (pp. 21–50). Hillsdale, NJ: Lawrence Erlbaum Associates.

Jones, F. F., & Scarpello, V. (1992, April). *Compensation system fairness: Is it the ends or the means?* Paper presented at the meeting of the Southern Management Association, New Orleans, LA.

Joy, V. L., & Witt, L. A. (1992). Delay of gratification as a moderator of the procedural justice-distributive justice relationship. *Group and Organization Management, 17,* 297–308.

Kidder, L. H., & Miller, S. (1991). What is "fair" in Japan? In H. Steensma & R. Vermunt (Eds.), *Social justice in human relations, Vol. 2: Societal and psychological consequences of justice and injustice* (pp. 139–154). New York: Plenum.

Kim, W. C., & Mauborgne, R. A. (1993). Procedural justice, attitudes, and subsidiary management compliance with multinationals' corporate strategic decisions. *Academy of Management Journal, 36,* 502–526.

Konovsky, M. A., & Cropanzano, R. (1993). Justice considerations in employee drug testing. In R. Cropanzano (Ed.), *Justice in the workplace: Approaching fairness in human resource management* (pp. 171–192). Hillsdale, NJ: Erlbaum.

Korsgaard, M. A., Roberson, L., & Rymph, R. D. (1998). What motivates fairness? The role of subordinate assertive behavior on managers' interactional fairness. *Journal of Applied Psychology, 83,* 731–744.

Lerner, M. J. (1980). *The belief in a just world.* New York: Plenum.

Leventhal, G. S., Karuza, J., & Fry, W. R. (1980). Beyond fairness: A theory of allocation preferences. In G. Mikula (Ed.), *Justice and social interaction* (pp. 167–218). New York: Springer-Verlag.

Levine, J. M., & Moreland, R. L. (1998). Small groups. In D. T. Gilbert, S. T. Fiske, & G. Lindzey (Eds.), *The handbook of social psychology (4th ed.)* (Vol. 2, pp. 415–469). New York: McGraw-Hill.

Lind, E. A. (1995). Justice and authority in organizations. In R. Cropanzano & M. Kacmar (Eds.), *Organizational politics, justice, and support: Managing the social climate of the workplace* (pp. 83–96). Westport, CT: Quorum.

Lind, E. A., Erickson, B. E., Friedland, N., & Dickensberger, M. (1978). Reactions to procedural models for adjudicative conflict resolution: A cross-national study. *Journal of Conflict Resolution, 22,* 318–341.

Lind, E. A., Greenberg, J., Scott, K. S., & Welchans, T. D. (2000). The winding road from employee to complainant: Situational and psychological determinants of wrongful termination lawsuits. *Administrative Science Quarterly, 45,* 557–590.

Lind, E. A., Huo, Y., & Tyler, T. R. (1994). And justice for all: Ethnicity, gender and preferences for dispute resolution procedures. *Law and Human Behavior, 18,* 269–290.

Lind, E. A., & Tyler, T. R. (1988). *The social psychology of procedural justice.* New York: Plenum.

Major, B. (1994). From social inequality to personal entitlement: The role of social comparisons, legitimacy appraisals and group membership. In M. P. Zanna (Ed.), *Advances in experimental social psychology* (Vol. 26, pp. 293–355). New York: Academic Press.

Merton, R. K., & Kitt, A. (1950). Contributions to the theory of reference group behavior. In R. K. Merton & P. F. Lazersfeld (Eds.), *Continuities in social research: Studies in the scope and method of "The American Soldier"* (pp. 123–156). New York: The Free Press.

Messick, D. M., Bloom, S., Boldizar, J. P., & Samuelson, C. D. (1985). Why we are fairer than others. *Journal of Experimental Social Psychology, 21,* 480–500.

Miles, J., & Greenberg, J. (1993). Cross-national differences in preferences for distributive justice norms: The challenge of establishing fair resource allocations in the European community. In J. B. Shaw, P. S. Kirkbride, & K. M. Rowland (Eds.), *Research in personnel and human resources management* (Supplement 3, pp. 133–156). Greenwich, CT: JAI Press.

Miller, D. T. (1999). The norm of self-interest. *American Psychologist, 54,* 153–160.

Montada, L., & Schneider, A. (1989). Justice and emotional reactions to the disadvantaged. *Social Justice Research, 3,* 313–344.

Murphy-Berman, V., Berman, J. J., Singh, P., Pachauri, A., & Kumar, P. (1984). Factors affecting allocation to needy and meritorious recipients: A cross-cultural comparison. *Journal of Personality and Social Psychology, 46,* 1267–1272.

Natua, R. (1983). Distributive behavior in a feminine culture. In J. B. Deregowski, S. Dziurawiee, & R. C. Annis (Eds.), *Explications in cross-cultural psychology: Selected papers from the sixth international conference of the International Association for Cross-Cultural Psychology* (pp. 371–380). Lisse, the Netherlands: Swets and Zeitlinger.

Novelli, L., Jr., Kirkman, B. L., & Shapiro, D. L. (1995). Effective implementation of organizational change: An organizational justice perspective. In C. L. Cooper & D. M. Rousseau (Eds.), *Trends in organizational behavior* (Vol. 2, pp. 15–36). New York: Wiley.

Ochs, J., & Roth, A. E. (1989). An experimental study of sequential bargaining. *American Economic Review, 79,* 335–385.

Opotow, S. (1990). Moral exclusion and injustice: An introduction. *Journal of Social Issues, 46,* 1–20.

Organ, D. W., & Moorman, R. H. (1993). Fairness and organizational citizenship behavior: What are the connections? *Social Justice Research, 6,* 5–18.

Peterson, R. S. (1999). Can you have too much of a good thing? The limits of voice for improving satisfaction with leaders. *Personality and Social Psychology Bulletin, 25,* 313–324.

Piaget, J. (1948). *The moral judgment of the child.* Glencoe, IL: Free Press.

Random House Unabridged Dictionary (2nd ed.). (1993). New York: Random House.

Rawls, J. (1971). *A theory of justice.* Cambridge, MA: Harvard University Press.

Rusbult, C. (1987). Responses to dissatisfaction in close relationships: The exit-voice-loyalty-neglect model. In D. Perlman & S. Duck (Eds.), *Intimate relationships: Development, dynamics, and deterioration* (pp. 209–237). Newbury Park, CA: Sage.

Rynes, S. L., McNatt, D. B., & Bretz, R. D. (1999). Academic research inside organizations: Inputs, processes, and outcomes. *Personnel Psychology, 52,* 869–898.

Rytina, S. (1986). Sociology and justice. In R. L. Cohen (Ed.), *Justice: Views from the social sciences.* New York: Plenum.

Shapiro, D. L., Buttner, H. B., & Barry, B. (1994). Explanations: What factors enhance their perceived adequacy? *Organizational Behavior and Human Decision Processes, 58,* 346–368.

Skarlicki, D. P., & Latham, G. P. (1996). Increasing citizenship behavior within a labor union: A test of organizational justice theory. *Journal of Applied Psychology, 81,* 161–169.

Smith, H. J., & Tyler, T. R. (1996). Justice and power: When will justice concerns encourage the advantaged to support policies which redistribute economic resources to the disadvantaged to willingly obey the law? *European Journal of Social Psychology, 26,* 171–200.

Steiner, D. D., & Gilliland, S. W. (1996). Fairness to reactions to personnel selection techniques in France and the United States. *Journal of Applied Psychology, 81,* 134–141.

Sugawara, I., & Huo, Y. J. (1994). Disputes in Japan: A cross-cultural test of the procedural justice model. *Social Justice Research, 7,* 129–144.

Sweeny, P. D., & McFarlin, D. B. (1997). Process and outcome: Gender differences in the assessment of justice. *Journal of Organizational Behavior, 18,* 83–98.

Thibaut, J., & Walker, L. (1975). *Procedural justice: A psychological analysis.* Hillsdale, NJ: Erlbaum.

Törnblom, K. Y. (1977). Distributive justice: Typology and propositions. *Human Relations, 30,* 1–24.

Tyler, T. R. (1994). Governing amid diversity. *Law and Society Review, 28,* 701–722.

Tyler, T. R., Boeckmann, R. J., Smith, J. J., & Huo, Y. J. (1997). *Social justice in a diverse society.* Boulder, CO: Westview Press.

Tyler, T. R., Huo, Y. J., & Smith, H. J. (1995). *Relative and absolute evaluations as a basis for self-esteem and group oriented behavior: Do we have to be better than others to feel good about ourselves?* Unpublished manuscript, University of California, Berkeley.

Walster, E., Walster, G. W., & Berscheid, E. (1978). *Equity: Theory and research.* Boston: Allyn & Bacon.

Wood, J. (1989). Theory and research concerning social comparisons of personal attributes. *Psychological Bulletin, 106,* 231–248.

Wright, R. (1994). *The moral animal: Why we are the way we are—the new science of evolutionary psychology.* New York: Pantheon.

Index

Page numbers in italics indicate figures.
Notes are cited with page number followed by note number.

Printed and bound by CPI Group (UK) Ltd, Croydon, CR0 4YY

23/04/2025

14660938-0003